TONI MORRISON ON
MOTHERS AND MOTHERHOOD

Funded by the Government of Canada
Financé par la gouvernement du Canada

Demeter Press
140 Holland Street West
P. O. Box 13022
Bradford, ON L3Z 2Y5
Tel: (905) 775-9089
Email: info@demeterpress.org
Website: www.demeterpress.org

Demeter Press logo based on the sculpture "Demeter" by Maria-Luise Bodirsky
<www.keramik-atelier.bodirsky.de>

Printed and Bound in Canada

Library and Archives Canada Cataloguing in Publication

        Toni Morrison on mothers and motherhood / Lee Baxter and Martha Satz, editors.

Includes bibliographical references.
ISBN 978-1-77258-104-1 (softcover)

        1. Morrison, Toni--Criticism and interpretation. 2. Morrison, Toni--Characters--Mothers. 3. Mothers in literature. 4. Motherhood in literature. I. Baxter, Lee, 1968-, editor II. Satz, Martha, 1943-, editor

PS3563.O8749Z896 2017   813'.54   C2017-903638-6

TONI MORRISON ON
MOTHERS AND MOTHERHOOD

EDITED BY
Lee Baxter and Martha Satz

DEMETER PRESS

To Miriam and Michael,
who everyday winningly reveal the motherwork I have done.
—Martha Satz

To Sooneiah and Aidan,
who have taught me as much as I've taught them.
—Lee Baxter

Table of Contents

CONTENTS

Acknowledgements

We would like to thank Andrea O'Reilly for her support throughout this project. We would also like to thank all the people with whom we have corresponded about this volume.

Lee would especially like to thank Andrea Robertson for her encouragement and support. While working on this project she has been particularly indebted to her mother, Norma Ducau, and her friends, especially throughout the editing process.

Martha would like to thank Debbie Needleman and Maresa Patterson for their valuable suggestions.

Introduction

MARTHA SATZ AND LEE BAXTER

T ONI MORRISON HAS NOTABLY ADVISED writers, "If there's a book that you want to read, but it hasn't been written yet, then you must write it" ("A Great Conversation"). And Morrison has followed her own advice, writing most centrally about Black women and girls and their formative and transformative female experiences, most particularly motherhood. Her work cultivates an examination of black motherhood that counters motherhood performed and advocated by the dominant culture.

Morrison writes of experiences that tell the stories that have been suppressed by white patriarchy. She expresses how African American culture prays, escapes, hurts, and repents. In other words, Morrison's work subverts the white gaze, as it offers an alternative history to the official narrative presented by white hegemony. And as already noted, her writing focuses on the everyday experiences of Black women and girls, who are placed at the centre of all of her novels. Although in *Song of Solomon*, to name just one example, the protagonist, Milkman, is male, the women—Pilate, Ruth, Corrie and Lena—function as foils throughout the story as they embody and depict the social and cultural pressures and their prescribed stereotypes of African American women.

Focusing on the experiences of Black women and girls, Morrison's writings subvert their historical exclusion and provide them with a voice that shares their everyday internal and external experiences. These experiences depict gender hierarchies and cultural expectations of what it is to be a woman, a wife, a mother, and a daughter. In so doing, Morrison, as Andrea O'Reilly argues,

1

"defines and positions maternal identity as a site of power for black women" (1). This position of power is used to instruct, protect, and empower their children in a racist, class-defined, and sexist world. But Morrison, in her work, also examines what happens when there is a deficiency of mothering and motherhood. In these books, the absence of a nurturing mother results in both personal and cultural damage. Morrison, therefore, advocates the importance of mothering as she highlights the effects of loss and anguish caused in its absence.

The works in this collection address a range of Morrison's novels, including *The Bluest Eye, Jazz, Song of Solomon, Home, Beloved, Paradise, Sula,* and *Love.* They examine and critique Morrison's challenges to the Eurocentric characterization of mothers, motherhood, and mothering. The essays emphasize how the women co-opt or challenge the dominant concepts of mothering and motherhood as stable notions. Furthermore, mothering and motherhood, as discussed in all of the essays, is not necessarily confined to the role that females play in raising children and taking care of family members. Stanlie James has described this form of nurturing as "othermothering," which can also include being nurtured by others on an individual or community level. She describes othermothering as an "acceptance of responsibility for a child not one's own, in an arrangement that may or may not be formal" (45).[1] Regardless of who raises the child or children, motherhood and mothering is complex and complicated.

This collection of essays focuses on the repressive and the inspiring facets of mothering and motherhood. The themes examined in the collection explore motherhood as experience, and mothering and motherhood as identity and subjectivity. Mothering and motherhood, as Andrea O'Reilly poignantly asserts within motherhood studies, bear separate meanings: "*motherhood* is used to signify the patriarchal institution of motherhood, while *mothering* refers to women's lived experiences of childrearing as they both conform to and/or resist the patriarchal institution of motherhood and its oppressive ideology" (2). And, as seen in this volume of essays, Morrison's depiction of motherhood, mothering, and othermothering is concerned with the women in Morrison's novels who counter the Eurocentric patriarchal institution of motherhood and their lived experiences of mothering, as well as how mothering effects a child's identity formation and agency.

This volume is timely, as it helps to further our understanding of gender, sexuality, power, community, identity, and media. News outlets and social media have played a huge role in disseminating images and news of racism and misogyny. The news has played and relayed images of shootings of black men by police, and of then presidential candidate Donald Trump accusing the Black Lives Matter movement of inciting violence against law-enforcement officers. We have also seen men in positions of power describing women using misogynistic language and defending their words as "two men in a locker-room just talking" and the continued opposition toward LGBTQ rights. Moreover, the government has slashed budgets making women's right to choose more and more difficult. Indeed, all of the papers in this volume provoke dialogue and debates on the raising of children and the ways they may be empowered. Through these debates, issues of othering, identity formation, maternal experience, patriarchal ideology, racism, and subjectivity all come to the forefront. By further opening up discussions on these issues, these essays offer the opportunity for us to better understand and respond to mothering/motherhood and address these various concerns. We have placed the chapters into three sections, which address Morrison's examination of othermothering, the intersectional oppressions that create "bad" mothers, and the effects of lack of mothering or poor mothering on children. We realize that these topics overlap but nevertheless feel that these three categories address the exploration of mothering/ motherhood in Morrison's work.

The first section, titled "Othermothering," examines how nonmothers, and alternative forms of mothering are advocated throughout Morrison's work. The term "othermothering" denotes "acceptance of responsibility for a child not one's own, in an arrangement that may or may not be formal" (James 45). We see this practice in her novels such as *Beloved, Paradise, Song of Solomon,* and *Home.* Susan Neal Mayberry explores "othermothering" in her chapter, "Masculine Othermothering in Toni Morrison's *Home.*" Mayberry argues that in her books, Morrison depicts forms of othermothering that include community mothering as well as "masculine othermothering" through Frank Money's character. Mayberry believes that "Frank Money's learned maternal bonding with the feminine allows him an African American manhood that enables him to become an effective othermother."

Similarly, Tosha Sampson-Choma examines othermothering in *Home*. This novel emphasizes not only that women are just as capable of everyday violence against children as men are, but that men too are just as capable of nurturing children as women are. Thus, Morrison challenges the normative perception of mothering and motherhood. Sampson-Choma contends that Frank functions as Ycidra's primary nurturer, while "their step-grandmother ... demeans, demoralizes and emotionally abuses" them. Predicating her argument on Patricia Hill Collins' concept of "othermother," Sampson-Choma argues that Frank's narrative provides an "opportunity to expand critical conversations on motherhood" as Frank both nurtures Ycidra but also "rewrites his own narrative in the discourse of brother-mother." This alternative form of mothering critiques and endorses "an Afro-American aesthetic," as the novel explores the "complexity of family relationships."

Alternative forms of mothering are central to all of Morrison's novels. Jill Goad's chapter, "'Not a Maternal Drudge ... Nor ... An Acid-Tongued Shrew': The Complexity of Ruth and Pilate in Toni Morrison's *Song of Solomon*," interrogates the broader stereotypes and cultural perceptions mirrored through Ruth and Pilate. The relationships with the men only serve to highlight the stereotypical characterization of Ruth and Pilate. Although this novel's protagonist is a man, Milkman, Ruth and Pilate explore the roles of black women in relation to their husbands, sons, fathers, nephews, and lovers with the ever present patriarchal white society. Ruth and Pilate are presented as opposing individuals: Ruth is a fragile woman whose identity is subsumed by her relationships with her father and son, Milkman, whereas Pilate is a self-created, independent woman. And, as Goad argues, Morrison's "characterization of Pilate speaks to societal judgments of women who do not fit a traditional mother and wife mould." In other words, women who do not fit into the traditional mould of "mother" or "motherhood" are castigated and punished by society.

Anna Hinton also examines Pilate's role in *Song of Solomon* in "'You've Already Got What You Need, Sugar': Southern and Maternal Identity in Toni Morrison's *Song of Solomon*." Hinton views Pilate's character as one who empowers others through motherwork because she retains her self-preservation through incorporating Southern traditions while living in the North. Pilate is considered as an outlaw, as she defines herself on her own terms. Hagar, on the other hand, rejects Pilate's mode of mothering and "desires what the heteronormative, capitalist, racist, and patriarchal culture tells her to desire." Pilate rejects the parameters set by white patriarchal society and thus maintains her individuality.

"Bad" mothering can be viewed as absent mothering or abusive (physical and/or emotional) mothering. The absence of mothers and child abuse can lead to children living with trauma, which causes them to make bad choices and live outside the community; they become seen as "bad" people. Morrison's work highlights the effects of the lack of nurturing and the lack of protecting one's child/children. Her novels destabilize and recognize the ambivalence of what it entails to be a mother. Veena Deo's chapter, "Studies in M(othering): Unpacking the 'Wicked Thing' in Toni Morrison's *A Mercy* and *Beloved*" examines the way mothers are represented in American history as products of social and cultural construction. Racism is intricately bound within the social and cultural construction of America.

Social and cultural hegemony is further examined in Lee Baxter's paper, "Rethinking, Rewriting Self and Other in Toni Morrison's *Love*." This essay examines identity formation through Julia Kristeva's alternative account of (m)othering in her work on mother and mothering, and patriarchal ideology. More specifically, Baxter considers the way patriarchy causes women to view one another as an other, thus creating a divide between women, mothers, and daughters. She posits that it is not until the Cosey "women recognize both their selves as other, as well as the other in the Other, that they can learn to love truly and break free from the idealized social constructs of femininity and maternity." Mothering in *Love* is both absent and present. The divide created between mothers and daughters is brought upon through "bad" mothering and is not overcome until the women accept themselves as Others and recognize that they need to mother themselves, love themselves, and pass on this self-empowerment to other women—to instruct, protect, and empower their children.

Maintaining one's individuality also means that one is secure in their identity. However, identities are constantly in flux and in question in Morrison's work. Identity formation in Morrison's work is more often than not interrupted by traumatic instances. Lauren Mitchell's "The Trauma of Second Birth: Double Consciousness, Rupture, and Toni Morrison's *Beloved*" and Kristin Distel's "'Are You Sure She Was Your Sister?': Sororal Love and Maternal Failure in Morrison's *Paradise*" examine the ways traumatic events distort one's relationship with one's self. Identity formation is halted with the violation of the body. Mitchell posits that there is a "dialectical relationship between Sethe's 'inner' and 'outer' stressors ... that result in ... a kind of rebirth." She discusses this through the lens of Hortense J. Spillers's recent work on "second birth." On the other hand, Distel explores the ways in which the attachment between sisters is a privileged relationship that provides a love that mothers fail to give. Her overall examination of *Paradise* views mother and sibling relationships as complex, where motherhood is marred by cruelty whereas bonds between sisters are not.

Rosanne Kennedy in her chapter "Racialized Intimacies and Alternative Kinship Relations: Toni Morrison's *Home*" examines the effects of growing up in households that mirror "the dominant aesthetic, cultural, and economic values of white society." Kennedy scrutinizes the ways the households in *Home* and *The Bluest Eye* embody racist ideas that end in "failed attempts at 'respectability'" and lead to alternative maternal and communal households.

In the section that investigates the lack of mothering, the essays examine the various ways mothers and community fail to provide safe spaces for children and empower them. The broader question, which these papers address, is how patriarchal ideology fails to ensure safety for the most vulnerable; how it creates a strict division between gender roles and racial hierarchies; and how it subjugates women and their various roles as mother, sister, daughter, and wife. In her examination of *The Bluest* Eye, Candice Pipes's paper,

"Failed Mothers and the Black Girl-Child Victim of Incestuous Rape in *The Bluest Eye* and *Push*," discusses the effects of incest in relation to gendered roles, identity formation, and patriarchal ideology. Pipes argues that the novel suggests that a "reordering of the black community is necessary to save black girl-children from incest." In other words, the reordering of the community exposes the falsehood that patriarchy ensures safety, in particular female safety, and allows for women and girls to form healthy identities with themselves and their female counterparts.

This subjugation causes women to find ways to subvert the heteronormative ideologies set out by the rule (law) of the father. However, by disrupting these ideologies, these women are further marginalized within their social spheres. They further marginalize themselves through problematic ethical acts, such as Sethe murdering her own child in *Beloved*, and Eva burning and killing Plum, and Sula cutting off her own finger in *Sula*. Martha Satz in "Mothering Oneself in *Sula*," explores how the ethical obligation, deontological, and care approaches are taken in *Sula*. These approaches result in the construct of a new mythology of human life. In particular, Satz argues that the Wright family and the Peace family are dialectic, which highlights two forms of mothering that cause the reader to respond to alternative forms of mothering.

Althea Tait examines trauma and how it is passed down from mother to daughter in her chapter "Black Motherhood, Beauty, and Soul ~~Murder~~ Wound." In particular, Tait analyzes how "conformity with Eurocentric forms of oppression" through forms of beauty causes an inner hate and fear that will become inhuman and ugly. These views are so entrenched that Black women cannot properly bond, which causes a deformed sense of identity.

In "From Sweetness to Toya Graham: Intersectionality and the (Im)Possibilities of Maternal Ethics," Jesse Goldberg argues that "motherhood cannot be raised to the level of universal experience, but rather it is always experienced intersectionally, and so what might be called a 'maternal ethics' is rendered both impossible on the level of universal imperatives and yet utterly material and necessary in an anti-Black, patriarchal world." More specifically, Goldberg examines the works of *Sula*, *Beloved*, and *God Help the*

MARTHA SATZ AND LEE BAXTER

Child in relation to the ethical demand that mothers are expected to undertake in order to protect their children.

Finally, Barbara Mattar's "'They Took My Milk': The Multiple Meanings of Breastmilk in Toni Morrison's *Beloved*" illustrates the "parallels between Sethe's agency as a lactating mother and our contemporary cultural meanings and interpretations towards this bodily fluid that can draw fascination, hunger, and disgust." Mattar argues that society needs a better cultural response in order "to reposition the lactating mother as the source of agency and informed decision maker about this aspect of her body and her relationship with her child."

In each of these essays, the readers will find the different ways Morrison's fiction constructs and responds to the thought-provoking notion of mothering and motherhood. Morrison's deft writing challenges her audience to look beyond the surface of beauty, beyond the authorized Eurocentric historical account of slavery and its generational traumas, and beyond the advised standards of how a mother should behave and/or nurture her children. She shows us what life is as a black parent navigating in a Eurocentric, patriarchal world. Morrison's work examines the difficult, terrifying, and sometimes horrifying difficulties of being a parent, a mother, a wife, a sister, but she does this by depicting hope through her portrayal of nurturing figures that range from Pilate to Frank Money—nurturing is gender blind. Mothering and motherhood, as we see within this volume of essays, are fluid concepts, in the sense that it is everyone's responsibility to nurture our children and ourselves as adults. We all need to be mothered and need to take time to mother ourselves.

ENDNOTE

[1]This has been examined and documented in such studies as Carol Stack's book *All Our Kin: Strategies for Survival in a Black Community* (1974); Priscilla Gibson's article, "Developmental Mothering in an African American Community: From Grandmothers to New Mothers Again"; Arlene Edwards's article "Community Mothering: The Relationship between Mothering and the Community Work of Black Women"; and Njoki Nathani Wane's article,

"Reflections on the Mutuality of Mothering: Women, Children, and Othermothering."

WORKS CITED

Edwards, Arlene. "Community Mothering: The Relationship between Mothering and the Community Work of Black Women." *Journal of the Association for Research on Mothering*, vol. 2, no. 2, 2000, pp. 87-100.

Gibson, Priscilla. "Developmental Mothering in an African American Community: From Grandmothers to New Mothers Again." *Journal of the Association for Research on Mothering*, vol. 2, no. 2, 2000, pp. 32-41.

O'Reilly, Andrea. "Introduction." *21st Century Motherhood: Experience, Identity, Policy, Agency*, edited by Andrea O'Reilly, Columbia University Press, 2010, pp. 1-20.

Morrison, Toni. "A Great Conversation between Toni Morrison and Junot Diaz." *Gradient Lair: Black Women + Art, Media Social Media, Socio-Politics & Culture*. 28 Dec, 2013, http://www.gradientlair.com/post/71459638476/toni-morrison-junot-diaz-talk-nypl. Accessed 17 May 2017.

James, Stanlie. "Mothering: A Possible Black Feminist Link to Social Transformations." *Theorizing Black Feminism: The Visionary Pragmatism of Black Women*, edited by Stanlie James and A. P. Busia, Routledge, 1999, pp. 44-54.

Stack, Carol. *All Our Kin: Strategies for Survival in a Black Community*. Harper Colophon Books, 1974.

Wane, Nathani Wane. "Reflections on the Mutuality of Mothering: Women, Children, and Othermothering." *Journal of the Association for Research on Mothering*, vol. 2, no. 2, 2000, pp. 105-116.

I.
"Othermothering"

Masculine Othermothering
in Toni Morrison's *Home*

SUSAN NEAL MAYBERRY

HAVING OFFENDED AN OLDER but vastly more ardent mother than I by deriding the innateness of maternal bonding upon giving birth to my son, I manage to break a young father's heart by blithely informing him: "Mother love does not come naturally." When that same father reminds me of my doubts five years later, I flatly deny having made light of maternal bonding. I had finally delivered a daughter after enduring all sorts of unnatural infertility treatments because I feared I might come to love my boy too much.

For almost fifty years Toni Morrison has stirred up more than her share of trouble in an effort to free mother love from such unbalanced oppositions—not by "lov[ing] nothing," but by helping both genders discern when an absence of love becomes "too much" as well as "know[ing] when to stop" loving too much (*Beloved* 92; 86, 216; 104). Validating in many of her novels a range of maternal reactions to all sorts of others, she endorses the notion of "othermothering" as an "acceptance of responsibility for a child not one's own, in an arrangement that may or may not be formal" (James 45). She also holds with community mothering, a related concept that encompasses women typically past childbearing years who have often previously othermothered and continue to care for adult community members (Wane 112; Edwards 88). Morrison's tenth novel *Home* (2012) extends these ideas to sanction what we may call "masculine othermothering"—a symbiotic model in which Frank Money's learned bonding with the feminine allows him an African American manhood that enables him to become an effective othermother.

13

As described by feminist critic Patricia Hill Collins, othermothering has been linked to traditional West African societies in which all the women in a household or village mothered all the children, regardless of biological ties. Mothering, thus, was not a "privatized nurturing 'occupation' reserved for biological mothers," nor was economic support of children the exclusive responsibility of men (45). Since mothering expressed itself as both nurturance and work, and childcare was viewed as the duty of the larger community, mothering, othermothering, and community mothering garnered power and status for women in West African culture. Because parenting duties remain organized as a collective activity, the practice still relieves "some of the stresses that can develop between children and parents [and] provides multiple role models for children; it [also] keeps the traditional African value systems of communal sharing and ownership alive" (Wane 113).

Since these West African cultural practices were retained by enslaved African Americans, they "gave rise to a distinct tradition of African American motherhood in which the custom of othermothering and community mothering was emphasized and elaborated" (O'Reilly 5):

> The experience of slavery saw the translation of othermothering to new settings, since the care of children was an expected task of enslaved Black women in addition to the field or house duties.... The familial instability of slavery engendered the adaptation of communality in the form of fostering children whose parents, particularly mothers, had been sold. This tradition of communality gave rise to the practice of othermothering. The survival of the concept is inherent to the survival of Black people as a whole ... since it allowed for the provision of care to extended family and non blood relations. (Edwards 80)

Manifested in many African American communities to this day, othermothering equips children with the psychological and social skills they need to survive the oppressive racism and sexism of a kyriarchal culture. These survival skills include a sense of stability, connections of kinship, feelings of self-worth, and knowledge of

African American social history, without which black children may succumb to what Morrison has long called the "white gaze"—constant negative messages from a dominant society that devalues them as human beings and disallows self-identity via a proud cultural inheritance. bell hooks deems othermothering "revolutionary," since "it takes place in opposition to the idea that parents, especially mothers, should be the only childrearers.... Even in families where the mother stayed home, she could also rely on people in the community to help" (144).

Morrison's novels reflect this "centrality of women in African-American extended families" by depicting the actualities of African American othermothering during and after slavery (Jenkins 206). Although Andrea O'Reilly's *Toni Morrison and Motherhood* widens the notion to include those grown women in Morrison's novels who never receive protection, nurturance, and cultural pride as daughters and thus become psychologically wounded adults, O'Reilly limits her analysis to the othermothering of adult women by other adult women.[1] Morrison's texts, in fact, disrupt these reified gender roles. Her (un)usual double-eyed look subverts both race and gender norms by questioning the primacy of female-oriented othermothering and asserting that males can be nurturers and culture bearers, too.

In a 1994 interview with Bill Moyers, Morrison was asked about the most crucial need in contemporary urban African American communities. She responded with a single word, "Love," and added, "We have to embrace ourselves." In the interview, without using the term, she commends male othermothering for converting bureaucratic agencies into agency for self- and other-regard: "I love those men I heard about in Chicago, black professional men who went every lunch hour to the playgrounds in Chicago's South Side to talk to those children. Not to be authoritarian, but just to get to know them, without the bureaucracy." Agreeing "absolutely" with Moyers that "The love [she is] talking about is the love inspired by moral imagination that takes us beyond blood," Morrison recounts a group of black businessmen who volunteer at local shelters to comfort crack babies: "They were spending time holding ... children who were ... [exposed to cocaine as fetuses]—holding them. Holding them. Now, I'm sure it does something for the baby, but think what it does for that man, to actually give up some time and hold a baby." As such, *Home* illustrates how experiences with othermothering effectively render black men better by tempering those more typically white American male rites of passage like making war and money.[2] Reflecting her ability to engage imaginatively with several subjects simultaneously, *Home* becomes "a kind of tiny Rosetta Stone to Toni Morrison's entire oeuvre" (*The New York Times*).[3] It also maps out new territory by disrupting normative narratives of masculinity more than any of her novels since *Song of Solomon*. *Home* reflects Michael Awkward's idea of a "nonmonolithic black masculinity" (33) that valorizes black feminism through nurturing activities while concurrently challenging the nuclear family model as a universal constant in American culture (33).

At the Toni Morrison Society's Fifth Biennial Conference in 2008, during which Morrison read the opening chapter of her then current book project, she commented that she had been planning for some time to examine the relationship between a brother and his sister. A Morrison Society colleague pronounced the ensuing novel *Home*, dedicated to Morrison's younger son Slade after sadly being delayed by his death in 2010, "right up [my masculinity studies] alley."[4] As Morrison contrasts the purportedly golden age of postwar 1950s with the violent reality of the Korean War, McCarthyism, and the routine emasculation of African American males, she offers Frank (otherwise known as "Smart") Money an alternative way to be a man as he comes to reassess Ycidra (nicknamed Cee) Money, "his original caring-for," in a new light (35). For a black veteran in 1952, the journey from a Northwest passage back to a reenvisioned home in Lotus, Georgia, becomes his greatest battle. But the fight to locate and love the feminine leaves Frank finally with his manhood intact.

Similar to the protagonists in Morrison's other narratives depicting male odysseys, Frank rejects Emerson's concept of the new white American male to adopt an African American manhood (see *Playing in the Dark*). We can link Frank's evolution as an othermother, then, to his personality formation, the death of that self, and a rebirth with the aid of a grounded female.[5] Claiming it *"was the third woman who changed everything,"* the one who except for three images *"had no competition in [his] mind,"* an adult Frank defines his past in terms of *"horses, a man's foot, and Ycidra trembling under [his] arm"* (68-69).[6] *Home* opens circa 1940 on a stud farm in taboo farmland five rocky miles outside Lotus, Georgia. After daring to crawl under a wire mesh fence despite ominous warning signs to the contrary, a twelve-year-old brother and his eight-year-old sister hold their breath in wonder while a black stallion finally dominates a rust-colored one, both sunny with sweat as they fight over "who controlled the mares and their foals" (*Paradise* 150). Here the black boy's first breathtaking revelation about what it means to be a man takes on tones of gender and racial power as it displays a coal black male horse overpowering a lighter-colored one while the colts and mares remain indifferent or look away. The boy remembers the horses as *"so beautiful. So brutal. And they stood like men"* (5).

Returning home, the siblings lose their way both literally and figuratively when they encounter a line of parked trucks, hear low voices, and witness a group of men dumping a body from a wheelbarrow into a shallow grave. The quivering black foot sticking out as dirt is shovelled over it, *"with its creamy pink and mud-streaked sole"* being whacked into the hole, shakes both children to the core: *"We could not see the faces of the men doing the burying, only their trousers; but we saw the edge of a spade drive the jerking foot down to join the rest of itself"* (4). Placing responsibility for coping with violence onto himself as big brother, Frank tries to absorb Cee's trembling, an act of what Morrison calls "anaconda love," which he will repeat throughout their childhood until Cee learns to rescue her own self. In her interview with Moyers, Morrison maintains that children "don't need all that overwhelming love.... I mean, that's just you being vain about it." *Home* emphatically defines such love as destructively "too much."

Frank's association of masculinity with accustomed violence and the magnificent sight of clashing horses that *"rose up like men ... Like men they stood"* actually begins in Bandera County, Texas. Born there in 1928, Frank, now four years old, and his family, including his pregnant mother, walk out in 1932, encouraged by the Great Depression and armed white vigilantes to "leave their little neighborhood on the edge of town: Twenty-four hours, they

were told, or else. 'Else' meaning 'die.'" Frank's recollections of
that time focus on an elderly black man who, sitting on his porch
steps, refuses to leave a beloved tree planted by his great-grand-
mother: "Elbows on knees, hands clasped, chewing tobacco, he
waited the whole night. Just after dawn at the twenty-fourth hour
he was beaten to death with pipes and rifle butts and tied to the
oldest magnolia tree in the county—the one that grew in his own
yard." Neighbours brave enough to sneak back and face hooded
men in order to bury him claim that "Mr. Crawford's eyes had
been carved out" (10). Frank's father, carrying the reins of the mare
they would never see again, ties up the flapping sole of Frank's
shoe with his own shoelace.

Memories of the mistreatment black men must tolerate, of ex-
haustion on the road and fetid leftovers from food pantries, are
mitigated by the manner in which his mother, giving birth on a
mattress in Church of the Redeemer's basement, names her daughter Ycidra, cherishing its sweet musical sound amid the belligerent
din of the crowd lining up for "*a tin plate of dry, hard cheese already showing green, pickled pigs' feet—its vinegar soaking stale
biscuits*" (40). The family's destination, however, contributes to
Frank's disillusionment because "*Any kid who had a mind would
lose it*" killing time in the small Georgia town, which becomes
for teenaged Frank "*worse than any battlefield*" (83-84). He and
two boyhood friends enlist to exchange what they believe to be
Lotus's mind-numbing boredom for the cold, flat days intermittently broken by risk and the mindless excitement of staying alive
in war-torn Korea.[7] But not before Frank assumes responsibility
for othermothering Cee. As his personality solidifies, nurturing his
baby sister and connecting the fiercely combative stallions with
how to think and behave as a male cause him to suppress memories
of the buried black man: "*I really forgot about the burial. I only
remembered the horses*" (5). Frank's equation of the horses and
masculine power aligns men with violence but also defines men
as protectors against violence as they repress their own feelings.

Akin to *Love's* fourteen-year-old Romen, Frank Money is born
with a natural propensity to care for people, although he doesn't
initially know what to do with it. Since both parents work six-
teen-hour days, Ida Money ultimately succumbing to fatal asthma

followed by the death of Luther from a stroke, the siblings rely on each other to figure out how to navigate short, razor-sharp affection, disapproval, silence, and how to imagine a future. Although he is inclined to privilege people over money, any training Smart Money receives in parenting comes from a materialistic step-grandmother, whose safe haven has been destroyed by three years of her second husband's homeless family crowding into her house, and from a grandfather who will do anything, or nothing, for peace. Whereas Grandfather Salem Money stays silent, Lenore's behaviour turns the traditional nurturing black grandmother into a prime example of destructive othermothering. Supposing herself "merely a strict step-grandmother, not a cruel one," she agrees to care for baby Cee, whose night cries she finds infuriating, only because the parents' additional wages mean that they may vacate sooner and because "the four-year-old brother [Frank] was clearly the real mother to the infant" (88).[8] Lenore projects her frustration, resentment at being inconvenienced, and the trickle-down effects of arbitrary abuse she has suffered toward her most exposed targets—her step-grandchildren, especially the little girl Cee.

Lenore's sadistic grandparenting combines emotional malice with unrelenting physical punishment, such as switchings for Cee's childhood awkwardness, for mishandling her chores, for spilling the shredded wheat and water that Lenore substitutes for milk: "Only the hatred in the eyes of [Cee's] brother kept Lenore from slapping her. He was always protecting her, soothing her as though she were his pet kitten" (88). An elitist as well as miserly, Lenore reminds the girl incessantly of her birth on the road. Cee compensates for her grandmother's frown at the "gutter child's" very entrance, the downturned lips at every small mistake, together with the tough, watchful community mothering Cee must contend with, by falling "for what Lenore called the first thing [Cee] saw wearing belted trousers instead of overalls" (47). In short, although the grandmother's approach to othermothering causes Cee's low self-esteem, the brother's alternative method of "too much" love, developed to atone for Lenore's mean care, cannot safeguard Cee from human "rats" like her future husband Principal (52).

Prohibited mild flirtations much less comprehension of male perversity by virtue of her big brother's presence, Cee wants the

knowledge, street savvy, and self-confidence that could have prevented Principal from marrying her at eighteen to get to drive Lenore's
Ford, from this prince of a lover introducing her to dull sex, and
from fanatic eugenicist Dr. Beauregard Scott experimenting on
her almost fatally at twenty. Because her brother never laughs at,
quarrels with, or condemns her, and can be counted on to shield
her from bad situations, an adult Cee neglects her responsibility
for addressing the frightening possibilities outside and inside that
she expects Frank to manage.

Bored at fourteen by a boys' baseball game, she sits nearby
picking off cherry red nail polish in hopes of appeasing Lenore
when she observes Frank carry his bat as he leaves the plate only
because his teammates object to his actions. Unaware that Frank
is circling the field, unconcerned until Frank swings the bat into
the legs of someone she has not noticed standing behind her, she
realizes after Frank has dragged her away that the strange man
was "flashing" her, a term that Frank must explain. As she begins
to tremble upon learning the truth, Frank puts "one hand on top
of her head, the other at her nape. His fingers, like balm, stopped
the trembling and the chill that accompanied it." Cee has always
heeded Frank's warnings about scary stuff "out there": she "recognized poisonous berries, shouted when in snake territory, learned
the medicinal uses of spiderwebs. His instructions were specific, his
cautions clear" (51-52). Sister and brother must learn separately,
however, that the arduous journey to establish an inside self is
both complex and solitary.

If Morrison shapes Frank's sites of memory in Texas and Georgia
by the permitted murder of black men provoking his excessive
defense of a girl, his formative experiences in Korea link the
legal slaughter of black men with pedophilia directed toward
a girl.[9] Smart Money repeatedly expresses his preoccupation
with supposed feminine weak spots he has no way of fixing: he
makes a collar for the rescued Doberman puppy that never leaves
Jackie's side; he cannot prevent *"the third woman who changed
everything"* from reaching up literally or figuratively because he
cannot take his eyes off the vulnerable flesh at the back of her
knees. Attracted to the small breakable thing within women more
than their beauty, intelligence, or personality, he seeks out the

something soft that lies inside each: "*Like a bird's breastbone, shaped and chosen to wish on. A little V, thinner than bone and lightly hinged, that I could break with a forefinger if I wanted to, but never did. Want to, I mean. Knowing it was there, hiding from me, was enough*" (68). Continued enabling of Cee, then, not only represents an abused boy's desire to cherish something forgiving, but also prevents the man from dealing with his potential for human depravity.[10] Continuing to emphasize the agonizing mystery of his interior monologue with italics, spacing, and the trope of the Talking Book, Morrison prevents even Frank from knowing the truth about his actions as a military guard in Korea until the end of the novel:

I have to tell the whole truth. I lied to you and I lied to me. I hid it from you because I hid it from me....

I shot the Korean girl in her face.

I am the one she touched.

I am the one who saw her smile.

I am the one she said "Yum-yum" to.

I am the one she aroused.

A child. A wee little girl.

I didn't think. I didn't have to.

Better she should die.

How could I let her live after she took me down to a place I didn't know was in me?

How could I like myself, even be myself if I surrendered to that place where I unzip my fly and let her taste me right then and there?

And again the next day and the next as long as she came scavenging.

What type of man is that? (133-134)

His helpless rage at the gruesome battlefield killing of his homeys Stuff and Mike, guilt over his own irrational killing spree in Korea, and the self-flagellation from a damaging relationship with Lily Jones enable Frank to repress his real shame. He gives up alcohol merely for another tranquilizer since living with Lily allows the little wishbone V to take up residence in his own breast. Wide open for a "forefinger that kept him on edge," he realizes that, without Sarah Williams's letter from Atlanta summoning him to "'Come fast. [Cee] be dead if you tarry,'" he would "still be hanging from [Lily's] apron strings" (68, 8, 69). Morrison's irony becomes clear as Frank miscalculates connecting the supposed safety of home with a tough materialist and social climber, not unlike Lenore. Fighting racism herself as she attempts to foster her career and purchase a house, Lily, known more forbiddingly as Lillian Florence Jones, has little empathy with or sympathy for pathetic cases of what we now call post-traumatic stress disorder (PTSD), in which apathy battles with bouts of self-directed violence. Recognized in the early 1980s, PTSD is a mental health condition triggered by experiencing or witnessing a terrifying event. Symptoms may include flashbacks, nightmares, and severe anxiety, as well as uncontrollable thoughts about the event.

Enlightenment, however, looks to locate Frank via the grounded female. Watching a nearly drowned girl vomiting blood makes him sick at the thought of whiskey; he bolts rather than shoots this time at the sight of a little girl with slanted eyes reaching for a cupcake at a church picnic. "Smart" Money needs to rescue the suffering female in himself. Claiming that black men underwent systemic "feminization" as slaves, Hortense Spillers views their embrace of the feminine as a way for males to achieve wholeness and self-actualization:

The black American male embodies the only American community of males which has had the specific occasion to

learn who the female is within itself, the infant child who
bears the life against the could-be fateful gamble, against
the odds of pulverization and murder, including her own.
It is the heritage of the mother that the African-American
male must regain as an aspect of his own personhood—the
power of "yes" to the "female" within. (80)

Embracing the mother within comes down to pinpointing that
balance of power. In the same way that Southern elders use "coon-
hunting" to separate *Song of Solomon's* Milkman from "the cocoon
that was 'personality'" (300) so he can discern life-preserving
instinct, Korea affirms for Frank that an aspect of masculinity
is the desire to dominate.[11] As this black brother struggles with
losing then recreating his identity, however, he clings to memories
of protecting his sister:

> *Down deep inside her lived my secret picture of myself—a*
> *strong good me tied to the memory of those horses and the*
> *burial of a stranger. Guarding her, finding a way through*
> *tall grass and out of that place, not being afraid of any-*
> *thing—snakes or wild old men. I wonder if succeeding at*
> *that was the buried seed of all the rest. In my little-boy heart*
> *I felt heroic and I knew that if they found us or touched*
> *her I would kill.* (104)

All of Morrison's successful male journeys entail incorporating the
feminine into the masculine. Finding a "home in this place" means
being smart about locating, then letting go of some brutal aspects
of the male self to accommodate the female and contain the killer
within (*Nobel Lecture* 28). Caring for a woman helps Milkman
Dead discover that "If you surrendered to the air, you could ride
it" (*Song of Solomon* 363); his experiences with othermothering
allow Frank Money to understand that being "*Hurt right down*
the middle" can keep you "*alive and well*" (*Home* 147).

Assuming responsibility for his sister, then, readies the brother
to approach personhood, a paradox Morrison offers in her 1993
Nobel Lecture in Literature when children ask an old griot, "Tell
us what it is to be a woman so we may know what it is to be a

man" (28). The final leg of Frank's odyssey to regeneration lets
him live out such truths. Informing the diversity of folk in Booker's
diner that he expresses an amalgamation of "Korea, Kentucky,
San Diego, Seattle, Georgia," Frank, nonetheless, has a few more
manifestations of black American masculinity to encounter and
merge with the mother's heritage before he can truly rescue Cee and
reconsider home (28). Significant experiences include discriminating
among laymen and clergy, trusting doubting Thomas, pummeling
a big pimp for personal joy, fending off in-training hoodlums, ap-
preciating the tragi-comedy of a still-drumming drummer, facing
down Frankenstein, and burying the living dead.

Morrison affirms this first black male signature (the centrality of
its church to the African American community) when Frank, trying
to focus on feeling nothing in order to escape the morphine sleep
of a Seattle, Washington, psychiatric ward and liberate Cee from
Beauregard Scott, absconds to the parsonage next to tiny AME
Zion for instruction. Reserving his blisteringly forthright condescension for a hopelessly racist American culture, Reverend John
Locke feeds and clothes the impossibly beleaguered product of a
miserably integrated military out of "the poor box," then drives
Frank to the bus station and directs him to the next stop on his
aboveground railroad (16). Pastor of a Baptist church in Portland,
Oregon, Reverend Jesse Maynard is as artfully class-conscious
about sanctioning segregation as communally-minded John Locke
is openly cynical about social revolution. If Locke's outspoken
sarcasm stabs savagely at doctors who "need to work on the dead
poor so they can help the live rich," Maynard displays silent but
glacial contempt toward a young, hale, but improperly clothed
veteran as "insult tax" for providing him (un)helpful information
copied from *The Negro Travelers' Green Book* (12, 22). Maynard's
reliance on this travel guide series published from 1936 to 1964 by
Victor H. Green exposes the minister's snobbery. Its information
useless to the needy with no money, the *Green Book* was intended
to provide African American motorists and tourists with the information necessary to board, dine, and sightsee comfortably and
safely during the era of segregation. While both sorts of clergymen
ultimately help with hand-outs, it is laid-off Chicago layman Billy
Watson who gives most liberally of himself because Jesus "did

that" (31). Learning that black preachers often reveal imperfect personal biases in their attempts to maintain supplicants, Frank discovers that even the church does not always make the man.

He does come to trust Doubting Thomas, however, when Billy's son Thomas confirms that black manhood depends a great deal upon mental readiness. Invited into the Watsons' Chicago home to meet the family and stay over, Frank notices the little boy lifting his left arm to shake hands, the right one limp by his side. Forced to relinquish carrying cap-pistols from the age of eight, his damaged arm a consequence of "Drive-by cop," Thomas has since invested his considerable talent into math competitions and reading books. If Frank initially laughs at the impudence of a bright eleven-year-old who assures him that he's good at everything and intends to go deep as well as far, Frank becomes embarrassed at the disabled child's response to Frank's attempt to dispense humility by asking "What sport you play?" Although Thomas accompanies his cold look with the perceptive observation that Frank should not drink, Thomas freely gives up his bedroom after approving Frank's reaction to having killed during the war: "'That's good. That it made you feel bad. I'm glad.' 'How come?' 'It means you're not a liar.'" Receiving an unreserved smile from freethinking Thomas when Frank concedes that the boy will, indeed, go deep, Frank learns a truth riveted in real childhood pain from the adult's tired question about what the child wants to be when he grows up: "Thomas turned the knob with his left hand and opened the door. 'A man,' he said and left" (32-33). Thomas, too, is working hard at turning his racially triggered handicap into masculine strength.

Sometimes, however, a metaphorical guardsman simply must get physical. Refusing to take the southbound bus because black porters provide sustenance on trains, Frank completes his experiences in Chicago with a breakfast cooked for the three males by Billy while Arlene Watson sleeps off the effects of her night shift. Then both men walk Thomas to school, after which the laid-off steelworker sacrifices possible daywork for Goodwill shopping with Frank. Proud enough of his new used attire to pin his army medal to his breast pocket, Frank—and Billy—are prevented police shakedown only when respect for Frank's service medal restrains marauding white officers.

Although this racial targeting may not have been worth comment, Frank does get down and dirty with a mean country boy during the rail ride home. Because Frank can now recall every detail of his painful wartime memories without being paralyzed, he actually enjoys some physical combat practice when the Georgian streamliner is forced to stop for repairs outside Chattanooga. Glared at when he winks at a shop woman in a wheelchair, he crosses the road to drink his Dr. Pepper and admire a flashy Cadillac. Hearing squeals from behind a rickety house that prompt expectations of a male aggressor showing off, Frank goes to find two females roiling dirt, watched over by a big man with bored eyes. When the flat-eyed man shoves Frank's chest, Frank gets ugly. Felling him with one swing, "Smart" Money punches him insensible, eager to shove the man's toothpick down his throat: "The thrill that came with each blow was wonderfully familiar. Unable to stop and unwilling to, Frank kept going even though the big man was unconscious. The women stopped clawing each other and pulled at Frank's collar." As two battered women try to revive their pimp, Frank ponders his rage "personal in its delight" unlike any emotion that accompanied killing in Korea. He stores away the memory, since he "might need that thrill to claim his sister" (101-102). Once again Morrison emphasizes that American culture aligns black men with violence while making those battered men feel responsible for protecting against violence, whether they locate themselves in James Dickey's redneck country of nine-fingered people or the inner city.

Black male city life in the South comes with its own set of physical challenges. Because, unlike Chicago, Atlanta's urban pace provides more time "to instruct one another, pray for one another, and chastise children in the pews of a hundred churches," Frank drops his guard. His amused affection causes him to miss "that reefer and gasoline smell, the rapid sneaker tread as well as the gang breath—the odor of scared children depending on group bravery. Not military but playground" (106). The gangsters-in-training get the better of him, although he breaks a few of their bones. Without the intercession of a ponytailed silhouette, he would have no means of summoning an independent Über. Here Morrison continues to contrast what she calls helpful "walking men" with more antagonistic male drivers. Unlike the midnight-walking, soft-talking Good Samaritan who anonymously stuffs some dollar bills in Frank's front pocket, one kind of paid driving aid is less concerned about helping Frank take a failing Cee home than about bloodstains on the back seat of his car; another driver fails to show up at all. As Morrison notes eloquently in *Jazz*, a black man must be both nurturing and guarded in the city: "Hospitality is gold in this City; you have to be clever to figure out how to be welcoming and defensive at the same time. When to love something and when to quit. If you don't know how, you can end up out of control or controlled by some outside thing" (9).

Home celebrates black masculinity as a balance between the masculine and the feminine that makes possible successful masculine othermothering. Staying alive on battlegrounds, civilian or military, requires the nurturing black male not only to stay connected to his church, to stay fit both mentally and physically, but to preserve his sustaining creative outlets because the strain from either warzone can get to be too much. Nursing his broken head, convinced now that Lily has merely "displaced his disorder, his rage and his shame" and has numbed him to emotional baggage, Frank wanders into a jazz club when he hears a trumpet's screech that matches his mood (108). Having insisted more than once that the novel must replace co-opted music in providing the black community with survival instruction, Morrison creates a tragi-comic scene that depicts the essential disruptions among African American sounds and the potent defensiveness of a sense of humour.

Frank Money prefers "bebop to blues and happy-making love songs" because "after Hiroshima, the musicians understood as early as anyone that Truman's bomb changed everything and only scat and bebop could say how." A dozen people crowd inside the smoke-filled room to listen intently to a trumpet, piano, and drums trying to say just how. Although the pianist and trumpeter, slick with sweat, are able to suspend the seemingly never-ending story, the drummer keeps on drumming. Finally recognizing that he is not going to stop, that having lost control "the rhythm was in charge," his comrades lift him from his seat and take him away, "his sticks moving to a beat both intricate and silent" (108-109). After the listeners clap their respect and sympathy, a female singer breaks into a scat that cheers everybody up until the joint empties and Frank boards the bus to a beautiful, chic, still uptown district of 1950s Atlanta.

As with our reaction to the still-drumming drummer who doesn't know when to stop, we do not know whether to laugh or cry when we meet the Buckhead Scotts. A strangely obnoxious mixture of *Beloved*'s (un)Enlightened schoolteacher and its Scots Quaker radical, Edward Bodwin, Dr. Beauregard Scott keeps his own counsel in the "large two-story house rising above a church-neat lawn" bought with Mrs. Beauregard Scott's money (58). Like *Beloved*'s depictions of pretentious white intellectuals, tropes of thick heads and unbending fronts signify *Home*'s most inflated male ego. Morrison describes her latest antisocial Scotsman[12] as a "small man with lots of silver hair," sitting "stiffly [in his home office] behind a wide neat desk." His camouflage of a kind doctor disguises a fanatically racist eugenics researcher similar to starchily collared schoolteacher and masks a vain misogynist who fancies himself a feisty champion of knightly causes like Brother Bodwin. Having survived by tiptoeing carefully around the potentially more powerful women whose voices he has, so far, succeeded in stifling (in short his peignoir-wearing, laudanum-loving lady of the manor, who never leaves it, and his two hydrocephalic daughters whom he has institutionalized for their swollen heads), another would-be Confederate warrior happily cripples women to honour his chivalric ideals. Self-righteous Dr. Scott relies on his "heavyweight Confederate" heritage and a locked but fully stocked bomb shelter to safeguard his righteous self-image (62-64). His darkly comic white male story represents all the sexism, racism, and classism Morrison's black othermothers struggle against.

Savagely satiric touches heighten the horror behind Dr. Beau's laboratory and the tragic results of disallowing the feminine. Morrison encapsulates Mrs. Scott's puerile, self-destructive essence, as well as the stout cook Sarah's benignly sturdy nature, with brief but emphatically ironic details. Called upon to care for all her finicky employer's needs, Sarah Williams explains Mrs. Scott as having a "tiny" laudanum craving. Aside from dabbling in delicate watercolours of flowers, the lady of the house spends her time watching the family-oriented television shows so popular in the fifties. Contemporary scholarship cautions us against turning the socially whitewashed 1950s into this sort of "nostalgia trap." With research that contributes significantly to the current debate on family values, sociologist Stephanie Coontz cuts through the kind of sentimental, ahistorical thinking that has created unrealistic expectations of the ideal family as she illustrates how "these myths distort the diverse experiences of other groups in America" and argues that they "don't even describe most white, middle-class families accurately" (6).[13] They certainly do not account for the masculine othermother.

When Frank spots the MD sign on the Buckhead lawn and is directed downstairs by Sarah, he trusts that learned instinct will balance violence with caution because he "couldn't let things get so out of control that it would endanger Cee." Responding to Beauregard Scott's threat to call the police by knocking the telephone from his hand, Frank calmly notes the kind of gun the slighter man pulls out of his desk drawer: "A .38. ... Clean and light. But the hand that held it shook." Scott points the pistol at what "in his fear ought to have been flaring nostrils, foaming lips, and the red-rimmed eyes of a savage. Instead he saw the quiet, even serene, face of a man not to be fooled with." After Scott pulls the trigger on an empty chamber, he runs for another phone but comes up short against Sarah purposefully pressing down its cradle while she locks his gaze "in an undecipherable stare" (109-112). Allied with a grounded female and restrained by his role as masculine othermother, Frank Money quickly and soundlessly gets his sister out of Beauregard Scott's big house.

Scott's Confederate cowardice is clear—as are Morrison's double entendres. Relieved by the absence of violence or theft (to Scott's mind merely the kidnapping of an easily replaceable employee), the royally white sham with no shame (or sexual potency) turns his aggression toward yet another black woman, one whom, since Sarah looks after his wife, he dares not dismiss yet, although he warns his cook not to overplay her hand. Dedicating his skills to racism, exposed as a henpecked husband, Morrison's great scientist grows fearful that Frank(enstein) is savage.[14] Like previous *Beloved* fanatics, the good doctor's insecurities about white male supremacy and his fear of women transform him into a monster. Although Beau Scott feels threatened as soon as Smart

Money walks in the door, Smart experiences the satisfaction of nonviolence: "not having to beat up the enemy to get what he wanted was somehow superior—sort of, well, smart" (114)—a huge step forward in the evolution of a competent masculine othermother.

Unlike his enemy, Frank's love for the feminine contains the monster. The most important lesson Smart Money absorbs from othermothering is the possibility of redemption by way of tough love defined as unmotivated respect. Truly rescuing Cee means rejecting anaconda love to embrace self- and othermothering so both Moneys can bury the living dead. "Country women who loved mean" and Cee herself help Frank see (121). After medicinal herbs help her recover from vaginal infection caused by Dr. Beau's experiments with specula and she undergoes the humility of being "sun-smacked," daily exposing the most vulnerable parts of her body to Mother Nature during one of the most defenseless times of her life, Cee develops a resolution and independence to rival that of the Lotus women with seen-it-all eyes. When Miss Ethel Fordham tells her that her "womb can never bear fruit," the woman passes along this news without sorrow or alarm, "as though she'd examined a Burpee seedling overcome by marauding rabbits" (128). Having to learn to feel anger, Cee must also come to accept her sterility and somehow keep on living. Because she learns to quilt and because she outright rejects her brother's pity, he can let his protective guard down in a good way, as he knows that she can fend for herself: Frank "had literally saved her life, but she neither missed nor wanted his fingers at the nape of her neck, telling her not to cry, that everything would be all right." Because Cee is "not going to hide from what's true just because it hurts," neither can Frank (131).[15] In this way, she figuratively saves his life, and he locates a more effective way to othermother from the others he is mothering.

Initially conflicted, Frank finally feels proud of women who rescue men (26, 69). Having managed to disengage Ycidra trembling under his arm, he now has only the memories of the horses and a man's foot left to weigh. The foot comes back to life as a mindful zombie. Initially skeptical, Frank ultimately permits a ghost's blue zoot-suit to extricate his personal shame and free him to othermother. Morrison calls on her readers to determine the history of this iconic dress, associated as it has been with power, danger, and the exotic, and with historically specific clashes between people of colour and white racists: "It had been enough of a fashion statement to interest riot cops on each coast" (34). *Home*'s sightings disclose a diminutive man wearing a style exaggerated and aggressive enough to act as signals of manhood that invite Smart Money's questions about what it means to be a man.

Juda Bennett argues that the blue-suited figure unveils a sartorial performance of masculinity, even as it resists sexual and political labels by remaining a cipher of gender, in this case a ghost. Because Frank no longer sees the ghost by the end of the novel, while it appears to Cee for the first time, Morrison ensures that her hero's journey emphasizes both genders yet simultaneously exposes gender itself as a constructed fiction. When Cee thinks that she sees a "small man in a funny suit swinging a watch chain. And grinning," we trust that a man's humanity has been restored, especially since his bones are carefully arranged in Cee's multi-coloured quilt so that he is interred upright and Frank's sanded wooden marker provides the tribute: "Here Stands A Man" (145). However, when we connect the grinning, watch-swinging ghost to Father Time, note its petite size and voicelessness, and confirm that Frank's perspective conflates the sacrificing black father, the sacrificed Korean child, and Cee's never-to-be-born daughter into one figure, we may read the zoot-suited zombie as the "transgendered manifestation of the Korean girl" (Bennett 158). His and her story, as relayed by the old black men on Fish Eye's porch, tells that tale.

Reinventing *Invisible Man's* Battle Royal and anticipating a brutal scene depicted in the film *Django Unchained* (2012), Morrison recaptures Frank's past via his memories of "*horses, a man's foot, and Ycidra trembling under [his] arm*" (68-69). The old uncles help him to remember the buried foot as Frank imagines white men at the stud farm where the horses stood like men abducting a black father and son, gambling on them to fight to the death. Instead of egregious violence, however, Morrison focuses on the psychological scarring of the participants. When the father commands his son to commit patricide, saying "Obey me, son, this one last time" and the son says "I can't take your life," the father rejoins: "This ain't life" (139). Despite that being "a devil's decision-making. Any way you decide is a sure trip to his hell," the son does it—and local blacks have to lead him out on a mule. Fish Eye informs Frank that the stallions he and Cee saw as children were sold to the slaughterhouse.

With her royal battle, Morrison finds the "heroism in a father's sacrifice, transforming him from passive victim to agent of his and his son's destiny." Like Sethe's hard choice in *Beloved*, "the father refuses to let the white racists wrest agency from him," and his becomes a ghost to be reckoned with (Bennett 153). Morrison puts her Moneys where her mouth is: "The purpose of education is to distill facts into wisdom" ("Toni Morrison Senior Day Address"). No longer mere witnesses of a single quivering, pink-coloured sole (soul) sticking up like an Achilles heel to suggest live burial, a brother and a sister act to honour the man and the home which have haunted both. [16]

His education into othermothering bequeaths Frank Money the wisdom to exchange commemorations of brutal studs for glimpses of a blasted but still thriving sweet bay tree. He will need more time to dislodge the hook of shame buried deep inside his chest at having violated the Korean girl, but in the meantime, there is worthwhile work to do. Putting the sister's story beside that of the brother renders *Home* Morrison's tribute to the black collective. If Cee reluctantly allows Frank to take her hand this time, guiding her over rough territory to the place of the bones, this time the sister refuses to cringe or close her eyes when she sees "the gentleman's" skull. After Frank carries his burden in his arms to place him gently beneath the undead sweet bay tree, it is Cee who hands Frank the shovel, touches his shoulder lightly, and says, "*Come on, brother. Let's go home*" (142-147).

Morrison's *Home* insists at last that while mothering by either gender may not be innate, it can become natural. When I forwarded an earlier draft of this essay to my friend Juda Bennett, author of *Toni Morrison and the Queer Pleasure of Ghosts* and sixty-something-year-old parent of a six-year-old daughter, Juda's reply was touchingly breath-taking. I hope that its revelations about masculine othermothering will mitigate my lack of modesty:

Hi,

Well, I do not have a second to read your essay because my partner is out of town and so I am a single parent this week for our six year old. I also can't do it because we are moving this week to a house that needs five contractors to come in the next week. And I also can't read it because I am on a Dean's search on campus and I have sixty applications to read....

BUT I read it because I made the mistake of reading your opening. How could I not read AND love this essay? I think it is important. I love every word of it: 1) the reference to Coontz, who we brought in for Women's History Month a few years ago 2) the playful wordplay on putting Moneys where mouth is 3) and mostly the important exploration of othermothering, which certainly speaks to this father

I love this and please tell me where it is going to appear. I think you write essays that make a difference, and I understand why Morrison wrote that letter to you. This is an essay that I wish I had written.

I am dashing this off without proofreading because I have a six year old pulling on my sleeve and I know you will understand. Last words: LOVE IT!

Juda

I was especially delighted to learn that not only did I not offend or disappoint somebody else by sharing my most recent pronouncement about the gender and racial complexities of mother love and the process of maternal attachment, but that, by means of our shared love for Toni Morrison's work, I bonded with a gay male othermother, who is clearly also working out how much is too much—or is not enough—and who is trying his best to know when to stop.

ENDNOTES

[1]O'Reilly specifically mentions Sethe and Baby Suggs; Violet and Alice. I would add the Convent women; L and the Cosey women; Rebekka and Lina; the Lotus women and Cee; Bride and Queen.

[2]See *Playing in the Dark: Whiteness and the Literary Imagination* for Morrison's theories about the formation of American (white) male identity.

[3]See promotional blubs for the 2013 Vintage paperback edition of *Home*.

[4]See Mayberry, *Can't I Love What I Criticize? The Masculine and Morrison* (2007).

[5]Joseph Campbell's seminal work on the similarities among cultural story patterns, *The Hero with a Thousand Faces*, includes the worldwide myth in which the boy travels through three family systems and then into the fourth and fifth realms of strange kingdoms and the nonliving as he is initiated into manhood. He learns that no matter where the hero goes to prove himself, he finds himself back home.

[6]Morrison uses italics to distinguish and emphasize Frank Money's interior monologue.

[7]The name of Frank's hometown represents one of *Home's* many allusions to Homer's *Odyssey*. The lotus-eaters of Greek mythology were a race of people living on an island near North Africa where the primary food source, narcotic lotus fruits and flowers, caused the island people to sleep in continuous, peaceful apathy. Having eaten the delicious but mind-numbing lotus in *The Odyssey* IX, Odysseus's men refuse to return to their domestic duties. Morrison's rendition of a modern black Odysseus, Frank confesses that only his sister in serious trouble could compel him to overcome his dread of returning to Lotus; he regards his attachment to Lily as "medicinal, like swallowing aspirin" (84, 107). Recent studies suggest that the blue water-lily of the Nile, already known to the Greeks as the blue lotus, was used as a soporific and in some processes took on psychotropic properties.

[8]Once more Morrison has some fun with name games in *Home*. If characters enjoy teasing "Smart" Money, who has none, about his nickname, readers understand that Frank's perception of the material puts people before things. We also appreciate Salem, biblical for "perfect peace," fantasizing like Poe's speaker in "The Raven" about forgetting Lenore forever.

[9]Morrison's first sympathetic portrait of a pedophile is not Frank Money, but Bill Cosey in *Love*. Both men suffer guilt over the

reverberations from laughing at a little girl "Raggedy as Lazarus" (*Love* 45).

[10]Morrison prepares us for this paradox in *Tar Baby* when two-year-old Michael, deliberately pinpricked by his mother, is found crouched singing to himself in the cabinet under his father's bathroom sink. Searching in the dark for something soft, he continues as an adult to prefer his mother and disappoint his father.

[11]Since "coon" is a well-known Southern epithet for a black person, the old men challenge Milkman with a means to comprehend the intrinsic nature of his community and himself. Coon or snipe hunting occurs as a night game during which sophisticated players take the uninitiated "out there" on a wild-goose chase to locate the prey that turns out to be themselves. The object involves a lesson in woodsman's skills or "street smarts."

[12]Morrison's name for *Beloved's* "Bodwin" recalls the urban insult for an egghead who has no social life.

[13]*The Way We Never Were* concludes that "there is no one family form that has ever protected people from poverty or social disruption, and no traditional arrangement that provides a workable model for how we might organize family relations in the modern world" (5).

[14]After carefully asking Cee where she was born; if she has children, is married, or belongs to a church congregation that jumps around, the belle with Daisy Buchanan's kind of money but a "voice ... like music" cavalierly informs her non-comprehending applicant: "I don't really understand my husband's work—or care to. He is more than a doctor; he is a scientist and conducts very important experiments. His inventions help people. He's no Dr. Frankenstein" (59-60). In case we miss the significance of that offhand allusion to Mary Shelley's researcher, or Cee's bewildered "Dr. who?", Morrison reemphasizes twice more that Dr. Beau applies for patents to control his inventions.

[15]In an interview titled "I Want to Feel What I Feel. Even If It's Not Happiness," Morrison does not flinch from questions about being a single mother, the death of her son, and why love doesn't last.

[16]Bennett argues that this scene-stealing character is "the most important ghost of Morison's career, in being born from the author's greatest loss [of Slade]" and that "this figure—as much as the

protagonist—gives meaning to the title of the novel, tying issues of visibility to a radical refashioning of the idea of home" (148-149).

WORKS CITED

Awkward, Michael. "Black Feminism and the Challenge of Black Heterosexual Male Desire." *Souls*, vol. 2, no. 4, Fall 2000, pp. 32-37.

Bennett, Juda. *Toni Morrison and the Queer Pleasure of Ghosts.* SUNY Press, 2014.

Brockes, Emma. "Toni Morrison: 'I Want to Feel What I Feel. Even If It's Not Happiness.'" *The Guardian*, 13 Apr. 2012, http://www.theguardian.com/books/2012/apr/13/toni-morrison-home-son-love. Accessed 21 May 2017.

Campbell, Joseph. *The Hero with a Thousand Faces*. 1949. Bollingen Series XVII, Princeton University Press, 1969.

Collins, Patricia Hill. "The Meaning of Motherhood in Black Culture and Black Mother-Daughter Friendships." *Double Stitch: Black Women Write About Mothers and Daughters*, edited by Patricia Bell-Scott et al., HarperPerennial, 1993, pp. 42-60.

Coontz, Stephanie. *The Way We Never Were: American Families and the Nostalgia Trap*. Basic Books, 1992.

Edwards, Arlene. "Community Mothering: The Relationship Between Mothering and the Community Work of Black Women." *Journal of The Association for Research on Mothering*, vol. 2, no. 2, Fall/Winter 2000, pp. 66-84.

hooks, bell. "Revolutionary Parenting." *Feminist Theory: From Margin to Center*. South End, 1984, pp. 133-147.

James, Stanlie. "Mothering: A Possible Black Feminist Link to Social Transformations." *Theorizing Black Feminism: The Visionary Pragmatism of Black Women*, edited by Stanlie James and A. P. Busia, Routledge, 1999, pp. 44-54.

Jenkins, Nina. "Black Women and the Meaning of Motherhood." *Redefining Motherhood: Changing Patterns and Identities*, edited by Sharon Abbey and Andrea O'Reilly, Second Story, 1998, pp. 201-213.

Mayberry, Susan Neal. *Can't I Love What I Criticize? The Masculine and Morrison*. University of Georgia Press, 2007.

Morrison, Toni. *Beloved*. 1987. Knopf, 1988.

Morrison, Toni. *Home*. 2012. Vintage International, 2013.

Morrison, Toni. *Jazz*. Knopf, 1982.

Morrison, Toni. *Love*. Knopf, 2003.

Morrison, Toni. *The Nobel Lecture in Literature*. 1993. Knopf, 2002.

Morrison, Toni. *Paradise*. 1997. Plume, 1999.

Morrison, Toni. *Playing in the Dark: Whiteness and the Literary Imagination*. 1990. Vintage, 1993.

Morrison, Toni. *Song of Solomon*. 1977. Everyman's Library, 1995.

Morrison, Toni. "Toni Morrison Senior Day Address." Vanderbilt, 8 May 2013, http://news.vanderbilt.edu/2013/05/senior-day-video-2013/. Accessed 21 May 2017.

Moyers, Bill. "Toni Morrison: A Writer's Work." *The Moyers Collection: A World of Ideas*. Films for the Humanities and Sciences, 1994.

O'Reilly, Andrea. *Toni Morrison and Motherhood: A Politics of the Heart*. SUNY Press, 2004.

Spillers, Hortense J. "Mama's Baby, Papa's Maybe: An American Grammar Book." *Diacritics*, vol. 17, no. 2, Summer 1987, pp. 65-81.

Wane, Njoki Nathani. "Reflections on the Mutuality of Mothering: Women, Children, and Othermothering." *Journal of The Association for Research on Mothering*, vol. 2, no. 2, Fall/Winter 2000, pp. 105-116.

"Not a Maternal Drudge ... Nor ... an Acid-Tongued Shrew"

The Complexity of Ruth and Pilate in Toni Morrison's *Song of Solomon*

JILL GOAD

IN TONI MORRISON'S *SONG OF SOLOMON*, the narrative is centred on a male protagonist, Milkman. Although Milkman is the focal character, he is not necessarily the most important, compelling, or dynamic, particularly in comparison to two women integral to the novel: Milkman's mother, Ruth, and his aunt, Pilate. Whereas Pilate has often been positively analyzed by critics for her connection to the past and resistance to material pursuits, Ruth is often critiqued for wanting money and status and remaining constrained by her father, husband, and son. Soophia Ahmad, for example, represents the general critical review of Ruth by indicting her meaningless life of privilege, which she does not use to better herself or her community (60). Gerry Brenner sees Ruth as undeserving of praise because her defining quality is obedience (103). Ahmad's contrasting perception of Pilate also represents this character's general critical reception; Pilate loves life and herself, and she has positive connections with both her past and culture (66). Brenner concurs that Pilate is characterized with "celebratory prose" (104). Although Ruth and Pilate possess opposing qualities, they are linked by simplistic critical treatment. Both women are often analyzed solely for their contributions to Milkman's growth instead of classified as characters whose roles in his changed perceptions are part of their identities, not the sole shaping force behind them. Additionally, Ruth and Pilate appear to be stereo-typical women characters. Through her connection to Milkman, Ruth embodies the Oedipal mother who, in Freudian theory, lives through and for her son and has no sense of self. The Freudian dyad Ruth and her father exist in, where she worships his power and he repudiates her powerlessness, is the basis for her status as Oedipal mother and obedient wife. Pilate's qualities render her the stereotypical matriarch, a term devised by Patricia Hill Collins to denote a black woman who does not adhere to traditional notions of femininity. The matriarch stereotype has emerged from dominant ideology as a means to blame black women for societal ills, such as fatherless homes and crime. I argue that Morrison uses Ruth's and Pilate's relationships with the men in their family, as well as their seemingly stereotypical characterizations, to interrogate the broader stereotypes and cultural perceptions they represent.

Ruth Dead favours Milkman over his sisters. She holds him up as a symbol of hope and family endurance, not seeing him as a separate, autonomous human in the process. Milkman is despicable for his dehumanization of Ruth, alternately scorning and ignoring his mother, but, arguably, it is her suffocating love and seeming desire to possess him that drive him away. Ruth breastfeeds her son long after it is considered appropriate, and she clings to him, as he represents for her the last sexual connection that she had with her husband. This characterization of Ruth initially renders her the stereotypical Oedipal mother, whose life is focused only on her male child as a means to compensate for her lack of power. The Oedipal mother—whose lack makes it impossible for the male child to see her as an autonomous figure— must be repudiated in order for the child to develop. The inclusion of Ruth's history, particularly the treatment of her by her husband and father, complicates her characterization. She cannot simply be seen as a platform for her child's development but as an example of the way mothers are expected to sacrifice themselves for their children. Ruth also represents the way women may be overshadowed by the powerful male figures in their lives.

Pilate is the other woman who made Milkman's existence possible. She cares for her nephew, but she is realistically cynical about receiving affection or acknowledgment in return. Pilate's ability to step back from Milkman, love him, and teach him how to move through the world without coddling him makes her the woman closest to him. However, Pilate's "overly aggressive, unfeminine" (Hill Collins 75) persona and her inability to sustain a romantic relationship with any man initially classify her as the matriarch, a black female archetype. The matriarch is a "failed mammy" (Hill Collins 75) because she is not a nurturer in the traditional sense of existing only to take care of her husband and children. In contrast to the mammy, the matriarch is not deferential to those who hold power over her. Pilate elicits Milkman's disdain and fear, feelings also embodied in her community, but she ultimately earns his love and respect long after she deserves it. Pilate's history creates a more sympathetic and complex portrait of her. Morrison's characterization of Pilate speaks to societal judgments of women who do not fit a traditional mother and wife mould.

Although Ruth's relationship to Milkman echoes the Oedipal complex, her behaviour may be traced to her relationship to her father, Dr. Foster. Jessica Benjamin's intersubjective theory, based on Freudian theory, notes all fathers choose their sons over their daughters: "The father recognizes himself in his son, sees him as the ideal boy he would have been; so identificatory love plays its part on the parent's side from the beginning" (109). The father can see himself in the son but cannot achieve recognition with a powerless, lacking woman—a dynamic reflected in the relationship between Ruth and her father. Ruth once saw Dr. Foster as the only person she needed, as her only friend, but acknowledges in adulthood that "He was not a good man ... he was an arrogant man, and often a foolish and destructive man" (124). Although the adult Ruth upholds her father as "the only person who ever really cared if I lived or died" (124), Dr. Foster may have only enjoyed her company because of the hero worship it provided him. He never encourages her to follow in his professional footsteps or pursue her economic independence. She is simply expected to marry and produce light-skinned children who do not resemble in colour or replicate the socioeconomic status of the "cannibals," as Dr. Foster refers to the black community in their town.

According to Freud, part of a child becoming independent is to reject the mother and the phallic lack she represents, in favour of the father and his phallic possession in order to become feminine (Benjamin 87). Lacan expands on Freud's argument by explaining the significance of the phallus: "[it] ... represents an illusion of wholeness and self-sufficiency" (qtd. in Sprengnether 197). The girl is drawn to this illusion to make up for her newly realized lack. Ruth's feelings toward her father reflect her search for wholeness. "I was small, but he was big" is what she tells Milkman to explain her childhood worship of Dr. Foster (124). Rolland Murray sees Ruth as "obsessed with the ... symbols of her father's authority" and "invest[ed] in her father's symbolic authority" (124). Ruth spends her childhood and young adulthood only wanting "to be in his presence, among his things, the things he used, had touched" (124). Dr. Foster and his possessions, which represent his wealth and power, draw Ruth in with the promise that contact can compensate for her lack. After marrying Macon Dead, Ruth continues to see her father as the only person who truly cares for her, which leads her in Macon's mind to consistently take her father's side against his. While Dr. Foster lies dying in his bed, Ruth fights to keep him alive long after his desire to live turns to "absolute hatred of this woman who would not grant him peace" (124). Furthermore, after her father's death, Ruth visits his grave to communicate with him. Ruth feels "fierce in the presence of death, heroic even, as she was at no other time. Its threat gave her direction, clarity, audacity" (64). Although Ruth loves her father, it is only when he is "small" in sickness and death that she can reverse their relationship and feel "big."

To further reinforce her position in a Freudian dynamic, Ruth keeps her son trapped in the Oedipus complex by breastfeeding him long after infancy. To maintain her connection with Milkman, Ruth hinders his ability to acquire his own identity separate from hers. In Freudian theory, when the little boy turns away from the Oedipus complex to develop, "object-cathexes are given up and replaced by identifications" (Freud 664). The original love-object, the mother's breast, has long been withdrawn, and the mother as love-object must be given up to make way for identification with the father or mother. By prolonging breastfeeding to maintain the mother-son connection, Ruth keeps Milkman in a state of arrested development and dependency, limiting his progression as heir to the Dead legacy. Ruth's desire to keep her son in a perpetual pre-Oedipal state means that "her son had never been a person to her, a separate real person. He had always been a passion" (131). For Ruth, her son represents not only proof that someone once wanted to touch her but also her triumph against her husband, Macon, who pressured her to abort her son. Milkman is her safe harbour from a loveless marriage and lack of companionship, and a link to her husband, though a conflicted one: "she regarded [Milkman] as a beautiful toy, a respite, a distraction, a physical pleasure as she nursed him ... he became a plain on which, like the cowboys and Indians in the movies, she and her husband fought" (132). Ruth can only earn violent recognition from Macon, so she looks to her son to see her lovingly. However, Ruth's rendering of Milkman as a symbol rather than a person ensures that he will reciprocate in kind.

For Ruth, Milkman "was first off a wished-for bond between herself and Macon, something to hold them together and reinstate their sex lives" (131). When this reinstatement does not occur, Ruth turns to her child for the closeness that she needs. Valerie Smith contends that "after she [Ruth] realizes that her husband will never again gratify her sexually, she uses Milkman to fulfill her yearnings" (35). As the Oedipal mother, however, Ruth may have other internalized motives for trying to maintain the lack of differentiation between her and her child. "For the woman the baby is a substitute for the missed penis" (Mitchell 7), and the male child promises a sense of fulfillment to the mother. Freud argues that mothers are under pressure to suppress their ambition, so they transfer it to their sons. As a result, what remains of the mother's masculinity complex can be satisfied (Sprengnether 84). Murray concurs that Ruth's extended breastfeeding is an attempt to achieve autonomy in her husband's oppressive house (128). Just as Ruth wants to be near her father's "bigness" despite her staying "small," she places all of her hopes for the future into her male child—something she does not do with her two daughters, whom she simply hopes will marry well.

The way the men in her life, Milkman and Macon, regard Ruth brings into sharp relief the idea that she is more than a symbolic figure. Instead, she has been worn down by being treated as an object. Macon and Milkman expect Ruth to fulfill supportive roles without wanting affection or attention in return. Moreover, they think nothing of discarding her when she does not behave in ways that fit their image and expectations of a wife and/or mother. In fact, the men see Ruth as "a silly, selfish, queer, faintly obscene woman" (123) of no consequence. Over time, their neglect erodes her sense of self; Ruth says of herself, "'I am not a strange woman. I am a small one'" (124). This statement mirrors the same feeling imposed upon her by her father.

Dr. Foster's "bigness" is the primary reason Macon wants to marry Ruth. Anticipating a business connection with the doctor, Macon sees Ruth as a means to gaining wealth and increasing his social status; for him, she is not as an autonomous individual. He also views Ruth's deference to her father as indicative of her subsequent obedience as a wife. Ruth's light skin and family name, both status symbols, ensures respect for Macon from the black community. When Ruth and Macon are married, his "hatred of his wife glittered and sparked in every word he spoke to her" (10). He cannot forgive her for picking her father over him and for tricking him into impregnating her. Macon sees himself as successful despite her. To Macon, Ruth's strangeness, which includes her clinginess with male family members and her social isolation, is a source of shame. Macon feels that his strict and hard-driving businesses approach compensate for Ruth's reputation and maintain his respect by the black community. However, Ruth's odd qualities result, in part, from Macon forbidding her from socializing with anyone he deems inferior, which encompasses every black family in their town. He also isolates her by barely acknowledging her presence, causing her to seek comfort with her son and her deceased father.

Macon has long denied Ruth intimacy and respect. He stops having sexual intercourse with her when she is twenty and withholds from her any closeness, which makes her wonder if she can endure her life. Ruth tells Milkman, "by the time I was thirty ... I think I was just afraid I'd die that way" (125)—unloved and with no physical contact. Macon tries to excuse the way he treats his wife by referring to the unnatural, incestuous behaviour he supposedly witnesses her engage in with Dr. Foster. To poison Milkman against his mother and to justify his physical and emotional abandonment and abuse of Ruth, Macon tells his son that he saw Ruth naked in bed with her dead father, kissing him. Additionally, Macon tells Milkman that Ruth's father has delivered her babies with "her legs wide open" (71). In Macon's stories, Ruth is the disturbed woman whose childhood adoration of her father has grown into something overtly, grotesquely sexual. Because of her unnatural behaviour, Macon argues that she does not deserve love, protection, or attention. Macon's stories of incest glaringly omit any indictment of Dr. Foster, whose paternal power would have made him culpable and Ruth the victim. Even though Macon's scapegoating of Ruth is blatantly self-serving, it has the desired effect of making Milkman see his mother as abject—"an obscene child playing dirty games with whatever male was near" (79). When Milkman remembers Ruth breastfeeding him well into childhood, he relates this memory to his father's accusations to justify emotionally abandoning his mother.

The one time that Ruth and Macon do have sex—after Pilate concocts a love potion for Ruth to give Macon—results in Milkman's conception. The intimacy quickly ends when Macon emerges from his stupor of arousal and actively tries to abort the child that he has helped create. Instead of resisting Macon's wish, Ruth injures herself. The image of her squatting over boiling water in an attempt to abort her fetus depicts the extent of her helplessness in her marriage. In this case, the disparate power dynamic between Macon and Ruth has moved from authority and obedience to abuse and quiet acquiescence.

Ruth is also seen as unimportant to her son. Through much of his life, Milkman does not hate his mother; it is more accurate to say that he does not think of her much at all, whether with concern, affection, or scorn. Joyce Wegs argues that "Milkman's rejection of … his mother … stems largely from [her] attempts to own him, to have dominion over him" (179). "Her steady beam of love was unsettling" (23) to her father, a sentiment reflected in Milkman's perception of Ruth. As Milkman reflects on the dynamic between him and Ruth, he coldly thinks the following: "He had never loved his mother, but had always known that she loved him. And that had always seemed right to him, the way it should be. Her confirmed, eternal love of him, love that he didn't even have to earn or deserve, seemed to him natural" (79). Milkman pulls away from what Ruth offers him, but he cannot imagine a life without this love, which he is never obligated to reciprocate. In effect, Ruth's nurturing is akin to smothering, but Milkman nevertheless expects and, to a certain extent, accepts her love.

The apathy Milkman has for his mother is most evident in a dream he has about her. In the dream, rapidly growing tulips slowly smother Ruth to death as she gardens, yet she smiles and fights them off as if they were "harmless butterflies," oblivious to the threat that the "bloody red heads" (105) present. Milkman, at the kitchen window, simply watches as Ruth breathes her last breath, swallowed by the flowers, which depicts, as Catherine Carr Lee argues, "his failure to accept commitment" (48). Although this scene characterizes Milkman as an emotionally disconnected son, it also speaks to Ruth's lifelong plight. From childhood to adulthood, she has lavished her attention on others, particularly the men in her life, but her nurturing allows them to flourish at her expense. So accustomed to the expectation to provide for others, Ruth has no sense of self-preservation when those whom she provides for threaten to consume her with their wants.

The only instance in which Milkman is responsive to his mother occurs when he strikes and threatens his father for hitting Ruth. However, Jan Furman believes that this is "less a display of regard for his mother's welfare than a startling instance of arrogance" (36). Milkman wants to express his masculine authority with this act by not exhibiting care; indeed, it is not "love for his mother" that makes him act against his father (75). Milkman's feeling of "righteous" (75) male egotism—it is his duty to protect those who are weaker—drives him to defend Ruth. He wants to show his family that he is in control of the conflicts that arise. In terms of the Oedipus complex, Milkman is taking the place of his father.

Milkman's defense of Ruth and the conversation that follows with Macon make him understand her more than he likely did through much of his life, but his perception of her still renders her less than a person:

> She was too insubstantial, too shadowy for love. But it was her vaporishness that made her more needful of defense. She was not a maternal drudge, her mind pressed flat, her shoulders hunched under the burden of housework and care of others, brutalized by a bear of a man. Nor was she the

acid-tongued shrew who defended herself with a vicious
vocabulary and a fast lip. Ruth was a pale but complicated
woman given to deviousness and ultra-fine manners. She
seemed to know a lot and understand very little. (75)

This description of Ruth depicts her as someone who is not a stereotype or empty symbol, not a platform for her son's development or
vessel for her husband's dissatisfaction. Instead, she is an educated,
refined woman with a rich inner life, whose external expression
has been unappreciated and suppressed by her father and her husband. Ruth represents what happens to women whose potential for
emotional and intellectual growth is stifled by dominant ideology's
intent to shelter them and place them into tightly defined roles. Her
true complexity—her values, feelings, and hopes—is suffocated by
people who never give her anything in return for her love. As Ruth
notes, her life has been a series of losses that have turned her into
"a spread-eagled footstool resigned to her fate" (132).

Pilate, Milkman's aunt, appears drastically different from Ruth
in circumstances, values, and appearance, but she is also subject
to being stereotyped. Pilate could initially be viewed as the black
matriarch defined by Patricia Hill Collins as "the 'bad' black
mother," whose aggression and lack of femininity "emasculate
[her] lovers and husbands." Because the matriarch works, her
children lack guidance and are badly behaved and unsuccessful
(75). The matriarch—an image created by dominant ideology to
blame black mothers for social problems in the black community
due to their lack of "womanliness" —is culpable in her children's
educational failures, legal trouble, and generational poverty. According to Hill Collins, "one source of the matriarch's failure is her
inability to model appropriate gender behavior" (76); too assertive
to be true women, matriarchs "are abandoned by their men, end
up impoverished, and are stigmatized as being unfeminine" (77).

Pilate's lack of femininity is evident in all facets of her life: she
has a child but no husband; she makes bootleg wine for money,
spends household money frivolously, and embraces unstructured
mealtimes catered to her family's cravings, even if that means de-
vouring nothing but bread and butter for dinner. Her hair is short,
she is taller than many men, and she wears dusty men's shoes.

Overall, she looks "odd, murky, and worst of all, unkempt" (20). Additionally, Pilate has a tendency to look directly into people's eyes when speaking to them and to never cry. Furthermore, she freely uses profanity and has no problem presenting her opinion bluntly. The black community views her as strong, powerful, and even supernatural. All of these elements classify Pilate as an atypical woman. She has had sex outside of marriage, earns money illegally, and does not take pleasure in structure and consistency. Pilate's appearance, body language, and diction all consist of stereotypically masculine characteristics.

Pilate's personal life and approach to emotion defy what is seen as typically feminine. After transitioning out of her youth, Pilate has no romantic male companionship—mainly because her missing navel frightens people—yet she harbours no resentment at this type of isolation. Although she is in touch with her history, Pilate is not given to emotional contemplation; she knows what will make her existence happy, and she tries to attain it. Her wants are simple: to spend time with her family, to provide her daughter and granddaughter with the material things they want, and to operate on her own schedule.

Pilate is viewed as having powers going beyond the abilities of a normal person, much less a woman, which further masculinizes her. That she birthed herself when her mother died in labour marks her as powerfully self-sufficient and is part of the reason why her community sees her shrouded in myth: "[Pilate] never bothered anybody, was helpful to everybody, but … was also believed to have the power to step out of her skin, set a bush afire from fifty yards, and turn a man into a ripe rutabaga" (94). Pilate's strength is further depicted when she threatens a man by holding a knife to when he attempts to hurt her daughter, Reba. According to Ruth, Pilate is the only person with power over Macon Dead. Aside from creating the potion for Macon that leads to Milkman's conception, Pilate intimidates her brother with a voodoo doll in his office after she hears that he wants to abort his child. Although Macon pretends to be unafraid, he makes sure to burn the doll until it is ashes. Even Milkman, a frequent visitor to Pilate's house, readily admits to fearing his aunt, especially after he saw her threaten violence with her knife, a phallic symbol that indicates her masculine power. Pilate also communes with her long-dead father, seeking his counsel and companionship—another aspect of her power.

The stereotypical matriarch's inability to be a role model keeps her family in poverty and ensures that they will not adhere to social mores, and Pilate's approach to household finances connects her to this archetypal figure. Dominant ideology holds the matriarch, in this case, Pilate, responsible for her family's shortcomings. Pilate's financial circumstances, the antithesis of her brother's, are based both on her lack of concern for material possessions and on the fluctuating nature of her liquor sales. When she earns money, it vanishes quickly, mostly because her daughter Reba uses it to buy gifts for her series of boyfriends and because she and Reba spoil Pilate's granddaughter, Hagar, with any possessions she wants, no matter how frivolous. As a result, Hagar does not understand that material goods will not assuage her true hunger. Hagar's spiritual emptiness as a result of Pilate's undisciplined spending is the harshest indictment against Pilate. Only Reba's luck at winning contests, which provides the family occasional food and money, keeps the three women from starving.

Pilate as matriarch is to blame for Reba and Hagar operating outside moral norms. Reba goes from boyfriend to boyfriend and is known as promiscuous, and Hagar engages in a years-long taboo sexual relationship with her cousin, which culminates in her repeated attempts to murder him when he grows bored with her. Hagar is perceived by the community as mentally unstable, and when Ruth meets her for the first time, she has the same assessment—"there was something truly askew in this girl" (138). Pilate as matriarch garners blame for Hagar's instability, believed to be the result of Reba's neglectful parenting, the product of a neglectful mother. In a show of moral laxity, Pilate does not discourage Hagar's relationship, despite being viewed by the community as distasteful. Furthermore, Pilate cannot save Hagar from her downfall as a result of her desire to look more like a white woman in order to earn Milkman's love. Hagar's shopping spree for clothes and beauty products, which drains the family's money, cannot alleviate her feelings of emptiness, and it leads to her illness and death. This final frivolous spending of household money reinforces Pilate's financial irresponsibility and stereotypical status. Nevertheless, her desire to use money to solve her family's emotional problems is a result of her deep love for her daughter and granddaughter.

Although Pilate is inherently stronger than Ruth Dead, she is subject to the same mistreatment by the men in her life: Macon and Milkman. The ill treatment, however, does not wear down or oppress her as it does Ruth, because Pilate exists far outside social norms. Whereas the two men punish Ruth for breaching the boundaries of her prescribed wife and mother role, they punish Pilate for defying their expectations of what a woman should be. Even more egregiously, although Pilate could be simplistically viewed as a stereotypical matriarch, she does not care about this classification. As a result, Macon and Milkman lay bare Pilate's weakness: fidelity to family, even at the expense of her dignity.

Milkman's abandonment of his aunt is emotional, but Macon's abandonment of his sister in his youth is both physical and emotional. He leaves Pilate behind in a cave to fend for herself after the two fight over whether to take or leave gold recovered after Macon's murder of an old man. Macon, motivated by greed, wants to prosper from the killing, but Pilate is apprehensive at committing this theft, feeling that "if you take a life, you own it. You responsible for it" (208). Despite the adult Pilate's reputation for violence, her youthful refusal to harm someone for personal gain characterizes her as more moral than the matriarch stereotype. In contrast, Macon is unwilling to choose family over money, a quality that drives him forward through his whole life. He clashes violently against Pilate's sentimentality and almost beats her unconscious, but she ultimately drives him away. As a result of leaving his sister behind, Macon forces Pilate into an existence that shapes her into the kind of person he hates: a woman whose youthful shunning of materiality and traditional gender roles has hardened into resistance to all societal norms. Alone after Macon leaves her in the cave, Pilate journeys from place to place and endures attempted molestation and being ostracized when her lack of navel is discovered. Consequently, she learns to depend only on herself, not a male authority figure, to survive.

In adulthood, Macon still refuses to reach out to his sister. He blames her as he does Ruth for financial shortcomings of his own making, and he expects the rest of the family to shun her on his behalf. Marilyn Sanders Mobley adds that "Macon forbids Milkman to visit his aunt Pilate because he is embarrassed by her eccentric ways, her unkempt appearance, and her stubborn persistence in making bootleg wine" (49). This admonition is consistent with Macon's strategy of trying to make Milkman an ally by poisoning him against the family's women. Smith contends that Macon finds Pilate's "sheer disregard for status, occupation, hygiene, and manners" (35) deeply offensive. In Macon's mind, Pilate shames the family name by existing far outside the capitalist system that he worships and by having no preoccupation with the image she projects. Macon warns Milkman against consorting with a woman who shuns materialism and androcentrism in favour of forging strong relationships because she "can't teach you a thing you can use in this world" (55). The worst offense Macon commits against his sister is that he encourages Milkman to rob Pilate so that the two men can enjoy what they believe Pilate has hoarded for years: the gold Macon was forced to abandon. He knows that Pilate could be harmed during the burglary, but in the face of a potential financial windfall, her safety does not matter. Ultimately, the burglary sets off a chain of events that culminates in Pilate's death—a risk Macon could have foreseen but likely did not care about.

Although Macon's treatment of Pilate results in her death, Milkman's treatment of his aunt may be more egregious. Pilate saved Milkman's life and served as a mother figure to him from the first time he visited her; according to Carr Lee, "Pilate is the only person to provide Milkman with what feels emotionally like a home" (50). Pilate is a caregiver, but she does not love Milkman possessively; she does not even seem to want anything from him except his company, which is different from the women, Ruth and Hagar, whom Milkman flees. Although Milkman should be grateful for his aunt, when he believes that Pilate has gold, he plots to rob her and injure her if she catches him in the act. He is prepared "to knock down an old lady who had cooked him his first perfect egg, who had shown him the sky ... told him stories, sung him songs ... and ... had brought him into the world when only a miracle could have" (209-210). Pilate reacts unexpectedly to the robbery, as she pretends to be a simple old woman and a victim of a prank by strangers in order to get her nephew out of jail. Humbling herself in front of the white police officers, she plays the "Aunt Jemima act" (209), a humiliating persona for a woman so self-sufficient. Pilate's sacrifice of her pride and her willingness to pretend to be the mammy that white culture expects her to be both reinforce her status as more than a matriarch. It is not until Pilate's selfless act, and after Milkman makes a journey to discover more about his family's history, that he realizes that he has done nothing for her or for his mother, not even the simplest act of kindness to reciprocate their love. His epiphany, however, comes too late to make up for decades of neglect.

Throughout *Song of Solomon*, Morrison posits Ruth and Pilate as two drastically different women with one common link—fidelity to certain male family members:

> They were so different, these two women. One black, the other lemony. One corseted, the other buck naked under her dress. One well read but ill traveled. The other had read only a geography book, but had been from one end of the country to the other. One wholly dependent on money for life, the other indifferent to it. But those were the meaningless things. Their similarities were profound. Both were vitally interested in Macon Dead's son, and both had close and supportive posthumous communication with their fathers. (139)

However, the most important links between these women are how they are subject to stereotyping from dominant ideology and how they are defined based on their relationships, or lack thereof, with men. Ruth's seeming adherence to the Freudian mother archetype and Pilate's seeming alliance with the matriarch image call into question the expectations placed on women. The rigidity of these expectations discount women's complexity and lead to punishment for those who do not obey. Ultimately, only the women's stories, rich with examination of their inner lives, can rescue them from being seen in limited terms. In the case of Ruth and Pilate, reading their stories allows for an interrogation of the ideologies that restrict them and an appreciation of the women's rebellions, even those that come from them simply living their lives.

WORKS CITED

Ahmad, Soophia. "Women Who Make a Man: Female Protagonists in Toni Morrison's *Song of Solomon.*" *Atenea*, vol. 28, no. 2, December 2008, pp. 59-73.

Benjamin, Jessica. *The Bonds of Love: Psychoanalysis, Feminism, and the Problem of Domination.* Pantheon Books, 1988.

Brenner, Gerry. "*Song of Solomon:* Rejecting Rank's Monomyth and Feminism." *Toni Morrison's Song of Solomon: A Casebook*, edited by Jan Furman, Oxford University Press 2003, pp. 95-110.

Furman, Jan. *Toni Morrison's Fiction.* University of South Carolina Press, 1996.

Hill Collins, Patricia. "Mammies, Matriarchs, and Other Controlling Images." *Black Feminist Thought: Knowledge, Consciousness, and the Politics of Empowerment.* Routledge, 2000.

Lee, Catherine Carr. "The South in Toni Morrison's *Song of Solomon*: Initiation, Healing, and Home." *Toni Morrison's Song of Solomon: A Casebook*, edited by Jan Furman. Oxford University Press, 2003, pp. 43-64.

Mitchell, Juliet. *Psychoanalysis and Feminism.* Vintage Books, 1974. Print.

Mobley, Marilyn Sanders. "Call and Response: Voice, Community, and Dialogic Structures in Toni Morrison's *Song of Solomon.*" *New Essays on Song of Solomon*, edited by Valerie Smith, Cambridge University Press, 1995, pp. 41-68.

Morrison, Toni. *Song of Solomon.* Penguin Books, 1977.

Murray, Rolland. "The Long Strut: *Song of Solomon* and the Emancipatory Limits of Black Patriarchy." *Callaloo* vol. 22, no. 1, Winter 1999, pp. 121-133.

Sprengnether, Madelon. *The Spectral Mother: Freud, Feminism, and Psychoanalysis.* Cornell University Press, 1990.

Smith, Valerie. "The Quest for and Discovery of Identity in Toni Morrison's *Song of Solomon.*" *Toni Morrison's Song of Solomon: A Casebook*, edited by Jan Furman, Oxford University Press, 2003, pp. 27-41.

Wegs, Joyce M. "Toni Morrison's *Song of Solomon*: A Blues Song." *Toni Morrison's Song of Solomon: A Casebook.*, edited by Jan Furman, Oxford University Press, 2003, pp. 165-184.

"You've Already Got What You Need, Sugar"

Southern and Maternal Identity in Toni Morrison's *Song of Solomon*

ANNA HINTON

THE MOTHERS IN TONI MORRISON'S fiction participate in a tradition of calling on wisdom and using practices born of Black women's bitter history in the U.S., particularly in the South, to develop self-confidence and self-love in themselves and in their children. However, Morrison's mothers appear unable to sufficiently do so. Pilate, in *Song of Solomon*, is an example. Pilate's granddaughter Hagar succumbs to despair after her cousin and lover Milkman leaves her for a woman who has "silky copper-colored hair" and "gray eyes" (Morrison 127), a woman closer to white standards of beauty. In turn, Hagar internalizes the racism and patriarchy embedded in Milkman's rejection, and tries to change herself into someone that Milkman would want. The task is impossible, and Hagar dies once she realizes the futility of her project.

Many critics blame Pilate's parenting for Hagar's fate; Pilate nurtures Hagar's materialism by indulging her every whim, leaving her unprepared to face rejection.[1] However, this argument ignores a central part of Hagar's characterization: Hagar is, and has always been, "prissy," "vain," "proud," and attracted to the "prosperous, conventional" middle-class lifestyle (Morrison 150). Hagar desires what the heteronormative, capitalist, racist, and patriarchal culture tells her to desire. Because of this, Hagar rejects Pilate's "out law" model of Black womanhood.[2] Pilate is the perfect woman for Hagar to emulate. Both family and community reject Pilate, yet she perseveres, thrives even. She has defined her values on her own terms and has shaped herself into the woman she wants to be. Pilate does not succumb to the mental and social degeneracy common to characters in African American literature who migrate to or who are born in the North. Instead, she seeks guidance and empowerment from her southern roots, sifting through childhood memories of the South for cultural knowledge and beseeching southern wisdom from other Black women to supplement her own. Pilate is empowered not only by her southern roots but also by motherwork, and she, in turn, empowers others through her motherwork. Self-made and self-sustaining, she is what Morrison calls "the ship *and* the safe harbor" (qtd. in Taylor-Guthrie 135 and 197);[3] she both builds and nurtures, and manages whatever circumstances befall her. This chapter argues that Pilate can be empowered and, in turn, can empower others through motherwork because she can do what Hagar and others in *Song of Solomon* cannot—to live in the North while retaining self-preservative southern traditions through what Zandria Robinson calls a "country cosmopolitan" attitude. Additionally, this chapter will conclude with a coda, a reading of a contemporary text in which the main character views mothering in a Pilate-like manner to reveal the power of this maternal paradigm.

The South has always been a key theme in Morrison's literature. For Morrison, the South is important as a space because it serves as a site of ancestral knowledge, discredited Black knowledge ("Rootedness" 342). But it was only toward the mid-1990s, after she published *Jazz*, that scholars began to seriously place Morrison's work within the southern literary canon (Denard i).[4] Since then, scholars have returned to Morrison's earlier works to analyze the characters' relationship to the South. In *Song of Solomon*, southern studies scholars tend to focus on how the South influences Milkman's development, and only discuss Pilate as a southerner and as a mother in relation to Milkman. This chapter, however, shifts the focus to Pilate. It opens with an analysis of Hagar and Pilate to reveal how instrumental region is to female character development, especially to the characters' development as mothers. This analysis also reveals that when scholars focus only on Pilate's effectiveness as an "othermother" to Hagar or Milkman, they reduce motherhood to a function that benefits others instead of an identity that can be mutually empowering and nurturing.

The South is crucial to Pilate's characterization as a strong maternal figure. She can only do motherwork—to preserve, nurture, bear culture, and heal in order "to protect ... children, physically and psychologically, teach [them] how to protect themselves, and [to] heal adults who were unprotected as children" (O'Reilly 26)—because of her connection to that region. Although many scholars have argued the importance of the South as a site of the ancestor in *Song of Solomon*, few, if any, have addressed how the intersections of region and motherhood shape identity and how Pilate's maternal identity, when discussed through both maternal studies and southern studies, speaks volumes to current discussions on identity politics.

Currently, cultural, ethnic, racial, and gender as identity categories are under critique. Many scholars argue that identity categories are constructed and that there is nothing inherently Black, white, woman, man, and so forth. Although these constructions might have been helpful in the past, they have proven insufficient and unstable. Reexamining the function and effectiveness of identity categories has also surfaced as a point of interest in southern studies. Changes in the South and what it means to be southern complicate notions of regional identity and subsequent discussions of region in southern literature. This is most clearly reflected in the shift to a "new South studies." New South studies questions what or who should be the proper subject of southern literature; it challenges the traditional southern studies model, which limits its focus to the deep South and to white men toward a model, and argues that issues of race, gender, and globalization need to be also discussed in terms of the South (Kreyling 5). New South studies also questions if an authentic southern identity, or a southern Black identity and tradition, still exists, and whether or not southerners should preserve aspects of old South traditions.[5] Some argue that a similar phenomenon is happening within the Black community, that more and more Black people do not value southern Black traditions and are, therefore, trying to disassociate themselves from them (Robinson 38). As Black southerners continue to migrate North, West, internationally, and then back South again, rejecting their southern heritage can and does discomfit them in their new homes. Morrison's novels reveal that she is aware of these trends and that she resists them. Her works suggest that the South is important as an ancestral home site and as a repository of valuable Black wisdom and knowledge, which is an important theme in *Song of Solomon* and is key to Pilate's motherwork.

Key to understanding how Pilate can be empowered by motherwork and can empower others through her motherwork is Zandria Robinson's concept of "country cosmopolitanism." Robinson defines country cosmopolitanism as the following:

> best-of-both-worlds blackness that addresses the embattled notion of racial authenticity in a post-black era by hearkening back to and modernizing rural, country tropes.... Implicit in country cosmopolitanism is a normalization of the class privileges of wealthier blacks, the patriarchal privileges of black men, and the sexual privileges of heterosexuals. Still, the strategy is also used to disrupt, usurp, and relocate the traditional boundaries and intersections of region and race. (17-18)

Pilate is a country cosmopolitan character both through and because of her motherwork. And although country cosmopolitanism, at times, perpetuates problematic race, class, and gender codes, Pilate as a mother resists and challenges them. Her inflection of country cosmopolitanism demands that oppressive class, race, and gender codes be questioned and rejected. She instead models the old "country tropes" of Black women who understood that dominant narratives about their worth were untrustworthy and who, therefore, created alternative stories and traditions that affirmed the Black, female self. Pilate uses this southern tradition to create "a both-of-best-words blackness," which she uses to empower her motherwork. In this way, Pilate can only do motherwork because she is a country cosmopolitan figure.

In many ways, Pilate is emblematic of the transient space that Black women presently occupy, and her struggles anticipate the doubt about identity that globalization raises. Pilate, whom Morrison marks as the epitome of successful Black motherwork, is a migrant, someone with no stable regional identity. Pilate says, "I was cut off from people early ... I was about twelve, I think"

(Morrison 241). At an early age, Pilate is displaced from the ancestral South. Although she sets out to find her family in Virginia, she is unsuccessful. However, she must earn a living and the only work that she is qualified to perform is day labour work, so she continues to move from place to place with other "pickers." Like past and present migrants, economic necessity keeps her transitory. As she moves from one place to another, her collection of rocks (souvenirs from the places that she has been) and her fourth-grade geography book are material reminders of her status as a migrant, as one without a stable regional identity.

Despite Pilate's physical isolation from the South as the site of the ancestor, Morrison still situates her as a strong maternal figure. She can effectively othermother and nurture both Hagar and Milkman.[6] In fact, Milkman seeks Pilate's home when he needs a sense of belonging; her "house [is] a haven" and "a safe harbor" (*Song of Solomon* 135). Moreover, she is the one who prepares Milkman for what scholars call his rites of initiation, his journey back to the South.[7] Pilate is even willing to kill for her children, as she stabs a man for "act[ing] mean to [her] little girl" Reba (Morrison 94). And Pilate, after noticing Ruth "was dying of lovelessness" (151), takes care of Ruth and even helps her to get pregnant and to stop Macon from killing their unborn son. Despite being displaced from the South, a space Morrison marks as crucial to successful motherwork, Pilate is still able to nurture, bear culture, protect, and heal as demonstrated in the above examples. Pilate can only do this, however, by constructing, from various fragments of Black women's southern traditions, a regional identity. In other words, she embodies a country cosmopolitan attitude.

Pilate can amalgamate a productive southern identity (country cosmopolitanism) and resist oppressive forces because early on she accesses the "ancient properties," the strength needed to survive. As a young woman, Pilate is rejected by each community she joins because her body, specifically her lack of a navel, positions her outside of the normate body:[8]

> After a while, she stopped worrying about her stomach, and stopped trying to hide it.... [Men] froze at the sight of that belly that looked like a back; became limp even, or cold, if

she happened to undress completely and walked straight toward them, showing them, deliberately, a stomach as blind as a knee.... It isolated her. Already without family, she was further isolated from her people, for, except for the relative bliss on the island, every other resource was denied her: partnership in marriage, confessional friendship, and communal religion. Men frowned, women whispered and shoved their children behind them. Finally, Pilate began to take offense. (148-149)

Here, Pilate (though for slightly different reasons) reflects the status many Black women face as migrants: she is isolated from communities of people to uplift her. Instead of allowing otherness to destroy her, she boldly flaunts her difference; she stops "worrying about her stomach" and "trying to hide it." She undertakes the process of self-empowerment and self-creation, which begins when she realizes that she will always have to deny her authentic self to forge and maintain new relationships, and she, therefore, chooses self-authenticity above everything and everyone—even romance. She chooses self-love and preservation. Pilate continues this process by "[throwing] away every assumption she ... learned and [beginning] at zero" (Morrison 149). She rejects the self-depreciating ideologies of racism, sexism, and ableism into which she was socialized.

Pilate can only do this because early caregiving (mothering) empowers her and provides an alternative paradigm—a distinctly southern maternal one—for her to model her life: "Those twelve years in Montour County, where she had been treated gently by a father and brother, and where she herself was in a position to help farm animals under her care, had taught her a preferable kind of behavior" (150). Although she is removed from the South and has few memories of the South, Pilate keeps and affirms the values of self-love and love for others that she learned as a child—values rooted in her ability to mother farm animals and to be a caregiver. Through motherwork, Pilate develops a fierce self-love despite social reprobation.

Moreover, Pilate's motherwork ensures that despite being socially ostracized and despite living outside of social norms, she is never completely isolated from others: "her alien's compassion for trou-bled people ripened her and—the consequence of the knowledge that she had made up or acquired—kept her just barely within the boundaries of the elaborately socialized world of black people" (Morrison 149). Pilate rejects the oppressive ideologies that people try to impose on her, but she does not reject people. Pilate's nat-ural proclivity toward motherwork, towards "troubled people" does not enable her to be completely isolated from others. "The knowledge that she had made up or acquired," her self-making, allows her to be both within society enough to care for others but sufficiently outside of society as not to let oppressive ideologies constrain her motherwork. Most importantly, the motherwork she does "ripens" her, a verb that suggests motherwork matures and empowers her but also that her motherwork is linked—through agrarian imagery—to the southern identity she has carved for herself. In turn, she can do motherwork that other mothers in *Song of Solomon* cannot.

For instance, Pilate is the opposite of Ruth. Pilate is able to "[come] into this city like she own[s] it" (125); she is fearless. Ruth, a mother who rejects the strength and power of southern ideals (like Hagar), has "no intelligence that [is] her own," and she is "a small [woman]" (137 and 124). Although motherhood empowers Ruth, her motherwork cannot empower others. For example, she preserves Milkman's life only with Pilate's help as an othermother. Ruth does not reconcile her identity as a north-ern-born Black woman with her southern heritage, and she abides by the rules of patriarchy. Consequently, she does not reap all of the benefits of motherwork "because woman cannot be ship and safe harbor in a patriarchal marriage that assumes women are inferior and assigns them exclusively to the reproductive realm of the home" (O'Reilly 25). This is clear when Ruth asks Pilate to help her save her unborn child from Macon's attempts to abort it; it is also clear when she feels ashamed that she nursed Milkman "until [he] was ... old" (Morrison 126), a practice that the text links to traditional southern Black motherhood.[9] The difference between Pilate's and Ruth's motherwork is that Pilate can resist patriarchal oppression because she embraces southern, Black (fe-male) traditions to empower herself, whereas Ruth allows Macon to impede her motherwork and she feels ashamed and dirty, instead of empowered, by her southern maternal practices. Pilate refuses to take a husband and abide by the rules of society if it means becoming a small woman and mother—like Ruth.

Pilate's country cosmopolitan attitude does not perpetuate the oppressive class, race, and gender codes that Robinson associates with it, and which hinder Ruth. She resists them, and this is most clearly demonstrated by the contrasting her against other migrant characters who do not embody a country cosmopolitan attitude. For instance, Ruth and Macon Dead represent how class complicates regional identity, a complication that contemporary Black migrants understand because of increased economic mobility. Macon Dead values property, patriarchy, and power. His family is a picture of Black middle-class respectability. As such, he is isolated from the Black community, except as an oppressive force, and from the South by choice. For him, the South, particularly as embodied by Pilate, represents a backward space. He avoids his "common bootlegger sister" and her home, where women lived unrestrained by bourgeois, heteronormative rules and rituals (Morrison 29). However, Macon yearns for this space, and passing by Pilate's house is enough to make Macon—a hard man—"[soften] under the weight of memory and music" (30). Unlike Pilate, Macon cannot create a "best-of-both-worlds black-ness" because he is encumbered by anti-Blackness, patriarchy, and classism, whereas Pilate resists all three. Instead of being a country cosmopolitan figure, Macon represents the struggle between rejecting what Morrison presents as a traditional Black identity and yearning for it.

However, the text does not take southern, Black identity for granted; it complicates this identity by how it depicts the South, represented in the fictional space of Shalimar, Virginia. For instance, the "old South" in *Song of Solomon* is more of a mythic than a real space. When Milkman visits Circe in the Dead's hometown, his ascent up the stairs is described as a dream: "He had had dreams as a child, dreams every child had, of the witch who chased him down dark alleys, between lawn trees, and finally into rooms from which he could not escape.... So when he saw the woman at the top of the stairs there was no way for him to resist climbing up toward her" (239). With Circe, Milkman encounters more of a spirit than a real person: "Perhaps this woman is Circe. But Circe is dead. This woman is alive ... she had to be dead. Not because of the wrinkles, and the face so old it could not be alive, but because out of the toothless mouth came the strong, mellifluent voice of a twenty-year-old girl" (240). This southern space is irresistible and inescapable. It is old yet fresh; however, just like a spirit or a dream, it is also immaterial and ephemeral. Moreover, the text's depiction of the South is further complicated by locating the fictional Shalimar, which the text self-consciously describes as a small town that does not even register on the available maps, within the real space of Virginia. In other words, it is a construction based on the history, habits, and conventions of a real place. Anticipating current questions of what and where is the authentic South,[10] *Song of Solomon* presents a South that is an amalgamation of the "real" South and a fantasy, or an idea, of the South.

Despite this (or because of this), Pilate can maintain the values that this *ideal* of the South represents, and she enacts them and makes them manifest wherever she is while still inhabiting the actual sociohistorical space in which she lives. For instance, Pilate's house on the "Southside" does not have the amenities of the other houses: "She had no electricity... [or] gas," and "they warmed themselves and cooked with wood and coal, pumped kitchen water ... through a pipeline from a well and lived pretty much as though progress was a word that meant walking a little farther on down the road" (27). Pilate rejects the materialism that is antithetical to the communal values *her* South represents. Moreover, her house, which is always associated with food, especially southern fruits like peaches, suggests the fecundity of the agrarian South and the womb. Unlike Macon, she does not shun the South but embraces it and creates it wherever she goes. Even as a migrant, she seeks out African American knowledge associated with the South, sharing with Ruth the following: "the main reason I stayed on [with a family] was a woman there I took to. A root worker. She taught me a lot and kept me from missin my own family" (142). Nevertheless, Pilate takes advantage of the socioeconomic realities of the time (mainly Prohibition and the Depression); she is an entrepreneur, a bootlegger. Her ability to manipulate the local police's race and gender bias to get Milkman out of jail reveals that she is also aware of contemporary politics.

Pilate is empowered by and empowers others through motherwork, and although it is important to analyze whether or not her motherwork is effective, the text suggests that, in some ways, effectiveness is immaterial. Motherwork is as much about the *process* of *self* development as it is about the act of developing others. For Morrison, reclaiming a Black southern identity, one divested of distracting identity politics, is pivotal to ensuring that Black women garner an empowering identity from motherhood, and country cosmopolitanism is one avenue to achieve this. This approach to motherhood and regional identity enables Pilate to define herself on her own terms in order to be, as Morrison says, a "complete human [being]" (qtd. in Taylor-Guthrie 135).

It is interesting to see how Pilate is "rewritten" in current literature and what that reveals about how Black women writers use the maternal paradigm present in *Song of Solomon* to talk about southern Black motherhood today. Therefore, this chapter concludes with a brief analysis of Natalie Baszile's *Queen Sugar*, which, arguably, provides a contemporary rendering of Pilate-like motherwork.[11] *Queen Sugar* is a novel about Charley, an African American widow and mother from California, who moves to Louisiana with her teenage daughter to run a sugarcane plantation she inherited. In *Queen Sugar*, most of the conflict centres on Charley as a Black woman trying to enter into the white, masculinist sugarcane industry in a supposedly "postracial" new South. Throughout her struggles, Charley's saving grace is her willingness to depend on the wisdom, strength, and empowerment that she receives from the southern Black women who nurture her—Miss Honey and, especially, Aunt Violet—and from her motherwork.

One of the most Pilate-like moments of motherwork in the novel occurs during a conversation between Aunt Violet and Charley. When Charley is ready to give up on her white love interest because he "compliments" Charley by ignorantly telling her that "You're not like other black people.... It's almost like you're not black at all" (282), Aunt Violet nurtures and directs Charley when she tells her:

You know why you're disappointed in Remy Newell, why you're so angry with yourself? Because you thought he was the complete package. Southern accent, progressive politics, and all. You forgot he's just a man.... But you've already got what you need, sugar.... Just keep doing what you're doing, Charley ... Take care of your child, get your fields planted, stay right with God, and you'll be just fine. (284-285)

Aunt Violet's advice to Charley is so clearly Pilate-like (with an additional addendum that perhaps Pilate, herself, needed) in that it demands that Charley not worry about social conventions, that she piece her life together on her own terms, and that she trust her ability to do so. Aunt Violet directs Charley to let her motherwork empower her and everything else will fall into place. This scene between Charley and Aunt Violet, as with Pilate's motherwork in *Song of Solomon*, reminds scholars that Black motherwork depends on Black women loving and defining themselves to be both ship and safe harbour. As prevailing conversations on Blackness and southernness continue to pressure what those identities mean, Morrison's maternal theory, articulated through a country cosmopolitan perspective, offers a paradigm that enables Black mothers to stabilize and to be empowered by both identities without internalizing the racism and sexism that is often interwoven into them. This reading of Pilate, region, and motherwork, along with the coda on *Queen Sugar*, nuances the way scholars use and understand Morrison's argument that Black mothers must be both ship and safe harbour: Morrison's Black mothers not only must be able to build and create for their children, but they must also be able to do so for themselves.

ENDNOTES

[1] For examples of these readings see: Harding and Martin 73-74; Samuels and Hudson-Weems 75; Storhoff 290-309; and Demetrakopoulos 97.

[2] In *Toni Morrison and Motherhood*, Andrea O'Reilly argues that Pilate in *Song of Solomon* and Eva in *Sula* are "outlaw[s] of the

institution of motherhood"; they do not abide by the rules of patriarchy (81).

³In *Conversations with Toni Morrison*, Morrison describes what it means to be ship and safe harbour in several interviews. In one, she says, "The problem [with education and a lucrative career] is not paying attention to the ancient properties—which for me means the ability to be 'the ship' *and* 'the safe harbor.' Our history as Black women is the history of women who could build a house *and* have some children, and there was no problem" (qtd. in Taylor-Guthrie 135). In another, Morrison says, "I tried hard to be both the ship and the safe harbor at the same time, to be able to make a house and be on the job market and still nurture the children. It's trying to make life enhanced by additional things rather than conflicted by additional things" (qtd. in Taylor-Guthrie 197).

⁴Carolyn Denard argues that part of the delay of considering Morrison a southern writer is because she was born in Ohio and her novels, up until the publication of *Jazz*, are set in the Midwest. However, this stance ignores the great influence Morrison's migrant parents had in shaping her identity and the amount of attention most of her novels pay to the South, despite the main characters being located elsewhere.

⁵Michaeel Kreyling argues that "there is an imperative to think new; on the other hand, one must not leave behind the old, enduring South, for doing that amounts to a kind of cultural suicide, a forfeiture of identity. Memory struggles with amnesia: what to remember and what to forget, and most importantly at what cost to whom" (5); and Zandria Robinson argues that Blacks in the South are pushing against stereotypes of southern Blackness that are pejorative while at the same time using southern Blackness as cultural capital for an authentic Blackness (32). This desire for authentic Blackness is mitigated by those who embody a post-racial paradigm that wishes to move beyond categories of race (38).

⁶O'Reilly explains, "Morrison's thinking on nurturance as an act of resistance builds upon the African American view of homeplace as a site of resistance. Homeplace, as discussed earlier, refers to a haven or refuge, where 'Black people could affirm one another and by so doing, heal many of the wounds inflicted by racist domination ... [a place where they] had the opportunity to grow and

develop, to nurture their spirits'" (33; bell hooks qtd. in O'Reilly.)
[7]In fact, the South in *Song of Solomon* is mainly discussed in light
of Milkman's journey back to the South as his ancestral home-
land. Scholars argue that Milkman's voyage to Virginia is a rite
of passage that transforms him from a spoiled, self-centered boy
to a culturally aware man. For instance, see Lee 43.
[8]Feminist disability studies scholar Rosemarie Garland-Thomson
coins the term "normate body" to define the standard by which
Western bodies measure themselves. This body is white, male, able,
Christian, and heterosexual. However, this body does not exist.
I use Garland-Thomson's term to suggest, or hint at, the ways in
which the intersections of gender, race, region, *and* disability have
been instrumental in Pilate developing the self-love that propels
her motherwork. Although outside of the scope of this chapter,
analyzing how disability shapes Morrison's mothers—Mrs. Breedlove in *The Bluest Eye*, for example, or Eva Peace in *Sula*—is a
fruitful project.
[9]Freddie, the janitor at Macon's firm, catches Ruth nursing Milkman
and says, "I be damn, Miss Rufie. When the last time I seen that?
I don't even know the last time I seen that. I mean, ain't nothing
wrong with it. I mean, old folks swear by it.... Used to be a lot of
womenfolk nurse they kids a long time down South" (Morrison 14).
[10]Kreyling notes that whereas the South was previously limited to
the Deep South of the north east, new South studies is considering
places such as Appalachia and Kansas as southern. And, in terms
of race, new South scholars, very tongue and cheek and harkening
on antebellum discourse, argue that the Mason-Dickson line is
anywhere south of Canada (7).
[11]There are many characters in *Queen Sugar* that parallel characters in *Song of Solomon*. For instance, Ralph Angel, as a selfish,
self-centered Black man who returns home to the South, parallels
Milkman.

WORKS CITED

Baszile, Natalie. *Queen Sugar*. Penguin, 2014.
Demetrakopoulos, Stephanie. *New Dimensions in Spirituality: A
Biracial and Bicultural Reading of the Novels of Toni Morrison.*

Greenwood, 1987.

Denard. Carolyn. "Toni Morrison and the American South: Introduction." *Studies in the Literary Imagination*, vol. 31, no. 2, 1998, pp. 1-21.

Kreyling, Michael. "Toward A New Southern Studies." *South Central Review*, vol. 22, no. 1, 2005, pp. 4-18.

Harding, Wendy, and Jacky Martin. *A World of Difference: An Inter-Cultural Study of Toni Morrison's Novels*. Greenwood, 1994.

Lee, Catherine Carr. "The South in Toni Morrison's *Song of Solomon*: Initiation, Healing, and Home." *Toni Morrison's Song of Solomon: A Casebook*, edited by Jan Furman, Oxford University Press, 2003, pp. 43-64.

Morrison, Toni. *Song of Solomon*. Plume, 1977.

O'Reilly, Andrea. *Toni Morrison and Motherhood: A Politics of the Heart*. State University of New York Press, 2004.

Robinson, Zandria. *This Ain't Chicago: Race, Class, and Regional Identity in the Post-Soul South*. University of North Carolina Press Books, 2014.

Samuels, Wilfred, and Clenora Hudson-Weems. *Toni Morrison*. Twayne, 1990. Print.

Storhoff, Gary. "Anaconda Love': Parental Enmeshment in Toni Morrison's *Song of Solomon*." *Style*, vol. 31, no. 2, 1997, pp. 290-309.

Taylor-Guthrie. Danille, editor. *Conversations with Toni Morrison*. University Press of Mississippi, 1994.

II.
"Bad" Mothering

Studies in M(othering)

Unpacking the "Wicked Thing" in Toni Morrison's *A Mercy* and *Beloved*

VEENA DEO

TONI MORRISON MARKS CRITICAL MOMENTS in American and African American history through her novels *A Mercy* (2008), before the nation took its shape from Old World and Enlightenment imaginings, and *Beloved* (1987), during and after the Civil War when the nation was ideologically torn asunder to reimagine itself as a multiethnic nation.[1] Although the sweep of history here is extensive, Morrison's project helps us ask questions about how and why her texts destabilize and animate the ambivalence of the term m(othering). Since mothering is a process, and mothers in these texts are in contexts of instability, migrations, and oppressive social forces, they are offered few clear resources and even fewer unambiguous choices to make. The social construction of motherhood, then, is deeply connected to the social and cultural construction of the American nation's anxiety and ambivalence about what it wants to be. The nation's ideological fissures and fault lines are narrativized in the lives of African American mothers and children as echoes of the complex and contradictory underpinnings of the nation, but with a difference. Black mothers are represented at key moments in American history as participating in the process of "othering" as an act of love and protection precisely when the nation is most fragmented, inhospitable to difference, or polarized.

The sign m(other) already has embedded in it the signifier for other. Whether approached psychoanalytically, where the mother splits into a good or bad mother in the process of individuation for an infant, or deconstructively, as I have done here, the slippage between the sign and the signifier prepares us for multiple

69

interpretations of the sign, whether from the perspective of the child or not.[2] The sign also gestures toward the more complicated ideas of home, nation, culture, and communication as in the idea of the motherland or the mother tongue. All intense attachments to the sign are implicit in the idea of home, nation, culture, and language; where one finds belonging is precisely the place where intense violence to one's self is also located.

But what or whose "wicked thing" is it to complicate safety of home and belonging?[3] Morrison writes Florens's mother as the one who defines wickedness at the end of the novel, *A Mercy*; she says, "to be given dominion over another is a hard thing; to wrest dominion over another is a wrong thing; to give dominion of yourself to another is a wicked thing" (167). The words "hard," "wrong," and "wicked" do not signify the same idea; rather they signify complexities with all forms of dominion in a nation aspiring to imagine itself politically and culturally as a multiethnic democracy from the perspectives of those in power and those who are not. In this chapter, I posit that Toni Morrison, in *A Mercy* (2008) and *Beloved* (1987), encourages readers to engage with her texts about the complex negotiations of culture at the intersections of time, place, gender, class, race, and nation at critical moments of American history by connecting the past and the present if the nation is to realize its aspirations.

These texts also cover considerable historical time in the racial history of the United States. It is noteworthy that they also gesture towards contemporary concerns for Morrison. In a 1987 interview with Melvyn Bragg, when *Beloved* was published, Toni Morrison said that she was not drawn to slavery as a subject matter at first; rather, she wanted to write about a very contemporary concern about "self-murder" and wanted to explore why "we self-sabotage ourselves." She was drawn to Margaret Garner's story to tell a contemporary story and then placed it in its appropriate time of slavery. Additionally, Toni Morrison's *A Mercy* was published in November 2008 when President Obama was elected president. At this moment in American history, the country had been in the new century for less than a decade and was looking once again to fulfill its emancipatory promise of equity and justice for all, in a rapidly changing landscape of new immigrants who were "browning"

America, while racism continued to terrorize black and brown youth. Also at this moment, the country had been at war against "terrorism" abroad, and attempted to fulfill its exceptional destiny of bringing democracy and freedom to the world. It is not unusual for Morrison to reach in to the past to make a point in the present.

The linkages between past and present are significant. Homi Bhabha theorizes the linkages effectively in his *The Location of Culture*. He argues that the "borderline work of culture" is not simply a "continuum of past and present" but rather "an insurgent act of cultural translation" (7). He writes further: "Such art does not merely recall the past as social cause or aesthetic precedent; it renews the past, refiguring it as a contingent 'in-between' space, that innovates and interrupts the performance of the present. The 'past-present' becomes part of the necessity, not the nostalgia, of living" (7).

As readers in the twenty-first century who have experienced the first African American, Barack Obama's, presidency, it is important for us to remember two things. First, there is extraordinary diversity within African America. In *The Making of African America: The Four Great Migrations* historian Ira Berlin writes, "In 2000, more than one in twenty black Americans was an immigrant; almost one in ten was an immigrant or a child of an immigrant," (7)[4] who did not share the history of enslavement but experiences virulent racism regardless. Secondly, immigrations from around the world make up American readership today. As such, it is important for us not only to understand how these texts innovate or "interrupt the performance of the present" (7) as Bhabha articulates in his *The Location of Culture* but to see how our textual engagements occur in the context of the United States' understandings of itself as a nation as well as our understanding of ourselves within this ever expanding nation (7).

Benedict Anderson's classic articulation of the nation as an imagined community is complicated in the context of the United States because of its historical concerns with race and racism. Anderson argues the following: "nationalism thinks in terms of historical destinies, while racism dreams of eternal contaminations, transmitted from the origins of time through an endless sequence of loathsome copulations: outside history." He further contends that

"The dreams of racism actually have their origin in ideologies of *class*, rather than in those of nation" and as such "justify domestic repression and domination" (149-150).

Patricia Hill Collins explains further the "paradox of American national identity" at the intersections of race, gender, class, and nation by exploring the experiences of black domestic workers to understand the constructions of the American body politic in her 2006 book *From Black Power to Hip Hop: Racism, Nationalism, and Feminism*. On the one hand, the American nation is constructed as an ideal patriarchal family with defined, gendered roles. On the other hand, Collins explains, "in American society, where family and racial lineage has long been used to distribute social rights and obligations, being born White American or Black American remains vitally important" (31). The black domestic worker may be seen to be "like" family, holding a contained second-class citizenship role but is never a member of the family no matter how many social and political movements have attempted to make permanent change in remaking America as a truly multiethnic nation, where everyone has a sense of belonging, not just in ethnically carved out spaces placed within racial hierarchies.

Following Etienne Balibar, Collins identifies the presence of both external racisms (expressed via practices of xenophobia or ethnic cleansing) and internal racisms (expressed via subordination of racial groups to maintain a standard of living) as interrelated phenomenon and integral to the founding moments of the American nation state (32). Additionally, the United States offers both a civic nationalism (where all people are equal before the law) as well as an ethnic nationalism (where groups internal to the nation recognize that first-class citizenship is reserved for white Americans). Collins writes, "the first-class White citizen, the foreign Indian [in his or her own land] who stands outside citizenship, and the second-class Black citizen—the relationship *among* these three groups became fixed as essential ingredients for a fundamentally racialized American national identity" (34). This racial triangle, Collins theorizes, "describes a template for conceptualizing American national identity" (35). This triangle is so tenacious that the presence of new immigrants may shift the terms about who is inside and who is outside, but the racial hierarchies continue:

"the paradox of American national identity that juxtaposes the democratic freedoms associated with individual rights to the reality of differential group treatment of Whites, indigenous peoples, and people of African descent thus reflects a complicated tension between the ideas of civic and ethnic nationalism" (Collins 36).

Such complex tensions within the nation mark the site of my reading of Toni Morrison's texts. In a patriarchal nation where race matters, how and why does a black mother become the site and the sign of violence in Morrison's texts? In what ways does this representation allow readers to understand "the borderline work of culture" and the "insurgent act of cultural translation" that Bhabha has identified?

According to Michael Ignatieff in his *Blood and Belonging: Journeys into the New Nationalism*, nationalists see national belonging as overriding all other forms of belonging—such as belonging to family, work or friends—because it offers security and protection. This is why one can sacrifice on the nation's behalf: "Where you belong is where you are safe; and where you are safe is where you belong. If nationalism is persuasive because it warrants violence, it is also persuasive because it offers protection from violence" (10). The moments of history signified by Morrison's texts place the black mother within the national landscape, where on the one hand, she has natural rights to her children in a Hobbesian sense,[5] but on the other hand, she has no legal rights to her own children, either because she is enslaved or because she can only count on self-support in a segregated and racist society. State institutions and social safety nets do not work for her, which forces her to react in the only ways she knows how to—individual action and self-support.

Morrison's texts, then, challenge readers to read and make meaning in the gaps her narratives open up between the black mother and her protective othering of her children as narrated in *A Mercy* and *Beloved*, as well as between America's expressed desire for coherence and its continued internal racial otherings. What the black mothers do in these texts in moments of national and personal crisis gestures at once toward fault lines in national imaginings as well as toward personal ethical decisions affected by those fault lines. If the nation built on the tenacious triangle articulated by Patricia Hill Collins is to be reimagined as a truly multiethnic and multicultural nation with no gaps between civic and ethnic nationalism, it is important for all of us within the national space to enter this narrative space and unpack its implications.

Institutional as well as personal violence is at the heart of both *A Mercy* and *Beloved*. Whereas *A Mercy* is a story about the underbelly of American exceptionalism or a vision of a failed utopia, a failed Eden in the new world as it was imagined, *Beloved* is a story about the hauntings of the institution of slavery, established exactly at the same time as the American nation emerged.

In *A Mercy*, Morrison offers through Lina, a Native woman, a parable of what the Native woman sees as the start of a fault line: the colonization of the land and its people by strangers whose understanding of the relationship of the land and its people is culturally and ideologically incommensurable to hers. The story that Lina narrates to Florens often is about the eagle who watches over her eggs in her nest high above ground to protect them from dangerous creatures preying on them. She is represented as a warrior mother who sharpens her talons on the rock and "her beak ... like the scythe of a war god." However, this same mother eagle has no defense against the "evil thoughts of man." In this particular case, the evil thoughts seem to belong to the new travellers who have come to the land, which they do not know but want to claim as their own. The traveller is enchanted by the land and its beauty and utters a desire unheard of before: "this is perfect. This is mine." The word "mine" has such a powerful resounding impact over the landscape that "the shells of the eagle's eggs quiver and one even cracks" (62). The eagle is taken aback by the strange word, its sound and meaning, and its unforeseen consequences; because of the incommensurability of it all, she attacks the traveller who then strikes her wing, and she loses the battle going in to a free fall. Florens, Lina's attentive listener, wants to know where the eagle is now, and Lina can only reply that she is still falling and falling forever. Florens barely breathes as she asks again, "and the eggs?" Lina responds, "they hatch alone." To Florens's follow-up urgent question, "do they live?" Lina responds with, "we have" (63). In that moment, Lina and Florens, Native American storyteller and African American listener, identify with each other in the margins of the emerging nation. Lina experiences this great loss as mother hunger, "to be one and to have one" (63). She recognizes it in herself as well as in Florens. It can also be read as the hunger for safety within one's family, the basic social organization that provides the first safety net. By extension, the family net is metonymically extended to tribe and nation, but not necessarily connected to land in the same way as the newcomers seem to think. They see it as a possession ranking above the people living on the land; it is a possession that can only be acquired by destroying or controlling people identified as "others," enemies, free labour, and so on.

Lina's specific cultural perspective names, frames, and articulates an understanding of a new reality of encountering words, ideologies, and conceptual frameworks that show large cultural discontinuities with real consequences, in which mothers cannot find their footing in the "falling forever" and daughters have to survive on their own with whatever cultural knowledge and consciousness they can gather. What are the children of this massive disruption and discontinuity likely to offer? Will violence to self and other be one answer? Will other hopeful strategies emerge? The answers are complicated.

Sethe and Florens, Morrison's strong narrative characters in *Beloved* and *A Mercy* respectively, share some things even with two centuries between them. They are both acutely aware of being abandoned by their mothers; they attach themselves emotionally to possessive love—love for a sexual partner, as Florens does to the blacksmith, or love for a child, as Sethe does to Beloved; they are both motivated to violent action when threatened by real (schoolteacher and slave catchers in *Beloved*) or imagined (fear of not being the exclusive object the blacksmith's love in *A Mercy*) danger; they both struggle physically and emotionally to articulate their stories of trauma; and they both experience the presence of a "wildness" beyond their control when they act in violence—Sethe trying to kill all her children and succeeding in killing Beloved, and Florens attacking the blacksmith and his protégé, Malaik.

Besides what Sethe and Florens share, their own mothers are similarly motivated by protective love towards their daughters although neither daughter hears words of comfort or wisdom from her mother. Florens's mother abandons her child by giving her away to a kinder white man. Sethe uses murder as a protective method to save her child from slavery. In either case, the trauma the mothers and daughters suffer continues to haunt them. In case of Sethe, Beloved literally reappears demanding attention and explanations for her murder, whereas Florens and her mother ache to communicate and explain themselves to each other because they know they will never meet again. This insurmountable distance between mothers and daughters marked by death or geographic space is ultimately affected by the social conditions beyond their control that define their world; for Sethe, it is the post-1850 Fugitive Slave Law world when the Civil War is near, and for Florens, it is the post-Bacon's Rebellion world in the late seventeenth century, when racial slavery is beginning to be solidified into law.

Morrison offers parallel narrative strategies to her primary narrators. Florens describes the new house that Jacob Vaark built as her "talking room" closer to the end of her narrative (161), and Sethe tells Denver that "I don't pray anymore. I just talk" (*Beloved* 35). For Sethe, talking is not the easiest thing she can do to process her traumas. Despite the difficulty she experiences in self-expression, she does give one poignant example, when she addresses her listener, Paul D, a man with a clear sense of right and wrong. He shows her a clipping of a newspaper and confronts her about her murder of Beloved. Sethe, however, cannot completely and fully articulate her side of the story even though the facts are simple—the slave catchers come to take away her and her children back into slavery and she simply does not allow her children to go back to Sweet Home and to the suffering that she knows to be there. In these facts lies a world of complicated rational and emotional negotiations about belonging, rights, and morality of all actions directed by her and toward her. Morrison writes, "Sethe knew that the circle she was making around the room, him, the subject, would remain one. That she could never close in, pin it down for anybody who had to ask. If they didn't get it right off—she could never explain" (163). Clearly, she cannot offer a rational explanation for this act.

Sethe and Paul D share much, but he cannot accept her actions and now sees her as someone "new," unlike what the Sweet Home girl had been—"prickly, mean-eyed … shy … and work-crazy."

They knew her as "Halle's girl," but about whom they all cared (164). Paul D tells her she was wrong to do what she did and that she has "two feet," and "not four," a reference to the inhumanity of her act. His words make a "forest [spring] up between them; trackless and quiet" (165). Paul D does not see her as a rightfully protective mother. This moral lack, which he points out, is a judgment she cannot grapple with easily. She knows her violence toward her children and self-sabotage is the result of violence done to her by individual people like the schoolteacher and his pupils as well as the institution of slavery. The tension within the narrative between right action and the double gesture of her violent act as both protection and political revenge requires superhuman strength to resolve. For both Sethe and Paul D, acceptance of each other, compassion, and forgiveness of self and other seem to be the only possible option to begin to overcome physical and psychological suffering.

In case of Florens in *A Mercy*, Morrison once again notes the physical agitation in the telling of the narrative. Florens etches her words with a nail on the walls and floors of the room; they are "careful words, closed up and wide open" and will "talk to themselves." They go "round and round, side to side, bottom to top, top to bottom all across the room" in a circular and chaotic manner" (161). To such contradictory and agitatedly written words, Florens gets attached in the telling. There is "no more room in this room ... [the] words cover the floor" (160). She even "sleep[s] among [her] words" (158). In this engagement, telling, and writing, Florens finds the strength to turn away from her obsessive storytelling directed at her lover, the blacksmith, to address her mother directly: "I cannot know what my mother is telling me. Nor can she know what I am wanting to tell her, Mãe, you can have pleasure now because the soles of my feet are hard as cypress" (161). The act of etching and writing offers her an insight that she is really trying to reach her mother, and she did not begin her writing with that recognition.

As if in response, Morrison offers the last section of the novel in the voice of Florens's mother from far away, making the need of such communication apparent as well as impossible. Morrison as the writer can imagine this communication, which in reality can never happen; as such, it becomes Morrison's "insurgent act of cultural translation" just as Bhabha theorized, as quoted above. Florens's mother knows the violence of sexual abuse in slavery: "There is no protection. To be female in this place is to be an open wound that cannot heal" (163). She explains her loss of self and culture in the New World in this manner: "language, dress, gods, dance, habits, decoration, song—all of it cooked together in the color of my skin. So it was as black that I was purchased by Senhor" (165). She recognizes that racial identity is merely a re- ductive identity created for her by the system of enslavement which is part of her forced migration to the New World. In Morrison's writing, mother and daughter signify their desire for connection and communication, with the knowledge that the present social institutions do not allow it.

Both Sethe and Florens desperately attempt to connect across time and space with the mothers and/or children from whom they are forever separated. Reading Morrison's *Beloved* and Nadine Gordimer's *Aila* together, Homi Bhabha makes the following re- marks: "To live in the unhomely world, to find its ambivalences and ambiguities enacted in the house of fiction, or its sundering and splitting performed in the work of art, is also to affirm a profound desire for social solidarity: 'I am looking for the join ... I want to join ... I want to join'" (*The Location of Culture* 18).[6]

The hunger for solidarity, connection, communication, and be- longing is so marked in both of Morrison's texts that the message for readers is clear—confronting the traumas; expressing guilt, anger, fear, and hatred, both nationally and institutionally; and imagining the missing pieces in the fabric of the nation's historical spaces may be the only way to move forward not only for char- acters in the texts but for readers in a multiethnic nation now in the twenty-first century.

In this matter, it is important to recall two moments in *A Mercy* and *Beloved*, which mark an arc of historical development for cross-cultural engagements. The first is Florens's acquisition of a double-consciousness, which is an assault on her humanity, and the second is Denver's birth, a new possibility; these engagements are complicated and contradictory. In both cases, these are cross-cul- tural and cross-racial encounters—the first marks a critical turning point in racialized identity formation and the second happens at the start of the Civil War in *Beloved*, when a white girl and a black girl unexpectedly do something "appropriately and well" (*Beloved* 85).

In *A Mercy* when Florens is tasked by Rebekka, her mistress, to find the blacksmith and return with him to help her heal from the smallpox she has contracted, she finds herself amid strangers whose help and support she desperately needs. Widow Ealing and her daughter Jane put her up for the night, feed her, and keep her safe because they feel sorry for an orphan child travelling by herself. Race at this point seems to be more fluid. The safe haven and life-sustaining nurturing that Florens finds in Widow Ealing's home is precisely when she encounters her lowest point too—being prodded and poked by unrelenting puritanical Christians who see her dark body as a sign that she is a minion of the devil. Early in American history, this conflation and eliding of meanings between the colour of one's skin and a moral lack is the first "wicked thing" that Florens begins to notice. Widow Ealing's daughter Jane—who is under the Puritans' scrutiny also because of her "wayward eye" (114) and who has to cut her body to show that she can bleed and is, therefore, a human being—understands aspects of her persecution. She also recognizes that part of the motivation of the community to destroy her family is simply its greed—they "crave" their family's "pasture" (109). The economic underpinning of the witch hunts is a sign of the lawlessness that Morrison writes early in the novel. Florens's experience with Widow Ealing and daughter Jane is at once positive and negative. After the community visitors enter Widow Ealing's house, they forget about her daughter and focus instead on Florens, proof to them that indeed, "The Black Man" is among them and the dark skinned girl is his minion (111). Their leader is presented with Rebekka's letter requesting Florens's safe passage, but they still examine her naked body for signs of what they fear—physical markings of Satan and his minions. In this encounter with the visitors who elide the black man/skin with Satan, Florens experiences the birth of a double-consciousness, which she has never experienced before. She notes, "No hate is there or scare or disgust but they are looking at me my body across distances without recognition" (113). She records this dehumanizing experience by saying, "something precious is leaving me. I am a thing apart" (115). Her letter protects her legally and underscores her belonging, but without the letter, she is a "weak calf abandon[ed] by the herd" (115). But this belonging is further racially hierarchized in the visitor's dehumanizing gaze at her body, which now reduces her to her skin colour alone. She is not simply a servant and one of the underclass abandoned by her mother; she is now not even human and becomes angry because of that. The dark skin she is born with is now coupled with an "inside dark [that] is small, feathered and toothy," and she wonders if her mother knows this and is the reason, perhaps, why she abandoned her (115).

Florens has not merely experienced Widow Ealing's house as both shelter and a prison; she has also seen daughter Jane's kindness and help in escaping from the village. It marks for her an emergent national fault line of racial identity formation. Jane packs her some food, sends her on her way away from these prodding people, kisses her on her forehead as a goodbye, but then thanks Florens by saying, "They look at you and forget about me" (114). Despite her physical disability, Jane's life is now different because the blackness of Florens's skin will be connected with the idea of the devil among the European settlers. Whether that would help her sense of belonging in the community is unclear, but she has found a momentary reprieve in her *whiteness* from the community who persecutes her because of her physical disability, her "wayward eye." Florens begins to believe that the darkness of night is her darkness and "is we [she and the blacksmith] ... is my home" (115). It connects her even more tightly to the blacksmith from whom she hopes to get an unconditional acceptance.

In *Beloved*, Morrison writes another cross-cultural engagement between Sethe and Amy Denver, a white indentured servant who is running away to Boston looking for "carmine" velvet (80). Denver, representing a promise for the future, loves to hear the story of her birth aided by Amy Denver after whom she is named. She helps in the creation of details of Sethe and Amy's interactions from "the scraps her mother and grandmother had told her" (78). Beloved is hungry for stories from and about Sethe, so Denver anticipates her questions and her desire for details and fills out the story: "Denver spoke, Beloved listened, and the two did the best they could to create what really happened, how it really was, something only Sethe knew because she alone had the mind for it and the time afterward to shape it: the quality of Amy's voice, her breath like burning wood" (78).

This suggests the idea of the mother and the two daughters as a triad, as they build the story of this encounter together, always revising it and renewing it for their own purposes. This triad is represented as a threnody at a later point in the narrative. This threnody, or their song of lament, has their desires and hopes interwoven as the story emerges from the interstices between and among them. In this telling, the essentials of the story—Amy heals Sethe's feet and her back and helps with the birth of Denver—are further embellished with Amy's song, her mother's lullaby, and her words, "my mama's song. She taught me it" (81). We see Amy's desire for carmine velvet and the details of Denver's birthing in a small boat in the river; we get a strong understanding that together Amy and Sethe had done something "appropriate and well" (84). Morrison continues further to give us a different perspective, "A paterroller passing would have sniggered to see two throw-away people, two lawless outlaws—a slave and a barefoot whitewoman with unpinned hair—wrapping a ten-minute old baby in the rags they wore" (84-85).

In a previous telling of the story of Denver's birth from her perspective, Denver in her green "bower" sees the miracle of her own birth primarily as a testimony to Amy's "friendliness," and narrates the backstory of Sethe's ordeal of running away (28). She explains that her mother's, Sethe's, feet were swollen, that she could go forward only because she had the memory of her mother in the rice fields of South Carolina and other enslaved Africans who "danced the antelope…. They shifted shapes and became something other. Some unchained, demanding other whose feet knew her pulse better than she did. Just like this one in her stomach" (31). The matrilineal linkage to an African dance from her mother to her unborn daughter continues to prod Sethe to survive. At that moment, Sethe is entirely spent and lying on the ground, but she describes her will to survive as primal, emerging out of the earth and turning her in to a snake, "all jaws and hungry" to bite the feet of whoever was approaching her (31). Sethe's desire to fight is complicated by her desire to seek help, trust, and hope for human solace. Hence, "instead of fangs and split tongue, out shot the truth" that she was running (31). This instinctive desire to to create community at this migratory moment for both women, regardless of the fact that the two would never meet again, suggests human possibilities and connections across boundaries—racial boundaries in this case. The ambivalent carmine red of Amy's velvet could be both the colour of death or birth and life, but in this case, it is clearly the latter. There is no doubt that these two "lawless outlaws" are positioned differently in society: the white woman has dreams of velvet and a good life; the black woman is running for her life and the survival of her children.

These two moments in *A Mercy* and *Beloved* follow the historic arc of the process of racialization in the United States for both black and white. One marks the beginning of the story of racialization in early America, and the other marks an almost unthinkable encounter at a moment when the states are about to go to war with one another over slavery and racial difference is institutionalized.

Echoing Patricia Hill Collins's analysis, Morrison establishes the foundational narrative of the nation in *A Mercy*. Morrison writes Lina, the Native woman in the novel, as the lone survivor of her people, who have been destroyed. She becomes a useful workhorse for Jacob and Rebekka Vaark, and she teaches Rebekka many things about Native knowledge. But she is cast aside easily after Jacob Vaark's death as if she were nothing, not even a servant. Morrison writes the desire of the characters for solidarity and belonging to a larger cross-cultural nation in an improvisational manner as complex and momentary experiences rather than sustained ones.

For instance, the house Jacob Vaark builds on his land—"befitting not a farmer, not even a trader, but a squire" (88)—is a site of ambition but also ambivalence and destruction. No one will live in it. It is an inheritance that will not be passed to any Vaark children, as they have all died before him. His only presence there is a brief one when he is dying. He insists that the women—Rebekka, Lina, Florens, and Sorrow—carry him inside the house where they place him on the floor just before he dies. The house is locked up, and no one is allowed in. When Florens sneaks in to etch and write in her "talking room" in Vaark's empty house, it is both an act of her insurgency because no one is allowed in, as well as her claim to the story of all the forced and indentured people who built America and are not allowed in to that house. In *Beloved*, the very first sentence of the novel is that 124 is "spiteful" and haunted—unhomely homes showing the underbelly of America's success story.

In *A Mercy*, Jacob Vaark is only briefly introduced as a good man, who treats people from different backgrounds well and with fairness. As a master of his household, he oversees a few people who help run his farm: Willard and Scully, the white indentured servants; Lina, the Native American woman who "was purchased outright and deliberately;" Rebekka, his mail-order bride, who came from England after he bought her passage on a boat; and Sorrow, a stray young woman whom Jacob gained in exchange for the lumber he got from the sawyer (33). Much as Vaark sees himself as a pragmatist who is kind and good, Morrison offers us enough contradictions between his self-perception and his actions for us to know that Vaark merely holds a promise of an Eden-like farm, where slaves, indentured servants, freedmen, and white landowners can all work cooperatively and maintain this surrogate "home" together. The fissures and fault lines are already present in the household along the lines of gender, race, class, and sexuality; these only widen dramatically after Jacob Vaark contracts smallpox and dies.

Human life was valued differently in the seventeenth century, and women had no rights of their own. As such, Jacob Vaark may see himself generously, but Morrison writes him out of the narrative very quickly, leaving mostly all women on the farm. And the transformation of Rebekka—from a friendly mistress to a woman who must assert her white privilege as a single woman of property and whose rights to property are tenuous—ultimately completes the fall of both Adam and Eve and their illusory Edenlike farm by the end of the story.

In *Beloved*, encounters between Amy Denver and Sethe are also improvisational and brief. Their encounter is in a transitional space very close to the river beyond which Sethe and her daughter would be in a free state. The encounter is also among marginalized women, but what emerges out of their encounter—a healthy Denver—ultimately offers some hope. Denver is also the one who steps over the threshold when Sethe is very ill. She finds help among well-meaning women and men, white and black. The improvisational nature of these cross-cultural brief encounters in both texts underscores the need for social, political, and cultural institutions of this nation to actually create bridges for better encounters, understandings, empathies, power sharing to create the kind of promise of America the foundational documents of the nation offer. Instead, readers and writers, co-creators of culture, often find ourselves back in familiar but separate spaces or politically polarized.

Morrison's texts engage us in complex ways. The tension Patricia Hill Collins identifies between civic and ethnic nationalisms is also the gap Morrison explores through her fiction. In bringing the conflicted, improvisational stories from the margins of gender, race, and class in *A Mercy* and *Beloved* to her readers, she urges us to listen with care and to seek these stories of Florens and her mother, Sethe and her daughters, Amy Denver and Rebekka Vaark, and Lina and even Beloved. If the tension and gap between civic and ethnic nationalisms is to ever be closed in the United States, we, too, have to step over the threshold of identity politics to engage with multiple narratives as well as the people around us

Toni Morrison destabilizes wickedness and evil from her very first novel, *The Bluest Eye*, helping readers indict Cholly Breedlove for his evil actions against his daughter while studying the larger forces that drive him to it. The texts under discussion here are part of Morrison's larger project of trying to explore the larger cultural circumstances that impact self-sabotage or any kind of morally questionable act by an individual. Sethe's killing of her daughter Beloved is not excused, but Morrison is also aware of the extraordinary pressures that make her political resistance against the oppressive institution of slavery, which owns her and her children, understandable. Morrison has expressed this ambivalent and contradictory idea in an interview: "It was absolutely the right thing to do ... but it's also the thing you have no right to do" (qtd. in Morgenstern 23).

A strong system of supremacy and hierarchies, past and present, can masquerade as heroic and nationalistic in a period of presidential elections and shifting political landscapes while poor women and men of all races, oppressed by a variety of issues and occupying the lowest order in the hierarchy, can be found negotiating in the margins of the nation for agency and lives of dignity. What then is the responsibility of twenty-first-century readers to see Morrison's texts as interruptions of "the performance of the present. The 'past-present'... [as] the necessity, not the nostalgia, of living" as Bhabha articulates in *The Location of Culture*? (7). By opening up the space between the mother and her othering, the space between the nation's desire for coherence and its internal otherings, these complex texts reminds us again to read in the gaps offered by these narratives and to stay cautious around arguments that merely reinforce binaries, no matter where they appear. The "wicked" is in adopting simple binaries, and Toni Morrison confirms that.

ENDNOTES

[1] Historian David Blight in his recent book, *Race and Reunion: The Civil War in American Memory*, argues that soon after the Emancipation Proclamation was signed, significant figures including politicians from the North and South, writers, poets, intellectuals, were involved in trying to privilege the healing and reunion of the states over recalling and acting on the emancipatory promises of the proclamation—assimilating the newly freed slaves in to the nation. Blight's study confirms that nationally, we have not embraced the emancipatory ideals of the Civil War despite the gains made by the Civil Rights Act several years after the end of the War.

[2] Jean Wyatt and Susan Strehle both discuss the formal and structural break between Florens's narration and the last section when her mother narrates in *A Mercy*. For my purpose here, the gap simply reinforces the political structures being put in place during the emergent system of slavery, which separated ethnic others as a form of control.

[3] The Oxford English Dictionary online offers the following definition and usages of the word "wicked": "Bad in moral character, disposition, or conduct; inclined or addicted to willful wrong-doing; practising or disposed to practise evil; morally depraved. (A term of wide application, but always of strong reprobation, implying a high degree of evil quality.)" Additionally, a

secondary reference is directly to "of a person (or a community of persons). The Wicked One, the Devil, Satan." Morrison's use of the word "wicked" in *A Mercy* seems to be reserved for someone like Florens, as she willfully and mindlessly attaches herself to the blacksmith, who later derides her for her willingness to be enslaved by such concepts as romantic love while leaving her autonomy behind. For readers of Morrison, therefore, attaching oneself to binaries without stepping back to read interstitially seems to have the same meaning.

[4]Ira Berlin in his book, *The Making of African America* argues for a reinterpretation of African American historiography to be more inclusive of all people of African descent who have immigrated to the United States from the diaspora after the 1965 *Immigration and Naturalization Act.* He argues, with other migration and post-colonial theorists, that a new nonlinear contrapuntal narrative of movement and stasis better explains the many forced and unforced migrations that tell the story of African America today. In this narrative the continual remaking of racism in the United States is further complicated by the internal negotiations and remaking of black identity through "routes" and "roots" as theorized by Paul Gilroy and others.

[5]Naomi Morgenstern in her article "Maternal Love/Maternal Violence: Inventing Ethics in Toni Morrison's *A Mercy*" quotes Thomas Hobbes to establish the foundational philosophical idea that in the absence of any contract, natural rights for her child belong to the mother; because she nourishes the child, she also has dominion over it. She discusses the fact that Morrison's black mothers occupy this Hobbesian political space because they may not know who the father is and because the institution of slavery was based on the slave status of the mother as transferring that same slave status to the children.

[6]Homi Bhabha in the introduction to his *The Location of Culture* quotes from page 213 of Morrison's *Beloved*.

WORKS CITED

Anderson, Benedict. *Imagined Communities: Reflections on the Origin and Spread of Nationalism.* 1983. Verso, 2006.

Berlin, Ira. *The Making of African America: The Four Great Migrations*. Penguin Books, 2010.

Bhabha, Homi K. *The Location of Culture*. Routledge, 1994.

Blight, David W. *Race and Reunion: The Civil War in American Memory*. Belknap Press of the Harvard University Press, 2001.

Collins, Patricia Hill. *From Black Power to Hip Hop: Racism, Nationalism, and Feminism*. Temple University Press, 2006.

Ignatieff, Michael. *Blood and Belonging: Journeys into the New Nationalism*. 1993. Noonday Press, 1995.

Morgenstern, Naomi. "Maternal Love/Maternal Violence: Inventing Ethics in Toni Morrison's *A Mercy*. *MELUS*, vol. 39, no. 1, 2014, pp. 7-29.

Morrison, Toni. *A Mercy*. Alfred A. Knopf, 2008.

Morrison, Toni. *The Bluest Eye*. 1970. Washington Square Press, 1972.

Morrison, Toni. *Beloved*. Alfred A. Knopf, 1987.

Profile of a Writer: Toni Morrison. Interview by Melvyn Bragg, directed by Alan Benson, "South Bank Show," Home Vision, 1987. Videocassette.

Strehle, Susan. "'I Am a Thing Apart': Toni Morrison, *A Mercy*, and American Exceptionalism." *Critique*, vol. 54, no.2, 2013, pp. 109-123.

"Wicked." *Oxford English Dictionary*, 2017, https://en.oxford-dictionaries.com/definition/wicked. Accessed 20 May 2017.

Wyatt, Jean. "Failed Messages, Maternal Loss, and Narrative Form in Toni Morrion's *A Mercy*." *Modern Fiction Studies*, vol. 58, no.1, 2012, pp. 128-151.

Rethinking, Rewriting Self and Other in Toni Morrison's *Love*

LEE BAXTER

TONI MORRISON'S NOVEL *LOVE* (2003) disrupts the ideological norms of family and, in particular, motherhood and mothering. *Love*'s narrative focuses on the history of the Cosey family, beginning in the 1800s through desegregation and up to the 1990s. Although the plot focuses predominantly on the patriarchal head of the family, Bill Cosey, the real story focuses on the women Cosey surrounds himself with. The women in Cosey's immediate family (May, Cosey's daughter-in-law, Christine, his granddaughter, and Heed, his second wife) fight against one another as Cosey stands on the sidelines laughing at their inability to communicate and build nurturing relationships with one another. The inability to communicate and develop nurturing relationships highlights the glaring absence of mothers, mothering, and motherhood within *Love*. Even when mothers are present, such as May, Christine's mother, they do not nurture or protect their children. The primary three women in the novel— Christine, Heed, and Junior—are abandoned, ignored, and/or twisted (physically and psychologically) by their lack of mothering. This absence of love and motherly nurturing causes a lack of self-love and of identity, and the inability to connect with others in meaningful relationships. Through presenting this inability to connect with another, Morrison challenges the dominant, or idealized, notion that family must constitute a stable environment, which includes unconditional love and committed relationships. Similar to Julia Kristeva's "Stabat Mater," Morrison considers an alternative account of (m)othering through an examination of "othering." This examination provides an alternative view of

88

women being defined by motherhood, in particular Christine and May. Moreover, it is not until the women recognize both their selves as other, as well as the other in the Other, that they can learn to love truly and break free from the idealized social constructs of femininity and maternity.

KRISTEVA: A BRIEF OVERVIEW

Kristeva's text "Stabat Mater" offers her readers complex descriptions of the mother-child bond that challenge social constructs no longer aligning with twentieth-century Western society. In particular, Kristeva explores the boundaries of human experience through the use of dialogic conversation that depicts the fluidity of boundaries between inside and outside, identity and nonidentity, love and hate, and subject and object. Although many psychoanalysts focus on the mother as object, Kristeva accentuates the mother as subject. Kristeva's methodology in "Stabat Mater" is laid out in two parallel columns. In one column, as a speaking subject, Kristeva explores the mother's role through her own experience as a mother and a child of a mother. In the other column, Kristeva writes as a reading subject examining and critiquing the Virgin Mary's role as (m)other in Western society. Kristeva's act of critical reading, writing, and self-reflection in relation to her role as mother and daughter parallel to the Virgin Mary's role solidifies Kristeva's identity as an active subject. However, the Virgin Mary, as becomes clear in her examination, is depicted in literature solely as an object that is revered and idealized through her symbolic role as Christ's mother. As Kristeva elucidates, the idealization of Mary as mother and woman no longer aligns with the images of twentieth- and twenty-first-century Western women.

Although some critics, such as Elizabeth Grosz and Domna Stanton, argue that Kristeva reinscribes cultural stereotypes of the maternal and motherhood, I, however, agree with Kelly Oliver, who states, "Kristeva, like other postmodernists, de-essentializes gender" (201). By breaking down gender boundaries, Kristeva also collapses the power dynamics between female and male roles. She questions why Freud and Lacan assert that it is the paternal threat that causes a child to leave the protective safe space of the maternal body. Through this question, Kristeva asks how children develop subjectivity, and argues that this development begins earlier than the mirror and the Oedipal stage. Kristeva further argues that maternal regulation comes prior to paternal Law. In so doing, she critiques the inadequate discourses around maternity, motherhood, and mothering.

The two columns form a conversation that explores traditional roles of motherhood, which are impossible standards for women to meet. Humans are far more complex than the portrayal of the Virgin Mary, who never speaks for herself; instead, she is depicted by men who have written her in text. Kristeva's dialogue between her and Mary reflects the break created by the social construction of what it means to be a mother, an individual, and a lover in contemporary society. Moreover, this dialogue produces an understanding of the subject and provides us with a critique of the networks of gendered power relations. Furthermore, these networks of power are seen through the ability to read and write the word and to read and write the world. Language and knowledge are not mutually exclusive (Kristeva, "Strabat Mater"; Valsiner). The world is intelligible through language and through the communication of our knowledge to one another. Communication, however, begins with the ability to read the world in which the language exists.

For instance, in her work "Revolution in Poetic Language," Kristeva introduces her definition of the semiotic. The semiotic is made up of the subject's nonreferential corporeal drives, such as affect, emotions, sensations, *chora*,[2] rhythms, and so forth. The semiotic is part of "how" meaning is made out of language, and is also a component of the construction of one's identity. In Kristeva's words: "We shall distinguish the semiotic (drives and their articulations) from the realm of signification, which is always that of a proposition or judgment, in other words, a realm of *positions*. This positionality ... is structured as a break in the signifying process, establishing the *identification* of the subject and its object as preconditions of propositionality" ("Revolution in Poetic Language" 98). This positionality refers to the cultural and subject positions within the social situation. Through this, Kristeva contends that the maternal body functions between nature and culture.

Arguing that the maternal should not be reduced to feminine, mother, or woman, Kristeva recognizes the mother's union to the infant and child, and divides the role of meeting the child's needs from love and desire. A woman loves and desires, as a mother loves and desires. In other words, each role identifies her as a social and speaking being. However, cultural expectations place the role of the maternal as "unsexed." Yet men and women, as Kristeva suggests, can perform the role of the maternal. That both men and women can carry out maternal duties in a nurturing, caring way breaks down the female-male gender boundaries, which creates the possibility of recognizing the Other as not so other, such as when Frank Money in *Home* nurtures his sister or when Paul D in *Beloved* nurtures Sethe.

In identifying the Other as not so other, Kristeva posits that the maternal body exemplifies the embodiment of the other through the maternal body. The maternal body depicts the maternal body as a body in the process of subjectivity. The maternal body is simultaneously subject and Other, and as such it is neither one nor two. This tension exposes the crisis in identity and difference. The maternal body represents self and other, a body that is in a state of a subject in process. As such, through the birth of another, the Other too becomes a subject in process. Kristeva contends that maternity is an example of love that stands outside the Law that can produce an ethics, or in Kristevian term a "herethics," which is not confined by social conformity. Describing that the mother's love for the child is simultaneously a love for herself depicts the mother and woman willing to surrender herself.

In surrendering herself to the child and other, the mother places herself in relation to her mother. As Kristeva explains: "Recovered childhood, dreamed peace restored, in sparks, flash of cells, instant of laughter, smiles in the blackness of dreams, at night, opaque joy that roots me in her bed, my mother's, and projects him, a son, a butterfly soaking up dew from her hand, there, nearby, in the night. Alone: she, I, and he" (*Tales of Love* 247). It is through this union (and reunion) that the mother is viewed as the primary source of identification; thus, identification is prior to the identification with paternal Law. In relation to *Love*, the women are associated only with paternal Law and, therefore, never identify with their mothers.

The primary identification with the mother's body is perhaps misplaced in the sense that the initial identification is with the mother's love: the two become indistinct and thus intertwined. The unconditional love of the mother is a love given to the other—the child "irremediably another" ("Stabat Mater" 112). In this recognition of the child as other, Kristeva (as a mother) also recognizes herself as other, an other that reproduces life and death as she recognizes her mortality and the child's mortality. Unfortunately, the mothers of Christine, Heed and Junior only view their children as Other. As such, the mothers and their children are incapable of recognizing the self as other. This lack of self-awareness reproduces feelings of hatred, which are reflected in their relationships with the self and with other women. Consequently, mother-child relationships are complex, as not only are mothers capable of love, but they are also capable of hate. As Kristeva notes concerning the birth of her child, she recognizes "the possibility—but not the certainty—for reaching out to the other, the ethical" (182) and posits the concept of "herethics."

The concept of herethics is founded on the idea of woman as mother in relation to the Other through love. The ethics in herethics addresses the "reaching out to the other" (182) by acknowledging the otherness of the Other as well as the otherness of the self. As Oliver suggests, "Herethics sets up one's obligations to the other as obligations to the self and obligations to the species. This ethics binds the subject to the other through love not Law. The model of ethical love is the mother's love for the child, which is a love for herself and a love for her own mother" (5). Kristeva's work, however, does not address the notion that a mother may not bond with her child and that she may feel little or no love for her child, as depicted in Morrison's novel *Love*. With no love for the child there is no love for the self. The bond between mother and her mother and between mother and her child is misshapen, which leaves the child with a sense of a lack in the self—a lack of identity. There is no love for self or other. I would suggest in *Love* that Junior's misshapen foot is a physical manifestation of her inability to connect with her mother and vice versa, which leads to Junior's lack of identity and her lack of responsibility to herself and others. Moreover, as Morrison portrays in many of her novels, including *Love*, children only develop subjectivity in relation to paternal Law.

Paternal Law brings the child into symbolic identity and positions her or him in the world of linguistic meaning. In so doing, the child enters into a life of desire and incompletion, continually seeking lost objects and creating a lack of plenitude in being. This is what Lacan calls "castration."[3] Castration is the child's recognition of the lack in the mother's maternal omnipotence. At this point, the mother, for the child, is no longer the sole provider of satisfaction, and causes the Law of the father to replace the mother.[4] Simultaneously, the Law declares "no" to the child, that she or he is not the mother's object of desire. Therefore, in accordance to Kristeva, herethics challenges patriarchal Law. Herethics unites the other as self with the other in another. In other words, by recognizing the self as another, one can then recognize the other in Others. Similar to Kristeva, Morrison recognizes the need to examine the fallacy of the Law, and how to overcome the sense of lack and reconnect with the sense of wholeness through the other. Consequently, many of Morrison's narratives not only challenge not only patriarchal Law but social constructs of mothering and motherhood.

Through challenging patriarchal constructs, as Kristeva depicts in "Stabat Mater," women can move outside the set boundaries set by the Law by recognizing one's self and other. Yet returning to a position of unconditional love (love of the mother, love of the other, and love of the self) is a difficult process, as Morrison conveys in novels such as *Beloved*, *Paradise*, and *Love*. Beyond it being a difficult process for the individual, the Law continuously imposes its presence through coercion, deceit, threats, and violent actions. For instance, in *Paradise*, the men in the town of Ruby violently attack the women in the Convent, blaming them for the unrest in Ruby. In *Beloved*, schoolteacher trespasses on Baby Suggs's property, asserting his power to take back what he deems is his property—Sethe and her children. In each instance, the men reinscribe the Law by subjugating others. These others lose their subjectivity, since they are positioned as objects within the male paternal gaze that imposes paternal Law within society.

At the end of *Beloved*, Sethe begins to pinpoint her loss of subjectivity through "her ma'am hurting her feelings" (321). Mirroring

Kristeva, Sethe's recognition is the beginning of her acknowledging herself as other. The recognition can be traced back the division between mother and child through paternal Law and the social hierarchical constructs devised to separate and make distinct boundaries through racial prejudices. In the final pages of the novel, Paul D ("the man who can walk into a house and make the women cry" [321]) has come to recognize the other in himself and offers to nurture Sethe and help her find the other in her self. Paul D articulates his understanding of the world and of others: "We need some kind of tomorrow ... You your best thing, Sethe. You are" (322). Paul D's statement and his willingness to care for her reflect Kristeva's notion that regardless of gender, both men and women can perform maternal duties while they simultaneously initiate the possibility of the recognition of the other as not so other.

In relation to Morrison's *Love*, the following question remains: how do Christine and Heed recognize their self as a subject? As a subject, I contend, people are mutually reliant on their understanding of self through recognizing differences in Others. This recognition allows us to challenge societal ideologies that all women strive to become mothers. Such a stance not only implies that all women are heterosexual but that all women who do not become mothers are somehow deficient or deviant. Through destabilizing the fixed notion of mothering, Morrison's work contends that no one prescribed performance of motherhood or mothering exists. Her characters refute the concept that a woman is a woman based on the (re)production of children.

LOVE

Love begins and ends with the disembodied voice of "L" (Love), the Cosey family's cook, confidant, protector, and surrogate mother of sorts. Although L is a ghost, she is also the omniscient narrator, who highlights the duality of mind and body, self and other, as she intermittently interjects throughout the narrative. Her interjections lead us through the love, hatred, desire, greed, and jealousy felt and depicted through Cosey's women. L also draws our attention to the Law—which is embodied by Bill Cosey—and how it has divided and shaped the lives of the Cosey women. Importantly,

L also suggests an alternative reading of female subjectivity and mothering through her interrogation of the way the Law can be subverted in order to return to the primary identification with one's unconditional love of the mother. This unconditional love reunites Heed and Christine when they recognize the other in each other as they acknowledge the mistreatment of their mothers, who sold and gave away their daughters all in the name of Bill Cosey.

Bill Cosey's character functions as a signifier for the Law. Cosey is similar to societal ideology (sexism, male dominance, class, and race), in the sense that he is simultaneously absent and present throughout the text. Although Cosey's physical body is absent, his physical presence is continuously evoked through the women's memories of him. Cosey's physical presence is also suggested through his portrait hanging above Heed's bed and in his study, which continues to smell of cigars and whisky thirty years after his death. For Heed and Christine, Cosey's physical presence is a felt presence that continues to deny them their friendship and their love for one another. Echoing Lacan, Cosey's felt presence positions both women, who were best friends before Cosey married Heed at the age of 11, in a state of desire and in-completion, as they continue to fight over the inheritance he left to his "sweet Cosey child" (88). This fighting stems from their continuous seeking of a lost object, love, yet the object of love that they desire is erroneously displaced onto Cosey's properties (the house and the resort).

Although on the surface Heed and Christine both desire to prove that the property Cosey left is hers alone, in reality, each woman seeks the love for the other, which was stolen when they were young girls. By displacing the real object, the women mistakenly pursue an object (Cosey's property) that they believe will provide them with their identity. It is not until Cosey's presence disappears that the women are released from paternal Law and surmount the lack, which created the divide, not only with their mothers but also with their sense of self. By overcoming this lack, Heed and Christine reconnect with their self and their feelings of unconditional love that generates a sense of wholeness in recognition of the self as other and the other. Consequently, many of Morrison's narratives challenge not only paternal Law but also social constructs.

According to Lacan, paternal Law brings the child into symbolic identity. Yet Christine and Heed are depicted as incomplete individuals whose identities are bound together through a mutual hatred of each another. Their hatred defines each as the Other not only to each other but also within their community. Their subjects are created by an imposed subjection, a forced identity. However, this form of subjectivity displays the women only as objects and not subjects themselves. The subject replicates particular qualities through which she or he associates and differentiates the self from other subjects. This differentiation, however, places the subject in a position in which she or he recognizes the self through the Other or through a social authority (ideology). In other words, the subject defines her or himself through the Other and accepts this definition of her or his identity. The acceptance of this identity is a form of expected obedience. Morrison exposes this obedience to underscore how social hierarchies (class, gender, race, and so forth) form symbolic identities through Heed and Christine. In relation to Cosey, the women recognize themselves through Cosey's love (and his property). This love is a love that Cosey withholds and uses to create a divide between the two women. This divide is symbolic of his viewing the women as objects rather than as subjects.

Christine and Heed are not allowed to develop a sense of independent autonomy, as each is forced to play a specific role defined by Cosey—Christine as granddaughter and Heed as child-wife. May's attempt to shield Christine from Cosey's questionable decisions and actions serves only to reinforce Christine's lack of subjectivity and to further isolate Christine and Heed from one another. Although one could argue that Christine's decision to move to the big city, to marry, to take up with Fruit, and to become Dr. Rio's mistress were declarations of her freedom from authority (society's and Cosey's), these decisions, in fact, depict Christine's endeavour to search for her identity and her subjectivity separate from Cosey and from May. However, each attempt to break free from paternal ideology only heightens Christine's awareness that she cannot escape paternal Law. In fact, Christine's subjectivity is tied to a paternal culture that defines gender and sex roles. Christine's relationship with Fruit causes her to change "her clothing," to sharpen "her language to activate slogans" and to hide "her inauthentic hair" in order not to "disappoint" Fruit (163). In the end, Christine's role reflects the roles of "a street-worker-baby-sitter-cook-mimeographing-marching-nut-and-raisin-carrying woman" (167). The words that are used to describe Christine reflect the stereotypes of feminine work.

This type of gender stereotyping is also displayed in the division of labour represented by L and May. While L cooks, May looks after all of the "household duties" in the hotel (102-103). May is portrayed as an industrious, hardworking woman who looks after the household needs, whereas Cosey assumes authority over the hotel through his good looks, his charm, and his money (103). This gender based division of labour mirrors the dominant forms of mothering—cooking, cleaning, and household duties—through the assignment of work and social relations within an historical context. Cosey, on the other hand, is the figurehead of Cosey's Hotel and Resort—"the best and best known vacation spot for colored folk on the East Coast ... guests from as far away as Michigan and NY couldn't wait to get down here" (5). He is a successful entrepreneur whose extroverted personality attracts clientele and musicians to his hotel. However, it is the women, L and May, who run the hotel. Moreover, L and May embody the social consciousness that women are subject to paternal Law, and, therefore, they resist individualism.[5] In other words, May does not recognize herself as a subject outside of paternal ideology, which, according to Patrice DiQuinzio indicates that she does not recognize others as subjects (7).

May reinforces paternal ideology by withholding her love from her daughter Christine and by further creating a rivalry between Christine and Heed (141). May does not nurture Christine except in the form of nurturing a hatred for Heed. Additionally, May relinquishes her responsibility of positively nurturing and taking care of Christine to L. After the death of May's husband (Cosey's son), Billy Boy, "Christine crawled under [L's] bed ... May looked on Billy Boy's death as more of an insult than a tragedy. Dry-eyed as a turtle, she left Christine to [L] to raise" (137). By relinquishing her obligation of raising Christine to another, May severs the bond between mother and daughter. By severing this bond, May divides Christine, the subject, from her unconditional love. Furthermore,

May's action instills within Christine a rejection of (m)other's love and therefore also separates her from the love of the other in herself. This is the beginning of Christine's indoctrination in paternal ideologies, which leads Christine to harm others as well as her self. As such, Christine's relationships "were organized around the pressing needs of men" (92). Although Christine sought "privacy" and "independence," she still repeatedly turned to men to fulfill her subjectivity. This form of subjectivity does not allow Christine to recognize herself as a subject. Mirroring Kristeva's argument, Christine does not see a reflection of herself in the Other, and, therefore, she remains an other in the sense that she does not see herself as subject until she can see through the eyes of an other.

Heed, too, does not recognize herself as a subject, since she is always placed within relation to the patriarchal gaze. After Cosey's death, his portrait continues to hang over Heed's bed, reminding her who is in charge. Like Christine, Heed is abandoned by her mother. Heed's abandonment positions her as complete object when her parents "sell" her to Cosey (184). Her family's and her best friend Christine's rejection instills self-hatred within Heed. This self-hatred is mirrored through her inability to recognize her self as anything other than an Other. Moreover, Heed's otherness is rooted in the paternal mores that are espoused by May and L. Instead of nurturing and explaining to Heed how her marriage to Cosey changes her relationship with Christine, Heed is repeatedly reproached and rebuked for her lack of education and her naiveté.

For instance, during Christine's sixteenth birthday dinner at Heed's home, Christine chides Heed for her incorrect grammar. This rebuke simultaneously exposes Christine's education and Heed's lack of it as well as Heed's lack of authority and agency within her own home. Heed's response to Christine culminates in Cosey taking Heed over his knee and spanking her as one would a small child for bad behaviour at the dining table. Heed becomes an object of ridicule in her own home. In order to regain a false sense of agency, Heed takes a young man to dance with her at Cosey's hotel. She flaunts him in front of all of the hotel guests to publically deride Cosey for spanking her. As well, she sets Christine's bed on fire. Heed's actions, however, only serve to further objectify her in the eyes of May, Christine, Cosey, and the community. By placing herself on display, Heed externalizes her sense of self as object. Therefore, instead of becoming the subject in the eyes of others, she mirrors her inner sense of self as object through everyone else. The repercussions of her actions cause May and Christine to distrust and hate her more, and they cause Cosey to turn away from her and return to his lover Celestial. Although, as already noted, the feelings of hatred between the girls is fuelled by May (141), Cosey also plays a role in destroying the relationship between Heed and Christine. L states: "I blame May for the hate she put in them, but I have to fault Mr. Cosey for the theft" (200).

The "theft" L refers to is the innocence that Cosey has stolen from Christine and Heed—an innocence connected not only to their love for one another but to severing the cords that tie the girls to the unconditional love of the mother, the self, and other. As J. Brooks Bouson contends, "Heed and Christine, as girls, share a deep and profound bond" (362). This bond is one of pure, unconditional love, which allows each girl to be "in touch with the 'sweet Cosey child' within" (362). The "sweet Cosey child" part of their self is "the authentic part of the self that transcends racial and social barrier of class and caste" (362). Although Bouson directly addresses class and racial barriers, I would add that the ability to connect with self-love (which is rooted in the relationship of self and other or mother and other) is also destroyed through their separation from each other. Their separation causes both women to spend their lives locked in a battle against each other. However, this battle also extends to a constant recognition that they cannot access their authentic selves, which causes their feelings of loneliness and melancholy (97, 133). These feelings stem from their loss of each other and their unconditional love—a love that no one else can replace.

Although Heed's marriage to Cosey is loveless and produces no children, Christine's love life is plentiful and produces multiple pregnancies, each of which she aborts. Women who are not or cannot become mothers are often stigmatized as inadequate, abnormal, and/or deviant within society. Although some positive shifts in attitudes toward women without children have occurred, the branding of women without children continues. In essence, the stigmatizations of women who do not have children amounts to the binary opposition of entrenched concepts of what it means to be a mother. In accordance with Kristeva's thinking, motherhood is a constructed and institutionalized systematic truth, and an essentialist paradigm, which idealizes mothers as selfless beings, whose sole focus is their children. The essentialist paradigm also oppresses a woman's sexuality through an assumption of heteronormativity and her sexual drive. Her sexual activity and pleasure are entwined with the product of becoming a mother as opposed to the mere pleasure of sex itself.

Under this paradigm, the townspeople have labelled Christine a selfish and a sexually promiscuous woman. Although Christine recognizes that her choice to terminate her pregnancies represents her autonomy, she also notes after her final abortion that "perhaps she should have stalled, even prevented" the abortion (164). Even though she decides that she does want to become a mother, the final termination (her seventh) causes Christine to contemplate her decision to remain childless as she is occasionally followed by "the unborn eye that ha[s] disappeared in a cloud of raspberry red" (164). However, Christine's reflection on motherhood is juxtaposed with Cosey's death: "The dirty one [Cosey] who introduced her to nasty and blamed it on her…. The powerful one who abandoned his own kin and transferred rule to her playmate [Heed]" (165). Christine's grandfather Cosey is the reminder and origin of her introduction to sexuality (even though at the time she did not fully recognize his act of masturbation as such), her loss of innocence, her loss of self-love, and her loss of Heed and the unconditional love they felt for one another. Similar to James M. Mellard's argument (260), Cosey is the origin of the "dirtiness" Christine and Heed both feel and fear will "leak into their ordinary lives" (Morrison 192).

While Christine can conceive, Heed is unable to bare children for Cosey. As repeatedly noted, one of the reasons for Cosey choosing Heed is her ability to produce a family for him (104). The one time when she may have been pregnant by another man, she loses the child (173). However, her desire to have a child leads her to dismiss her miscarriage and to convince herself that she is pregnant, which stems from her feeling that to become a mother would mean that she would no longer have to "prove" anything

(173). However, after eleven months of pretending to be pregnant, L slaps her and forces Heed to "wake up" and admit that her "oven's cold" (174). This realization further reinforces Heed's feelings of defectiveness, of lack. Heed's inability to reproduce diminishes her status to that of an object of ridicule within the community and causes Cosey to further recoil from her. Her feelings of lack are also tied to her absence of authority within the household and her inheritance. Similar to Christine, Cosey, as a signifier of the Law, is the origin of Heed's introduction to sex, the loss of her innocence and childhood, her loss of self-love, and her loss of Christine. Cosey's paternal touch contaminates Christine and Heed.

During Christine and Heed's postmortem conversation, they trace the origins of their contamination, the loss of the other, and the loss of their self-love. They recognize that their lack of self love is rooted in Cosey's inappropriately touching Heed and to Christine's witnessing Cosey masturbate after touching Heed. During this discussion, Morrison does not identify who says what, which renders the women's words and feelings interchangeable: "He took all my childhood away from me, girl." / "He took all of you away from me" (194). Both sentences represent the effects of Cosey's actions on both Christine and Heed. By recalling the origin of their divide, Cosey and paternal Law lead them back to their original love for the other. In other words, the women remember what love is prior to their introduction to the Law. Echoing Kristeva's contention that the ethical is "reaching out to the other" (182) and understanding that space exists between the otherness of the Other and the otherness of the self, Christine and Heed acknowledge their subjectivity and dispel the notion of the self as other and the other as Other. In other words, it is at this moment of identification that Christine and Heed can nurture the self and the Other through the acknowledgement of their separate identity and their love for self and the Other. They also acknowledge and recognize that their mothers were part of perpetuating the patriarchal system (184). Morrison's novel highlights how this system places women subordinate to men and fatherhood, as it divides women and divides their subjectivity causing them to dissociate their self as Other.

At the end of the novel, Cosey is reduced to nothing more than a dead man. With the loss of his "physical" presence, Cosey's power dissipates over Heed and Christine as they confront his legacy in the ruins of the hotel. Heed's crossing over aligns her with Love, unseen but not unheard. The ability to communicate within the space between the otherness facilitates Christine's and Heed's return to their original state of selfless love, a state prior to paternal Law. They return to the Law of the mother. In this state, their love that crosses boundaries, such as class and gender, as it moves outside the dominant patriarchal system.

Following Kristeva, Morrison's novel is a creative work that provides a space for imaginative exploration that moves outside the patriarchal system. In other words, her novels paradoxically explore the notion of motherhood without the characters always being biological mothers. Although on the surface the novel appears to be about Cosey, it is actually a novel that examines and rewrites the importance of mothering and motherhood in a nontraditional sense. Neither Christine nor Heed become mothers; nevertheless, their love for each other disrupts the conventional social and cultural constructions of mothering through their return to matriarchal Law (or in Kristevian terms herethics), which denotes unconditional love through the recognition of self as other and other as self.

ENDNOTES

[1] Lacan's mirror stage uses the lower case "o" to denote the ego and an Ideal-I for the subject. The Ideal-I is the "other" within the subject's understanding of her or his as "I." Whereas, the use of the capital "O"—"the Other" —signifies "other people," or other subjects the individual meets in social life. "The Other" also represents language and the customs within society that is organized under the law.

[2] *Chora* is the Greek word for an enclosed space, or womb. This is a person's developmental stage when one cannot distinguish self from that of the mother. At this stage, one is solely governed by her or his drives—perceptions, feelings, needs—without recognition of boundaries.

[3]For Lacan, the penis and phallus are not the same. The penis is the biological organ, whereas the phallus invokes other signifiers. Castration is the loss of the phallus, the entry into law and language, which causes a break between physical experiences and language. In other words, there is a loss of oneself to others through the loss of a relation to things.

[4]Lacan argues that the mother is the initial Big Other. She is not viewed as the Law but rather a single source of desire that gives complete pleasure through milk, comfort, safety, and so forth.

[5]This statement is not as cut and dry as it would appear, as L is a complex representation of both upholding maternal love as well as paternal Law.

WORKS CITED

Bouson, J. Brooks. "Uncovering 'the Beloved' in the Warring and Lawless Women in Toni Morrison's *Love*." *Midwest* Quarterly, vol. 49, no. 4, summer 2008, pp. 358-373.

DiQuizno, Patrice. *The Impossibility of Motherhood: Feminism, Individualism and the Problem of Mothering*. Routledge, 1999.

Grosz, Elizabeth. *Sexual Subversions: Three French Feminists*. Allen & Unwin, 1989.

Kristeva, Julia. "Revolution in Poetic Language." *The Kristeva Reader*, edited by Toril Moi, Columbia University Press, 1986, pp. 89-136.

Kristeva, Julia. "Stabat Mater." *The Kristeva Reader*, edited by Toril Moi, Columbia University Press, 1986, pp. 160-185.

Kristeva, Julie. *Tales of Love*. Translated by Leon Roudiez, Columbia University Press, 1987.

Lacan, Jacques. *Seminar XX: Encore!*, Trans. Bruce Fink, W. Norton, 1975.

Lacan, Jacques. *The Seminar of Jacuqes Lacan, Book III: The Psychoses*, Trans. Russell Grigg, edited by J.A. Miller, W. Norton, 2000.

Mellard, James M. "Unimaginable Acts Imagined: Fathers, Family Myth, and the Postmodern Crisis of Paternal Authority in Toni Morrison's *Love*." *Mississippi Quarterly*, vol. v, no.1, Jan. 2010, pp. 233-264.

Morrison, Toni. *Beloved*. 1987. Vintage, 2004.

Morrison, Toni. *Love*. Vintage, 2005.

Morrison, Toni. *Paradise*. Alfred A. Knopf Incorporated. 1998.

Oliver, Kelly. *Ethics, Politics, and Difference in Julia Kristeva's Writing*. Routledge, Inc., 1993.

Stanton, Domna. "Difference on Trial: A Critique of the Maternal Metaphor in Cixous, Irigaray and Kristeva." *The Poetics of Gender*, edited by Nancy K. Miller, Columbia University Press, 1986, pp. 157-182.

Valsiner, Jaan. *A Guided Science: History of Psychology in the Mirror of Its Making*. Transaction Publishers, 2012.

The Trauma of Second Birth

Double Consciousness, Rupture, and Toni Morrison's *Beloved*

LAUREN A. MITCHELL

Toni Morrison's *BELOVED* BRAIDS historical truth and a gothic ghost story into the narrative of Sethe, a Black, formerly enslaved mother, whose trauma is spiritually, emotionally, and even materially haunting. Inspired by the true story of Margaret Garner, the novel connects through a process of "re-memory" to a series of harrowing events that fold Sethe's past into her present by way of triggering images, events, and emotional artifacts. The literal haunting of the novel by what becomes known as "the baby ghost" originates after Sethe's escape to freedom. After experiencing the exhilaration of becoming an independent subject and of loving her children as much as she wants, as hers, for the first time, Sethe sees her former slave owner, named schoolteacher, coming to collect his "lost property." Overwhelmed with the horror of being brought back to the plantation, Sweet Home, Sethe attempts to murder her four children in the shed behind her house to spare them slavery. She fails in all but one: the nameless baby girl, known by the only word Sethe could afford to be written on her tombstone: "Beloved."

Although the death of the baby sets in motion a series of events that propel the novel forward, what inspires Sethe's reactionary violence is the trauma she suffered while enslaved. Shortly after giving birth to her third child and pregnant with her fourth, she is forcibly held down by her schoolteacher's nephews, and nursed. It is a bizarre iteration of "rape"—a word generally meant to categorize a violation of a particular type of penetrative sexual encounter—which is both fetishistic and dehumanizing. In turn, the novel requalifies that rape can be such that the violation of Sethe's body extends beyond sex to determine a power structure. In this essay, I centre my attention on the rape as the catalyzing force, and result, of the hegemonic power structures that work to reconstruct Sethe's identity.

Sethe's story occurs through a multifocal narration that, at times, undermines her as a traditional subject, where the insidious merging of memory and of trauma revises the underpinnings of her identity. What results is a reflection of Sethe's gaze back upon herself as it is informed by how her oppressors cast her as an object. Because this is fundamentally discordant with her own self-consciousness, it forces her toward a multifocal awareness of her subject position. It is a recursive gaze that continually edits and affirms her identity as it has been informed by the struggles of the Black, maternal, and recently enslaved body. This self-reflexivity enacts both W.E.B. Du Bois's theory of double consciousness and a rupture in identity that, through Julie Kristeva's theory of abjection, can be likened to the physical and psychological after effect of birth. I posit that there is a dialectical relationship between Sethe's "inner" and "outer" stressors (her strong sense of identity as a mother, and the anguish and trauma facilitated by her imposed position as a slave, respectively). The result of the inner and outer stressors is tantamount to a kind of rebirth which as I will discuss is typified by Hortense J. Spillers's recent work on "second birth."

Morrison writes the rape of the breast as the scene to which there is always a return, as it is embedded in the cyclical structure of the novel. In so doing, I argue that *Beloved* makes identity scenic through memory. Scenic memory is inspired by re-memory in its temporal structure—an interjection of the present into the past. I consider scenic memory in relation to *the* point of rupture during a traumatic event: the moment that lands at the centre of re-memory. In other words, although Sethe is no longer enslaved, the primary scene of her trauma—the rape of the breast—interrupts the possibility of freedom long after the Civil War has ended. Although *Beloved* takes place about a decade after the war, Sethe's consciousness remains at the precipice of slavery and freedom, and therefore her narrative offers though her re-memory a duality of selves and identities that shifts throughout the novel. Here, I use

Beloved to highlight a dialectical exchange of identity creation and recreation, which occurs through encounters with trauma.

Although Sethe must confront trauma in a number of ways—and thus her identity is shaped by her trauma—I focus here on her rape as the scenic rupture point through which the rest of the story filters. I posit that to understand *Beloved*, we must understand a two-folded formation of identity that occurs through Sethe's rape. The event of the assault itself extends past the dialectical exchange of internalized pressure (the physical and psychological vulnerability that is inherent to Sethe's subject position as a slave) versus external rupture due to a specific event—during her dehumanizing rape. This essay reads the idea of double consciousness as discussed by W.E.B. Du Bois in terms of its application to trauma theory, and, as I will explain, facilitates a psychic framework by which we can interpret a tension located internally within the subject as a site of fragmentation under hegemonic pressure, as a kind of "stress fracture" in identity creation. On the other hand, a traumatic event—Sethe's rape—evokes an external rupture vis-a-vis a major life event, not unlike the physical and metaphorical rupture that occurs during a physical birth. This rupture causes a paradoxical relationship that divides subjectivity into a "before" trauma and an "after" trauma yet, at the same time, causes a kind of centrifugal narratological pull that through Sethe's re-memory collapses the temporal boundaries of the past and present, as the scene to which there is always return. Scenic memory, then, both divides Sethe's life into "before" and "after" and, at the same time, engulfs her daily reality.

The external rupture of birth offers both a physiological and a psychic basis for Sethe's crucial rupture in identity. Hortense J. Spillers's recent interpretation of Du Bois's double consciousness as a second birth provides a crucial link between these internal and external folds of identity manipulation through trauma. Here, Spillers works in tandem with Du Bois's double consciousness, where a traumatic encounter causes the subject—in this case, Sethe—becomes aware of her potential as an objectified being or as a resource. I place Otto Rank's *The Trauma of Birth* in conversation with Spillers and *Beloved* to explore and revisit the idea of double consciousness, especially given that Rank views psychological rebirth as a process of self-creation (Rank 3). Although I push against his position that the titular trauma of being born is the apex trauma of human life, here I use his work in conversation Spillers's second birth, in which the cyclical nature of traumatic memory, or re-memory, creates what I consider a "scenic identity:" one that always returns to the moment of Sethe's rape, as she sees herself reborn, or recast as an object.[1]

As she experiences herself as an object to someone else, the trauma of her second birth becomes the point of departure for her re-memory. The structure of the novel—the way that Sethe's assault reappears insidiously through re-memory—emphasizes how double consciousness is an uncanny redundancy of selves as a point of recursion, a limitless potential to multiply her selves during her psychic second birth.

SCENIC MEMORY AND IDENTITY

As *Beloved* is considered one of the great masterpieces in the contemporary canon, it has inspired almost an entire field of study on re-memory—and other iterations of how memory haunts the present—that has reached a powerful, interdisciplinary status.[2] Sethe defines re-memory within the novel as places and events of the past that fold into the present irrespective of temporal boundaries, triggered by images or moments. She says, "even if I don't think it, even if I die, the picture of what I did, or knew, or saw is still out there. Right in the place where it happened" (36). Re-memory sits at the intersection between activity and image, with "thought pictures" (36) provoking a return to memories as they flood the present tense. It is an active form of memory, especially as it relates to trauma. Conceptually, re-memory finds a home in studies of politics and psychoanalysis in addition to the literary field where it originated.

Most significant to this essay, *Beloved* works in parallel to trauma studies and reflects the narratives extensively studied by scholar Cathy Caruth. Her work focuses primarily on narratives of post-traumatic stress disorder (PTSD), a trauma response that becomes triggered by a specific scene of violence, which deconstructs temporal boundaries and creates a sense of timelessness through repetition. Like Sethe, Caruth aligns trauma primarily with image, as she argues that, "o be traumatized is precisely to be possessed by an image or event" (4-5). She goes on to write that "history occurs as a symptom" (5). These narratives have been historically understood as memories that appear in a kind of repetition.

To that end, the structure of the *Beloved* is crucial to the way that the reader is meant to interpret Sethe's trauma, her history, as endlessly repetitive. Not only does memory work in *Beloved* for the purposes of the story, but it also encompasses the very fabric of the plot itself, which looks backward as much as it does forward; the plot is cyclical, just as memory is cyclical. Morrison's prose works in service of a nonlinear temporality even as the novel moves forward, which reflective of memory's associated constellations— or re-memory, where Sethe is triggered by her environment and catapulted back into her trauma. In one of the opening scenes of *Beloved*, Sethe moves through mundane chores—running through fields to reach the water pump, washing sap from her legs. But then Morrison writes, "[her] brain was devious.... Suddenly there was Sweet Home rolling, rolling, rolling out before her yes, and although there was not a leaf on that farm that did not make her want to scream, it rolled itself out before her in shameless beauty" (6). In this introduction to Sethe, Morrison feeds us with distractions of a beautiful landscape, while at the same time making Sethe's daily routine anguished by memories.

Traumas in *Beloved* are unflinchingly and immediately addressed so that they do not stage a melodramatic intervention; rather, the rape and murder of Sethe's past are defined immediately as givens and thus triggered by a "then something" (6), over which Sethe has no control. Morrison goes on to write, "Nothing else would be in her mind. The picture of the men coming to nurse her was as lifeless as the nerves in her back where her skin buckled like a washboard" (4). There is an insistence in this passage on "looking away" from the full force of the trauma. As Caruth writes, it is "[a] history [that] can be grasped only in the very inaccessibility of its occurrence.... It is the fundamental dislocation implied by all traumatic experience that is both its testimony to the event and to the impossibility of its direct access" (8-9).The traumas remain present in their sensation but in a kind of environmental ambiance that always remains in the periphery. The scene of violent rupture that has separated Sethe's life into a "before rape" and "after rape" has already occurred. The reader can only bear witness to the memories rather than the event itself. The memory of the assault is highlighted in the context of its absence; the times when Sethe does *not* think about her rape as rarer than the ones she does. The scene is described with reference to the assault, but without specifically naming it: we only know that something happened, but we do not understanding what, exactly, it was.

Similarly, the landscape itself triggers her memory of horrors she has seen, although in her reflection, her re-memory, the images come in as shadowy, missing pieces. She recalls the sycamore branches grown heavy with the bodies of lynched Black teenagers, yet it is the beautiful landscape she thinks of first: "It shamed her—remembering the wonderful soughing trees rather than the boys. Try as she might make it otherwise, the sycamores beat out the children every time and she could not forgive her memory for that" (6). The sight of trees carries with them an aura of suffering and regret for Sethe: she can remember the trees so clearly but not the boys. There are many things for which she cannot forgive herself, as she resists memories of a beautiful hell. "It never looked as terrible as it was and it made her wonder if hell was a pretty place too. Fire and brimstone all right, but hidden in lacy groves. Boys hanging from the most beautiful sycamores in the world" (6).

Sethe's "inaccessible history" (to use Caruth's term) follows her at all times; the reader learns the details through the obliquely referenced shards of memory in dialogue rather than through being catapulted back to any one long or specific scene. Glimpses of Sethe's rape appear through her re-memory, or scenic memory, as these glimpses are contextualized through specific environmental renderings: the barn, the trees, the butter churn, the hole in the dirt floor. Trauma makes it difficult to look directly at an event itself; rather, it comes in the form of hints, of absences, of peripheral vision. By telling us that Sethe is not seeing this image of the men coming to nurse her—the vision of herself as a predator's prey—or by focusing on the beautiful sycamore trees filled with their strange, hellish fruit, Morrison is directing out attention to the constant and exhausting efforts for Sethe to see her life beyond the context of its trauma.

DOUBLE CONSCIOUSNESS AND REBIRTH:
RECURSIVE IDENTITY FORMATION

Many theorists have described the inception of trauma as primarily an event: a catalyzing moment that divides into a "before" and an "after." Caruth's work in particular has offered crucial insight into the intersecting fields of literature and trauma studies. Her study on traumatic memory's timelessness offers crucial insight about re-memory as a psychological function derived from the poetics of literature. However, I wish to push against the sharply defined perimeters of her claim that "to be traumatized is precisely to be possessed by an image or event" (emphasis added). While this may be one important articulation of a certain kind of evental trauma, it risks being totalizing. Current social science and medical research has confirmed what was known experientially by people who experience racism on a day-to-day basis: it may be necessary to widen the definition of PTSD to be more inclusive of life-long stressors that often come in hand with oppression.[3]

In line with that, I reframe trauma in *Beloved* as equally caused by a slow-burning, life-long oppression that creates the conditions for traumatic events. Rather than approaching trauma as distilled down to a single, horrific moment, through DuBois's double consciousness, a clear framework emerges that shifts attention to the hegemonic pressures forcing fragmentation to occur and that places fragmentation—the "stress fracture" of self, as I mentioned earlier—as the root, and not the result, of trauma. In *Beloved*, Blackness is representative of an inescapable hierarchy of personhood. In *The Souls of Black Folk*, Du Bois writes the following: "the Negro is a sort of seventh son, born with a veil, and gifted with second-sight in this American world—a world which yields him no true self-consciousness, but only lets him see himself through the revelation of the other world. It is a peculiar sensation, this double-consciousness, this sense of always looking at one's self through the eyes of others" (2). Double consciousness is reflective of the much theorized oppression of "the gaze" and of otherness, although DuBois presents an especially damaging possibility: the "self" becomes a failed subject position, as the subject is only allowed to see herself in the context of the other from under a "veil."

Double consciousness leaves an opening for a transition in identity that is nonconsensual and is a result of a racialized power dynamic. Sethe's time in slavery has made her vulnerable to being considered an object and a commodity, which allows for multiple levels of abusive treatment. Often, trauma is thought of in terms of catastrophic events. (Even the structure of this essay centres on the rape as a core event leading to all other horrifying events in the novel.) Although the rape is pivotal event of the novel—although it has happened "off-stage," in the past rather than the present—Sethe's re-memory guides us to the hegemonic openings that would make it possible, even acceptable, to schoolteacher. The rape does not occur in isolation as a random act of violence; it is an artifact of the subject position, which arose from slavery that facilitated her attack.

The moment that anticipates Sethe's rape occurs while schoolteacher teaches his students, including his nephews, about the characteristics of Blacks. She overhears a student say her name during a lesson and moves to where she can hear their conversation. "No, no," Schoolteacher says. "That's not the way. I told you to put her human characteristics on the left; her animal ones on the right. And don't forget to line them up." Horrified, Sethe walks backward and says, "[I] didn't even look behind me to find out where I was headed "(193). This lesson stands as part of a long history of pathologizing Blackness as something other than human. Here, schoolteacher imposes an animal identity on Sethe, which is so abjectly disturbing to her that she walks backward out of the room. To encounter herself as an "object" in a teaching lesson on the difference between animals and humans rather than as herself is a shock to Sethe. The lesson on her "animal qualities," in essence, gives later permission for Sethe to be milked by schoolteacher's nephews, as if she were livestock. The insult of schoolteacher's lesson and the animal nature of the assault are points of rage for Sethe throughout the novel. In one of her reflections on the rape, she laments, "They handled me like I was the cow, no, the goat, back behind the stable because it was too nasty to stay in with the horses. But I wasn't too nasty to cook their food or take care of Mrs. Garner" (200).

Juxtaposed against pivotal, jarring encounter with schoolteacher and his students are the basic human dignities (which can be categorized as "unimpressive necessities") offered by Sethe's previous slave owner, Mr. Garner. The Garners' behaviour is amplified to a form of kindness by the absence of overtly violent cruelty. Mr. Garner allows Sethe to choose her husband, to stay with her children, and, most importantly, to nurse them for as long she needed—"a blessing she was reckless enough to take for granted, lean on, as though Sweet Home really was one" (23). In considering this quote, I cannot emphasize enough that *Beloved* does not extend a redemption narrative to the Garners for their "niceness" to their slaves. Rather, we see that prior to the point where Sethe walks in on schoolteacher's lesson, she is okay enough to abide by the static, daily subjection of slavery, in which trauma takes on a long-view of oppression. Prior to the rape, Sethe can cope with her position as a slave in part because she has enough brittle agency to withstand the dangerous precocity of her objectified position. Sethe's double consciousness under the Garners works within a paradigm of logistical functionality, which provides some comfort in her day-to-day life, without explicit threats of imminent danger (though certainly many implicit ones).

Rather than approaching trauma as a specific force that separates the self into a "before trauma" and "after trauma" split, double consciousness offers a different framework. Seeing the self as a chronic object, without an attainable subjective consciousness, there is an inversion: trauma facilitates a kind of fragmentation and that fragmentation is an uncontrollable, separating, and anxious splitting of the self. But what of the identity whose subject position is abject and is therefore forced into fragmentation?

Du Bois's double consciousness is entrenched in Black identity, and therefore lends itself explicitly to Sethe's narrative. However, there is also potential for a double consciousness, or, at the very least, a doubling in double consciousness, as we look to the identity formation of Sethe in her role as "mother." *Beloved* provides a recursive definition for double consciousness, not a "coupling" or "twoness," but a potential for exponential repetition. The potential for Sethe to encounter herself as object, rather than as self-sufficient subject, is, indeed, limitless, particularly at the tense junction of multiple subordinate—though notably not submissive—identities (woman, slave, mother, who may offer indefinite potential to create new slaves). Looking at this potential for repetition as a "second" birth begets a recursive tendency in identity formation, insofar as this confrontation of identity as other has the capacity to happen more than once. As *Beloved* is a text so entrenched in narrative and identity development, it is indeed a profound and hurtful rupture, as Sethe begins to see herself reflected so incorrectly in the gaze of the schoolteacher.

THE TRAUMA OF SECOND BIRTH

When Sethe overhears schoolteacher during his lesson, she becomes acutely aware that she is not entitled to her own selfhood. In turn, her slave status is one fraught with vulnerability and has left her open to attack. But Sethe's rape, the scenic centre of the novel, marks a rupture that incites action—she must leave Sweet Home. She must send her children away. Her second birth is a result of a violence in identity formation, perhaps only becoming a site of resilience later—a hollow victory, if any at all, after everything she suffers.

Spillers's "second birth" concept, or rebirth, connects the predisposed pressure of double consciousness on the identity placed on Sethe as a cross between "nonself" and a commodity with the eventual identity rupture of the rape. Her slave status, and therefore the need for her to be doubly-conscious of herself, creates the condition for trauma, as it places her always the risk of physical harm. Shaking the term "rebirth" loose from its spiritual origins of catharsis and redemption (Spillers), it commands that Sethe has to maintain a double awareness of herself and of how others may see her as an object. The exhausting, constant need to rectify the narrative under which she is subordinate—a slave and, thus, property—with her own desires to be an independent subject creates a cognitive framework that demands she constantly step outside of herself. This becomes painfully acute after her rape, which has the effect of splitting her identity into a "before" and "after" the trauma.

To the extent that a clear picture of the rape emerges, it is through the provocation of Paul D, a close friend from Sweet Home who becomes Sethe's lover. His presence summons the release of tacit memories—ones that haunt her but have been unarticulated in specific terms. He reminds Sethe of the details of this assault. She was she seen as prey by schoolteacher's nephews, and as it was happening, though, she could not look down upon herself. During her assault, her husband watches from a loft in the barn, outside of her field of vision:

> I am full God damn it of two boys with mossy teeth, one sucking on my breast the other holding me down, their book-reading teacher watching and writing it up. I am full of that, God damn it, I can't go back and add more. Add my husband to it, watching, above me in the loft—hiding close by—the one place he thought no one would look for him, looking down on what I couldn't look at all. (70)

The multiplicity of gazes within this passage underscores a nonconsensual performativity in Sethe's rape, making her trauma extend past her as an individual toward becoming a collective anguish. This, in turn, begets a recursive tendency in the trauma: her "second birth" has the potential to multiply itself. Her husband, watching her being raped from an unseen place, also experiences her trauma: he sees what she could not and looks at what she could not. The performed body's turmoil is now the spectator's turmoil, as Sethe cannot look at her abused body as the rape occurs. Later, she is severely whipped and beaten by schoolteacher for telling Mrs. Garner, the lady of the house. She names the resulting twisted scars on her back a "chokecherry tree;" a euphemism for what Paul D will later call a "revolting clump" (21) after they begin their sexual relationship.

There is a sense of impotence here in *Beloved* in the narrative of rebirth; by reacknowledging the anguish of being watched and not being saved, Sethe's trauma is reawakened. This is the event that sparks a shift in Sethe; this is the rebirth that forces her to leave the plantation. Although he is a witness and not a recipient of the trauma, her husband crumbles. Philosopher Kelly Oliver has written that the act of witnessing constructs a new subjectivity for the witness, which in itself can cause fragmentation and trauma (18-19). Sethe's trauma forces Halle to acknowledge his own. The false promise of Sweet Home as a potentially safe place—a plantation where oppression is insidious, but not explicit—is broken. His sense of self is disrupted in the face of Sethe's rape.

Halle is removed from the narrative. He hides from Sethe who must then run alone. He is later seen by Paul D, who smears butter from the butter turn over his face as if a return to the richness of the milk he experienced in infancy. The image comes to Sethe like a wave: "There is also my husband squatting by the churn smearing the butter as well as its clabber all over his face because the milk they took is on his mind" (70). The fragmentation that Halle experienced by witnessing his wife's trauma forces his own kind of rupture, a literal rebirth that causes him to regress back into a nonverbal, babylike state embodied in an adult man. Sethe's trauma inspires not only her own rebirth but the rebirth of her husband, which catapults him backward. As Otto Rank has written, "the expulsion from the blissful intrauterine state—separation from the mother—is inevitably traumatic" (3).

In *The Trauma of Birth*, Rank argues that the subject has a predisposition toward trauma simply by being born. E. James Lieberman writes that in Rank's work, "Trauma is the prototype for all anxiety crises: weaning, walking, the Oedipal conflict, willing and choosing anything important, such as living creatively, and, finally, dying" (xi). To Rank, the existence of trauma is implicit upon leaving the comfort of the womb, and the anxious exercise of life is the constant attempt to achieve the comfort experienced preconsciously. The rupture that is birth, whether it be a psychic or physiological birth, is a force that works by external pressure that exists beyond our control. In other words, it is eventual. The rupture delineates a specific point of "before" and "after" the event.

The process of becoming a mother brings with it a stark shift in identity, which is summoned by way of an embodied explosion—in no uncertain terms, birth is even under the best of circumstances defined by a series abject bodily processes. In her theory of abjection, Julia Kristeva writes, "It is as if the skin, a fragile container, no longer guaranteed the integrity of one's 'own and clean self' but, scraped or transparent, invisible or taut, gave way before the dejection of its contents" (53). The classic example of the abject is vomit: it comes from the body of the subject and was once a part of it. Once violently removed or disembodied, the effluvia (vomit or otherwise) is rejected and promptly disassociated from the subject's body. In other words, it is left behind, no longer a part of the subject's body, and yet a separate entity in the world that was a result of his or her involuntary action (for example: she vomited, but the vomit is not her). The abject is the removal of the self from self, so to speak, so that the subject's ownership of the abject substance is disavowed. It is literally and figuratively sticky, a part of ourselves for which we cannot shirk a responsibility we do not want.

If birth is seen as a purely physical process, it is explicitly a process of abjection, inclusive of blood, placenta, amniotic fluid, and a litany of other expelled bodily substances. Even the birth of the baby signifies abjection: an exiting of one body from another, complete with the general effluvia of the maternal body—a process of fluidity as it were, finally culminating in the doubling of bodies. Maternity offers a positive possibility to the abject. Sethe is proud to be a mother, and it is not maternity itself that causes her anguish but the rupture of her own rebirth.

In the context of a second birth, abjection marks a messy blurring of selves and an attempt for Sethe to both distance from and cling to her newly formed abject identity. In the psychic abject, second birth places the subject in the aftermath of the rupture and in an uncomfortable confrontation with the self, as if it were a familiar stranger. Kristeva writes, "The abject confronts us ... within our personal archeology with our earliest attempts to release the hold of *maternal* identity even before existing outside of her.... It is a violent, clumsy breaking away with its constant risk of falling back under the sway of a power securing as it is stifling" (13).

It cannot be ignored that the rape, the scenic centre of the novel, occurs when adult men forcibly suckle Sethe's breastmilk, which is another fluid that categorically falls under "abject" but is one that because of its positive associations (feeding babies), Sethe explicitly associates with herself. She coos the phrase "milk enough for all," as she feeds her family. Because of the rape, her breast milk is, figuratively, soured by the nephews. The food for her family is stolen and she now has a negative connotation of her ability to feed her family. As Sethe turns away from her rape, her face moving toward the ceiling, away from her attackers, she attempts to disassociate from the trauma, but her breast milk never quite becomes "the" breast milk, which would indicate a separation between her milk and her-self. She says, "They stole *my* milk" (17, emphasis added). Sethe does not treat her breast milk as one would treat an abject substance like vomit: expelled and ignored. Neither the breast milk nor the actions of the nephews can be stripped from Sethe's re-memory. Rather, her identity is bound in the milk as a physical confirmation of her ability to be a good mother.

Although I would be remiss if I were to only locate birth within a narrative of trauma, many women (perhaps, too many women) will cite pain, fear, and apprehension when thinking of birth, especially during their first birth experience, where the entire process is unfamiliar, unknown, often medicalized, and overly politicized. Although giving birth is not inherently physically traumatic for all women, I call attention here to the sharp line dividing "birth" from "pregnancy," which is precisely the move to a double consciousness: the "birth" of another human being summons a recursive and irrevocable splitting of identity of the woman, who becomes "mother" in addition to the subject she was before. To her child, she will only be known as mother—a point of anguish for Denver, who hurts at the thought that her mother had a life before she existed—and her identity will be divided. And thus, with the arguable "trauma" of the birth itself comes the trauma involved with the tension of adopting this new, socially and psychically fraught identity of being "mother."

Rank writes that "in attempting to reconstruct for the first time from analytic experiences the to all appearances purely physical birth trauma with its prodigious psychical consequences for the whole development of mankind, we are led to recognize in the birth trauma the ultimate biological basis of the psychical" (xvii). Although Rank's "birth trauma" refers to the subject who was once baby, and although his work has been critiqued for its eagerness to lean on a biological argument,[4] the biologically abject process of birth applies to both mother and child. "Mother" stands at the precipice of tensions in identity, an inescapable seeing of oneself being seen. This new subject position can be seen in light of how psychoanalytically discordant desire becomes for the mother, wherein the baby stands at a bizarre impasse of "abject," and that if it were completely reduced to a process of body, everything that exits in the mother's body would be dissociated with her immediate identity and would, in turn, be rejected. Yet the process of birth becomes oddly desirous, as the mother desires the love of the abject-turned-separate being. She will spend her life in its service, as the baby will spend her life in the service of her own independence.

How can we not see some trauma in this new formation of identity—a rupture?

A MOTHER TO HERSELF

The greater metaphor of rupture and Spillers's "second birth" concept both mobilize the stakes of the physical body within the identity formation of the psychic body. Rupture holds both a literal sense and a psychoanalytic one. Sethe's ruptures do not coincide directly with her experiences with childbirth as dividing herself into an identity of "premother" and "mother." When *Beloved* begins and ends, Sethe is a mother—and this is a strong, positive part of her identity. Feeding her children, loving her children—especially in freedom when she could "love them as much as [she] wanted" (Morrison 162)—and being awed and proud of her "crawling already?" baby girl are all points of pleasure in her narrative. In many ways, the rare times she gets to be joyful about her children are when the novel grazes happiness. It is crucial to consider second birth as a psychological function rather than a material (physical) one. The "rupture" of second birth and the "trauma" of being born do not necessarily have to do with Sethe's children (at least, not in this essay): they have to do with Sethe herself. Her key scene of trauma results in the birth of a new self—a new subjectivity that returns to the scene of its birth as if it were a punctuation mark in Sethe's life.

119

Her trauma is a byproduct of her maternity but not the explicit cause of it. Morrison locates her maternity in an unorthodox way, inasmuch as it contributes to her sense of double consciousness but not necessarily to her rebirth—which if we are to subscribe to the metaphoric rupture of birth and maternal identity is very ironic indeed. Maternity contributes to the potential for Sethe's internalized fracturing rather than the major shift in identity that it so often is. Trauma is what causes Sethe to be born; a messy, liquid urgency that marks a change in her identity. Through that view, Sethe becomes mother to herself.

ENDNOTES

[1]The concept of "scenic memory" has taken on several definitions. Most recently, researchers at the Sigmund Freud Institute in Frankfurt published a study on how children of Holocaust survivors process trauma. They define scenic memory as "a concept that stresses the non-verbal, unconscious communication between the generations... [a] highly symbolic and metaphorical expression of the extreme trauma handed down to the patient by the parents" (207). Janette Dillon has also recast the term to fit an analysis of the early modern theatrical stage, framing "scenic memory" in terms of iconography—images or icons placed on stage that signify collective meaning to an audience of people. My definition of "scenic memory" connects these two definitions such that "the icon" becomes a trigger for and symbol of trauma at the same time.
[2]Notably, a whole volume of essays entitled *Toni Morrison: Memory and Meaning*. This essay has been particularly influenced by the work of Nicola King in, M*emory, Narrative, Identity: Remembering the Self* (2000).
[3]I am particularly indebted to the work of Dottie Lebron and her staff at the McSilver Institute for Poverty, Policy, and Research at the NYU Silver School of Social Work for her report entitled *Facts Matter! Black Lives Matter! The Trauma of Racism*.
[4]See E. James Lieberman's introduction to the 1993 edition of *Trauma of Birth*, where he not only speculates that Rank leverages a presumed biological argument, but also suggests that this biological argument stems from Rank's insecurity: "[It was] per-

haps because he lacked a medical degree with which to bolster his authority" (xi).

WORKS CITED

Caruth, Cathy. "Introduction." *Trauma: Explorations in Memory*, edited by Cathy Caruth, Johns Hopkins University Press, 1995, pp 3-12.

Dillon, Janette. "Scenic Memory." *The Arts of Remembrance in Early Modern England: Memorial Cultures of the Post-Reformation*, edited by Thomas Rist, Routledge, 2016, pp 195-2010.

DuBois, W.E.B. *The Souls of Black Folk.* Dover Thrift Editions, 1994.

King, Nicola. *Memory, Narrative, Identity Remembering the Self.* Edinburgh University Press, 2000.

Kristeva, Julia. *Powers of Horror: An Essay on Abjection.* Columbia University Press, 1982.

Lebron, Dottie, et al. *Facts Matter! Black Lives Matter! The Trauma of Racism.* McSilver Institute for Poverty Policy and Research at the NYU Silver School of Social Work, 2015.

Morrison, Toni. *Beloved.* Plume by the Penguin Group, 1988.

Oliver, Kelly. *Witnessing: Beyond Recognition.* University of Minnesota Press, 2001.

Rank, Otto. *The Trauma of Birth.* 1929. Dover, 1993.

Lieberman, James. Introduction. *The Trauma of Birth*, by Otto Rank, 1929, Dover, 1993, pp. i-xx.

Seward, Adrienne Lanier, and Tally, Justine, editors. *Toni Morrison: Memory and Meaning*, University Press of Mississippi, 2014.

Spillers, Hortense J. "Born Again": Faulkner and the Second Birth." *Fifty Years after Faulkner*, edited by Jay Watson and Ann J. Abadie, University of Mississippi Press, 2016, pp 57-78. Kindle Edition.

"Are You Sure She Was Your Sister?"

Sororal Love and Maternal Failure in Toni Morrison's *Paradise*

KRISTIN M. DISTEL

ONI MORRISON'S *PARADISE* (1997) examines the concepts of motherhood and sisterhood from myriad perspectives. Various aspects of mothers, maternity, and normative, prescribed gender roles have traumatized each of the five women who live at the Convent, which is the novel's name for the structure that was once an embezzler's mansion, later a Catholic girls' school, and eventually the home of five abused women. The following chapter focuses primarily on Seneca, whose mother abandoned her when she was five years old; this instance of a failure to mother is significant because it is paradigmatic of maternal cruelty observable in much of *Paradise*. Examining Seneca as a victim of failed maternity also allows readers to grasp the sacredness of the bond between sisters.[1] Seneca believes that her mother, Jean, was actually her sister until one of the Convent women realizes that although mothers are capable of abandoning their children, sisters do not desert one another. Specifically, one of the women asks Seneca, "Are you sure she was your sister? Maybe she was your mother. *Why?* Because a mother might, but no sister would do such a thing" (265, emphasis added).

This chapter explores the ways in which the aforementioned excerpt illustrates the sanctity of attachment between sisters and privileges the manner in which sisters can provide love that mothers fail to give. I will also address the bonds of solidarity among the five women within the physical structure of the Convent—a space in which the terms "Mother" and "Sister" are used in formal, religious contexts yet still fail to provide meaningful acceptance and love. Ultimately, my chapter examines the mother-sibling dynamic between Seneca and Jean to demonstrate that in *Paradise*, motherhood is marked by cruelty in ways that bonds between sisters are not. Finally, this chapter suggests that when Seneca believes her sororal bond with Jean has been violated by Jean's desertion, Seneca experiences shame and trauma that give rise to the novel's emphasis on solidarity

SENECA, JEAN, AND MOTHER/SISTER DUPLICITY

To understand Seneca's character and the importance of sororal bonds for her, a brief summary of Seneca and the mother/sister confusion in the novel are necessary. Three examples within the text are particularly important: Jean's act of abandoning Seneca; Seneca's learning that Jean was her mother; and finally, Jean's encountering Seneca after the Convent women have been murdered and subsequently resurrected.[2]

Readers first encounter Seneca during one of the novel's many instances of external analepsis. The text describes the abandoned five-year-old Seneca, who "spent four nights and five days knocking on every door in her building" after Jean has left her (126). On the third day, Seneca decides that Jean has left because of Seneca's own misbehaviour, and she determines that cleanliness and goodness will bring her sister home:

> She cleaned her teeth and washed her ears carefully. She also flushed the toilet right away, as soon as she used it, and folded her socks inside her shoes.... Those were her prayers: if she did everything right without being told, either Jean would walk in or when she knocked on one of the apartment doors, there she'd be! ... Meantime, the nights were terrible. On the fourth day, [she] brushed her eighteen milk teeth until the toothbrush was pink with blood. (127)

Seneca, "demoralized by unanswered prayers, bleeding gums and hunger ... gave up goodness, ... and opened the bread box" that contained the forbidden Lorna Doone cookies, which Jean was sure Seneca would eat (127-128). Leaning against the box is a note written in red lipstick that ostensibly explains Jean's desertion; Seneca can only read two words of the letter—her own name and Jean's. Seneca finally relinquishes hope of her sister's return on the sixth day, admitting to a caseworker, who arrives at the apartment, that she has been abandoned. Until Seneca is twenty years old, she believes that Jean is her sister; it will become apparent in this chapter that it is the violation of the sororal bond, perhaps more so than the actual act of abandonment, that so grieves and pains Seneca.

The novel emphasizes storytelling and confessional-style divulgences as a means of combating trauma. Connie, the Convent's maternal figure and "a new and revised Reverend Mother" prompts the five battered, neglected Convent women to participate in what she terms "loud dreaming" sessions, in which Connie traces outlines of the women's naked, abused bodies on the basement floor (265, 264). These sessions compel the women to reveal to one another their traumatic histories; the sessions also allow the women to exorcise the ghosts that haunt them. Seneca tells the four other Convent women about the abandonment she experienced as a child while she draws neat red lines on her painted form, which represent Seneca's habit of cutting herself. Here, it is necessary to return to the passage that I first explored in this chapter's introduction. One of the Convent women asks Seneca, "Are you sure she was your sister? Maybe she was your mother. *Why?* Because a mother might, but no sister would do such a thing. Seneca capped her tube" (265, emphasis added). This exchange—or realization, rather—causes an ontological shift within Seneca's character. Hereafter, her lived experience as an abused and abandoned child does not mark her in the same way as it has heretofore in the text. She no longer needs to engage in self-harm, and she is no longer a victim of a broken sororal bond. Rather, she is the daughter of a mother who harmed her child psychologically—something that is actually quite normative in terms of this novel's model of motherhood.

The third scene that merits mention in terms of mother/sister confusion between Jean and Seneca appears on the novel's final pages, in which Jean spots a resurrected Seneca. Seneca's hands are streaming with blood. As Gigi (one of the Convent women) tends to the wounds, Jean attempts to jog Seneca's memory: "'Don't you remember me?' Seneca looked up, the bright lights turning her eyes black. 'Should I? From where?'" (317). She calls Seneca by name, identifies herself as Jean (but omits a designation of either mother or sister), and even reminds Seneca of the housing project in which they lived, although she accidentally calls the street by the wrong name (317).

This final scene shows that Seneca has seized the power that is inherent within the mother-child relationship. Andrea O'Reilly posits that this encounter (and indeed all the parent-child encounters in the novel's conclusion) does not signify reconciliation (169). O'Reilly argues that the women do not "reclaim the reproductive— mother and/or daughter—identity they had lost" (169). I would point out, though, that in the case of Seneca and Jean, there is no identity to be reclaimed; there is only Jean's lie to be exposed and her power as mother to divest. According to Kathleen Woodward, shame stemming from a traumatic childhood often does not lead to an empowered adulthood or transformative knowledge (213), and *Paradise* may indeed support this assertion. However, I would argue that knowledge and the ability to wield power are not mutually exclusive, and Seneca is able to appropriate (and indeed has appropriated) her traumatic experiences as a means by which to obtain and exert power and, eventually, to achieve solidarity within a community of women.

In keeping with the consistently marginalized nature of her character, Seneca is not truly the subject of her own chapter; the text subjugates her within her own narrative of abandonment and trauma (Morrison 81-138). That is, readers only learn about Seneca's history of abuse and abandonment within the larger, framing metanarrative of Sweetie Fleetwood, a young mother whom Seneca sees while Sweetie is (albeit temporarily) abandoning her own children. Thus, the text juxtaposes the extended examination of a mother who is actually leaving her children with the comparatively brief story of Seneca, who believes that her sister abandoned her, only to learn later that the supposed sister was actually her mother. In its complexity, the novel iterates once again in Seneca's chapter that the mother-child relationship is sometimes marked by desertion and neglect, whereas no such markers of cruelty appear in relationships between sisters.

SHAME, GENDERED TRAUMA, AND SOLIDARITY

I turn now to Sandra Bartky's "The Pedagogy of Shame," which not only provides an excellent overview of the differences between shame and guilt but also gives a useful explanation of the gendered nature of shame.[3] An extended examination of Bartky's theory will be illustrative of the shame that is inherent to transgressive maternal/sororal relationships and to the novel's interest in questioning religious paradigms, both of which are explicitly gendered. According to Bartky, shame, morality, gender, and feelings of guilt exist within a dialectical relationship; shame, she argues:

> Requires, if not an actual audience before whom [one's] deficiencies are paraded, then an internalized audience with the capacity to judge, ... hence internalized standards of judgment. Shame ... involves the distressed apprehension of oneself as a lesser creature. Guilt, by contrast, refers not to the subject's nature but to her actions: typically, it is called forth by the active violation of principles which a person values and by which she feels herself bound.... Shame is called forth by the apprehension of some serious flaw in the self, guilt by the consciousness that one has committed a transgression. (227)

One can infer from Bartky's statement that shame is characteristically more complex and perhaps more harmful than are feelings of guilt. Because guilt focuses on actions, rather than on inherent shortcomings or "some serious flaw in the self," shame can be said to represent one's perceived sense of worth. That is, although our actions do not necessarily indicate or reflect who we are as people (both individually and as part of a larger community), shame is meant to suggest something about one's value as a person. Bartky persuasively argues that "Shame requires the recognition that I am, in some important sense, what I am seen to be" (227). When one internalizes the judgment of another, especially in regards to one's own sense of worthiness, shame often results; in such instances, one's locus of identity and sense of value are dangerously located outside the self. Kathleen Woodward argues that while guilt is often thought to be a more complex and mature emotion than shame, shame "persists beyond childhood" and can result in what she has termed "traumatic shame ... shame that cannot be transformed into knowledge" (213). It will become apparent that Seneca falls victim to the type of internalization Bartky discusses, especially in her acts of self-harm.

Bartky also notes that shame affects men and women differently simply because shame is used more actively and more aggressively to punish and regulate women's bodies, beliefs, and activities. She argues not only that "women typically are more shame-prone than men" (226) but also that "women's shame is more than merely an effect of subordination but, within the larger universe of patriarchal social relations, a corporeal disclosure of self in situation" (226). Thus, although shame affects both men and women, the means by which shame is wielded as a weapon of social control is highly gendered.

Within the context of *Paradise*, it is important to consider shame alongside the concept of solidarity. All five women in the Convent have experienced gender-based shaming; after the loud dreaming session in which they confront the painted images of their abused bodies, their response to past corporeal shame is a powerful sense of solidarity. Chandra Talpade Mohanty's definition of solidarity points out the fundamental flaw of "sisterhood" and positions solidarity as a means by which women can react meaningfully against the patriarchal social structures to which Bartky refers. Thus, solidarity functions as a means by which women can neutralize and reject shame.

Mohanty's definition of solidarity is essential to an understanding of the shame-solidarity intersection I am presenting here. Mohanty writes, "Rather than assuming an enforced commonality of oppression, the practice of solidarity foregrounds communities of people who have chosen to work and fight together" (7). As numerous feminist theorists have demonstrated, such a model of solidarity has largely replaced the rather outdated concept of sisterhood. Victoria Burrows's argument regarding the need for a revision of the sisterhood model is especially powerful, as she illustrates that sisterhood has its foundations in the normative, patriarchal family structure (11). For most of the Convent women, the family unit is the source of their shame. For Seneca in particular, sisterhood would strip her of agency and return her to the site of her shame and abandonment. A politics of solidarity meets the needs of each Convent woman, as evidenced by the transformative loud dreaming session, which J. Brooks Bouson's excellent work on shame in Morrison's novels has termed "a collective sharing of trauma ... [that] has the potential to heal" (*Quiet* 210).

Of course, race further complicates the issue of shame in Morrison's novels, particularly within the confines of the individual family unit. On the subject of familial shame, Brooks Bouson argues that families within Morrison's oeuvre (though particularly in *The Bluest Eye*) sometimes shame one another in response to the family's real or perceived shortcomings (*Embodied* 59). Within the Convent, however, in which one unidentified "white girl" lives among four black women (3), racial differences do not seem to impede the women's solidarity or their ability to subdue shame with their collective sense of purpose.

"A MOTHER MIGHT, BUT NO SISTER WOULD DO SUCH A THING"

The purpose of this chapter is not to suggest that sisters are incapable of inflicting cruelty upon one another. The novel does not support a claim that sororal bonds are perfect. However, such attachments *are* sacred; perfection and sacredness are not mutually exclusive concepts in this novel. It is fundamentally true, however, that sororal bonds do not bear the same markers of cruelty observable in mother-child relationships. Certainly, nearly all characters (especially those who are marked by a history of trauma and abuse) are capable of acting unkindly toward one another; sisters are no exception. However, the tenet of the mother-sister paradigm within *Paradise* seems to be that mothers, not sisters, are willing to act cruelly toward their children and to inflict deep psychological harm. This is especially true when a mother, Jean in particular, values self-preservation over the wellbeing of her daughter.[4]

That Seneca stops painting blood onto the image of her body and "cap[s] her tube" of paint indicates that she accepts the suggestion that Jean was her mother, not her sister (265). Her impulse to commit self-harm ceases when she realizes that the bond of sororal love has not been violated. The sacredness of the sister bond is restored. Because abandonment is within the purview of maternal behaviour in this novel, Seneca is relieved (emotionally and mentally) to find that Jean's abandoning her is an act of a mother leaving a child, not of a sister deserting another. This knowledge is restorative and healing; it relieves Seneca of the compulsion to harm her own body. It erases her shame and fosters a sense of solidarity.[5]

ABANDONMENT AND TRANSGRESSIVE MOTHERHOOD

The fact that abandonment is condemnable is a basic tenet of much of Morrison's work; indeed, many characters within her oeuvre have been abandoned, or at the very least, they fear desertion and denounce it as unpardonable. This is perhaps most concisely and powerfully evidenced in *Song of Solomon*, in which Pilate recalls the words of her child's father: "You can't just fly on off and leave a body" (147, 208, and 332). This passage, which Pilate reflects on and repeats several times in the novel, helps explain why she has kept a bag of human bones with her throughout her life: abandonment is an unacceptable form of cruelty. Desertion by mothers is particularly complicated because it indicates an aberrant performance of gender identity. Edith Frampton's analysis of breastfeeding and the body in Morrison's novels usefully positions female embodiment as fundamental to the understanding of maternal relationships: "Morrison's work foregrounds not simply the maternal symbolic but also the materiality of motherhood and the subjectivities it engenders" (160). The experience of motherhood and daughterhood intersects with abandonment in complex ways, inflicting the abandoned female body with insuperable feelings of shame and trauma.

Indeed, abandonment marks many of the mother-child relationships in *Paradise*. Mavis, for example, has abandoned her three children after accidentally causing the deaths of her young twins. Gigi has no relationship with her mother, and her father is imprisoned. While taking her fiancé to meet her mother, Pallas (also called Divine) stumbles upon her mother and her own fiancé having sexual intercourse. Connie, whom the maternal Mary

Magna rescued from child prostitution on the streets of Brazil, so fears Mary Magna's death (the ultimate form of abandonment) that Connie uses supernatural abilities, called "stepping in," to prolong Mary Magna's life. In describing Mary Magna to Mavis, who has recently arrived at the Convent, Connie says, "She is my mother. Your mother too" (48). Extending Mary Magna's life, then, is a means by which to establish a secure, lasting sense of motherhood within the novel—an effort that is ultimately doomed to fail. Indeed, Mary Magna dies shortly thereafter. As Linda Wagner-Martin suggests, "Throughout the narrative, [*Paradise*] calls out for family unity, and particularly for mother-daughter strength" (111). It is precisely in this area, though, that the narrative evinces the failure of mothers to establish nurturing relationships with their daughters; the female characters—the novel's daughters—are desperate for maternal guidance and acceptance. The equitable substitute they find, however, is solidarity within their female community.

Because so many of the mother-child relationships within the novel are tragic and abusive in various ways, the text succeeds in destabilizing the concept of maternal instinct. Indeed, the mothers in *Paradise* belie the notion that women are natural caregivers and innately selfless protectors of their children. On this subject, Kimberly Yates argues the following: "Morrison uses her mother characters to rupture the assumed relationship between mother as female biological creator and mother as responsible nurturer.... She questions the concept of maternal instinct by portraying a range of mothers and women who may or may not want to be mothers" (22). Yates is certainly correct in asserting that Morrison's work reveals maternal instinct to be a social construct rather than an innate quality. I would argue, though, that *Paradise* problematizes a belief in maternal instinct even more fully than Yates has acknowledged in her discussion of Morrison's early work. The mothers in *Paradise* do not simply reject motherhood or determine that maternity does not suit them in some way; rather, through abandonment and mistreatment, they cause their children (their daughters, particularly) to become the social "other." Because of shame and trauma, these daughters cannot function in a normative manner; they require the separatist space of the Convent. In essence, the novel normalizes maternal behaviour that would typically be thought transgressive.

One could certainly argue that Jean herself is a figure of pity and that perhaps she left Seneca because she had no resources with which to care for her daughter. The text never reveals the reasons behind Jean's abandoning her daughter, and, indeed, Jean's departure is ironically marked by both cruelty and care. Adrienne Rich claims in *Of Woman Born* that "Every mother has known overwhelming, unacceptable anger at her children" (224). Jean and Seneca's relationship was also likely marked by Jean's own experiences with trauma, which, according to Amos and her colleagues, might have been galvanized when Jean became a mother, thus prompting her to raise Seneca as her sister; a rejection of motherhood is also a rejection of attachment to the child as a daughter (1444). Indeed, at the age of fourteen, Jean was still a child when she gave birth to Seneca. It is possible (and given that Jean looks into the quality of the foster home into which Seneca has been placed, it is also likely) that Jean hoped a kindly person and one who could provide for her child's needs would take Seneca into her home. Perhaps Jean was simply desperate, or perhaps she was angry and selfish. In either case, it is true that the act of abandoning Seneca is marked with some signifiers of normative maternal love: Jean leaves a table full of food as well as a note presumably explaining her desertion. This does not explain, though, Jean's leading Seneca to believe that they were sisters rather than mother and daughter. Furthermore, and perhaps more tellingly, Jean is aware that Seneca (again, a five-year-old child) cannot read the note that her mother/sister has left.

THE INTERSECTION OF POWER, SHAME, AND TRAUMA

Here, it is important to turn briefly to Michel Foucault's concepts of power and the creation of docile bodies. In choosing to leave her daughter, Jean has exerted a mother's ultimate power over her child, and this abandonment has caused Seneca's body to be both dangerously docile and vulnerable. Indeed, the lack of protection from a maternal figure allows others to take advantage of Seneca's body, often by violent and sexual means. During the course of Seneca's childhood and adolescence, she is sexually abused by a foster brother and by a string of boyfriends. Strangers frequently grope her and flash their genitals at her (261), and she is sexually exploited (for payment) by a woman named Norma Keene Fox, who subjects Seneca to "abject humiliation" (137). Kelly Reames notes that these instances of abuse have made Seneca "ever-agreeable, lest she be unloved again" (46). This interpretation of Seneca's character is valid, but it does not account for Seneca's sense of shame that originated with Jean's desertion. Seneca internalizes her abusers' actions and decides that she must be to blame for their appropriation of her body. This is a direct correlation with Bartky's argument that shame indicates an internalization of others' standards of judgment (227). In "Foucault, Feminism, and the Modernization of Patriarchal Power" Sandra Bartky argues that "The depth of ... women's shame is a measure of the extent to which all women have internalized patriarchal standards of bodily acceptability" (77). Seneca's foster families value her because she never cries, because she is a "docile body." She does not cry, however, because her internalized shame and frequent self-harm have replaced normative demonstrations of emotion.

Jean and other mothers in this novel exert what Amy Allen has termed "power-over," which divests the subject—in this case, the daughter—of identity and agency (123). In keeping with the Foucauldian tradition, the body is the site of the struggle for power. Judith Butler argues that in discussions of power and control, "The subject who emerges here is still no sovereign, is still not one who is free to appropriate or not appropriate the effects of power that come its way, or that can be figured to possess or to lack basic rights or properties" (192-193). While Seneca believes that Jean is her sister, there is no capacity in which Seneca can appropriate Jean's power; in privileging solidarity, the novel positions sororal relationships as a site of equal power dynamics. It is not until the loud dreaming session and, eventually, the posthumous encounter with Jean that Seneca can reject the shame of her bleeding, starving five-year-old body. Indeed, Seneca's wounds suddenly stop bleeding when Jean confronts her—a belated restoration of Seneca's shamed body.

The novel's mothers reject the concept of female solidarity because it is naturally anathema to the desire to wield control. As the women of the Convent begin to eschew their respective feelings of shame and come to terms with their traumatic experiences, they display what Amy Allen calls "power-with," which is the act of working alongside others to achieve collective power and to re-alize common goals (126). The mother-daughter relationships in *Paradise* lack a sense of solidarity, of a shared goal. Sisters share goals, and they share one another's suffering; this is power-*with* (126). During the loud dreaming session, the unnamed Convent woman realizes that Jean could not be Seneca's sister because Jean wields and misuses power over Seneca. She does not share in Seneca's suffering as a subjugated female body and thus fails to exhibit a sense of solidarity, which is the novel's fundamental criterion for sororal bonds.

THE CONVENT: "SISTER," "MOTHER," AND THE FAILED PARADIGM OF CHRISTIAN DUALISM

Morrison's body of work frequently calls into question the overly simplistic binaries common to Western religion, specifically Chris-tianity. Morrison's propensity is particularly evident in *Paradise*, which destabilizes Christian dualisms of good and evil and the religious connotations of the terms "Sister" and "Mother."[6] As previously mentioned, the Convent, repurposed as the women's eventual home, once served as a school—Christ the King School for Native Girls—and it is here that Mary Magna brings Connie to live after rescuing her from systemic sexual abuse. Within the confines of the school's avowed Catholic belief system, the schoolgirls and their teachers/caretakers frequently use the epistemologically bur-dened terms "Sister" and "Mother." However, because Morrison endeavours to make normative religious tenets both non-normative and subject to interrogation, these terms fail to provide stability to Connie or to the other residents of the school.

Most of the girls who live there are deeply unhappy with the strict (and indeed foreign) religious teachings. Their unhappiness is evidenced by the girls' many attempts to flee the school. As the girls individually escape or simply leave when they are of age, the school falls into disuse. The religious overtones inherent to the physical structure of the Convent, however, remain, especially as the novel positions Connie as the ersatz mother and spiritual guide to the women living there. Connie appropriates the sacred space of the Convent and privileges moral relativism, autonomy, and solidarity among women. Her acts of kindness and her expressions of maternal love expose the flawed model of "Sisters" and "Mothers" in the Catholic tradition in that an adherence to Christian dualism would not have allowed her to help such women as Seneca, Pallas, Mavis, and Gigi in any meaningful way.

In examining Connie's liminal role in the nominally religious space, Justyna Sempruch states, "Suspending the sublime model of the virginal life, Consolata 'runs' the convent in a permanent erasure of the nun in herself, in a disabling state of being non-mother, no-body" (101). It is certainly true that Connie eventually rejects the religious connotations of the term "Mother," although she substitutes the Catholic trope of maternity with her role as a maternal figure to the Convent women. This is perhaps most evident when fifteen-year-old Pallas arrives to the Convent after fleeing her mother's home and being subsequently raped by a group of men. Immediately upon meeting Connie, Pallas climbs into her lap; Connie rocks Pallas and says, "Poor little one, poor, poor little one. They hurt my poor little one" (173). It is not until Connie rejects the school's Catholic teachings and embraces non-Western religious practices that she is able to provide love and meaningful support to those who need it.

Linda Wagner-Martin suggests that the novel's emphasis on "the love preached in Christianity can help … the women gathered in the Convent … find ultimate satisfaction in lives lived *for* and *with* others" (115, emphasis in the original). It seems, though, that the text's emphasis on female solidarity actually rejects Christianity and instead privileges relativism; the men who murder the Convent women in the novel's opening lines are avowedly Christian, and the tiny town of Ruby is the site of multiple Christian churches. Such formal iterations of religion are unable to meet the Convent women's needs for love and acceptance (Baillie 175). Instead, the Convent "becomes a palimpsest of failed white and black patriarchal designs," and Morrison certainly identifies Western religion as one of those "patriarchal designs," especially through the beginning the novel with purportedly Christian men murdering five women

(Dobbs 113). The novel substitutes the dangerously appropriated model of Christian binaries, including the terms "Mother" and "Sister," with the gnostic and deeply maternal figure of Piedade, "a black Madonna" (Baillie 175). The novel closes with this non-normative image of maternal protection; Piedade is the figurehead of the protected space the Convent women have long sought.

CONCLUSION

The attachment inherent within the sororal bond is crucial throughout Morrison's oeuvre, but it is especially fundamental to an understanding of *Paradise* and its complex explorations of sisters, solidarity, and the flawed model of female relationships provided by Christian theology. In her examination of sibling bonds in Morrison's first five novels, Connie R. Schomburg argues the following:

> Morrison explores and indeed redefines the boundaries of sibling relationships, making it clear that the word 'sister' applies not only to the supportive, sustaining biological bonds between Claudia and Frieda MacTeer, but also to the emotional bonds between Sula and Nel, to the unhampered-by-the-grave bond shared by Denver and Beloved, and, most importantly, to the larger community of women with whom Morrison's female characters must find a connection in order to find wholeness. (156)

The culmination of the paradigm that Schomburg has identified is found in *Paradise*, in which a relationship between sisters is sacred, far more so than maternal attachment could be. In *Paradise*, the maternal model is inherently flawed, a mere imitation of the sanctity fundamental to the sororal bond. In capping her tube of paint and determining that she no longer needs to slice open her skin or punish her own body, Seneca eschews the sense of shame that grew out of her "sister's" rejection, out of the supposedly broken sororal covenant.

Paradise violates Morrison's well-known concept of "motherlove," most viscerally represented in *Beloved*, and replaces it with steadfast "sisterlove," with a sense of solidarity that is inherent to the sororal relationship. Sororal kinships privilege solidarity and reject shame, whereas loyalty is noncompulsory within mother-child bonds. Adrienne Rich claims, "The mother's self-hatred and low expectations are the binding-rags for the psyche of the daughter.... The cry of [the] female child in us need not be shameful or regressive" (243, 225). Until she learned that Jean was her mother, Seneca's childish cry *was* comprised of shame. Prior to the transformative "loud dreaming" session, Seneca bore the shame of being "demoralized" by Jean's desertion—an abandonment that was, she was sure, the result of her own shortcomings (127). In Bartky's terms, Seneca's childish "defects... [came] suddenly and horribly to light" (227). Upon learning that her mother, not her sister, had abandoned her, those "defects" that led to Jean's desertion are no longer Seneca's. They are no longer a source or shame. Jean's act of abandoning Seneca is comprehensible because, within the construct of this novel, mothers leave. Sisters, those who are bound by sororal love and solidarity, do not.

ENDNOTES

[1] The novel's emphasis on the bonds between sisters is evident even in its front matter: Morrison has dedicated the book to Lois, her last living sibling.

[2] I would direct readers to my chapter, "Gendered Travel and Quiescence in Toni Morrison's *Paradise*," for an extended examination of resurrection in the novel (*Women's Utopian and Dystopian Fiction*, edited by Sharon R. Wilson). See also Justine Tally's *Paradise Reconsidered: Toni Morrison's (Hi)stories and Truths*, in which Tally argues for that the Convent women return as revenants in the novel's conclusion.

[3] A large portion of Bartky's article does indeed examine shame within the classroom setting, though her argument is easily and effectively extended to social spheres outside of the classroom. Bartky notes, "All social ensembles are 'pedagogical' in an extended sense" (225), a logical claim that allows the meaningful application of her findings to Morrison's novel.

[4] Jean's rejection of her daughter stands in stark contrast to the

model of selfless, ruthlessly protective love seen in Sethe (*Beloved*) or Pilate (*Song of Solomon*).

[5] Although Seneca is relieved to learn that her mother, not her sister, abandoned her, the novel certainly does not condone mothers who desert their children. Rather, it acknowledges that deserting one's children is within the scope of normative motherhood because, in this text, selfishness and self-preservation are part of the maternal experience.

[6] It is important to consider the novel's preface, which is an excerpt of the Egyptian poem "Thunder, Perfect Mind," part of *The Nag Hammadi*. The poem criticizes overly simplistic concepts of good and evil and instead privileges divine female power. This preface is part of the *Beloved/Jazz/Paradise* trilogy and "A sign of Morrison's transferred allegiance from the authority of the Bible to that of the gnostic text, the epigraph evidences a new relationship to self" (Le Fustec para. 38-39).

WORKS CITED

Allen, Amy. *The Power of Feminist Theory: Domination, Resistance, Solidarity.* Westview, 1999.

Amos, Jackie, et al. "Entrapped Mother, Entrapped Child: Agonic Mode, Hierarchy and Appeasement in Intergenerational Abuse and Neglect." *Journal of Child & Family Studies*, vol. 24, no. 5, 2015, pp. 1442-1450.

Baillie, Justine. *Toni Morrison and the Literary Tradition: The Invention of an Aesthetic.* Bloomsbury, 2013.

Bartky, Sandra. "Foucault, Feminism, and the Modernization of Patriarchal Power." *Feminism and Foucault: Reflections on Resistance*, edited by Irene Diamond and Lee Quinby, Northeastern University Press, 1988, pp. 61-86.

Bartky Sandra. "The Pedagogies of Shame." *Feminisms and Pedagogies of Everyday Life*, edited by Carmen Luke, SUNY Press, 1996, pp. 225-241.

Bouson, J. Brooks. *Embodied Shame: Uncovering Female Shame in Contemporary Women's Writing.* State University of New York Press, 2009.

Bouson, J. Brooks. *Quiet as It's Kept: Shame, Trauma, and Race in the Novels of Toni Morrison.* State University of New York Press, 2000.

Burrows, Victoria. *Whiteness and Trauma: The Mother-Daughter Knot in the Fiction of Jean Rhys, Jamaica Kincaid and Toni Morrison.* Palgrave Macmillan, 2004.

Butler, Judith. "Bodies and Power Revisited." *Feminism and the Final Foucault,* edited by Dianna Taylor and Karen Vintges, University of Illinois Press, 2004, pp. 183-194.

Distel, Kristin. "Gendered Travel and Quiescence in Toni Morrison's *Paradise.*" *Women's Utopian and Dystopian Fiction,* edited by Sharon R. Wilson, Cambridge Scholars Publishing, 2013, pp. 133-153.

Dobbs, Cynthia. "Diasporic Designs of House, Home, and Haven in Toni Morrison's *Paradise.*" *MELUS: The Journal of the Society for the Study of the Multi-Ethnic Literature of the United States,* vol. 36, no. 2, 2011, pp. 109-126.

Foucault, Michel. *Discipline and Punish: The Birth of the Prison.* Translated by Alan Sheridan, Vintage, 2012.

Frampton, Edith. "'You Just Can't Fly on Off and Leave a Body': The Intercorporeal Breastfeeding Subject of Toni Morrison's Fiction." *Women: A Cultural Review,* vol. 16, no. 2, 2005, pp. 141-163.

Le Fustec, Claude. "'Never Break Them in Two. Never Put One Over the Other. Eve Is Mary's Mother. Mary Is the Daughter of Eve': Toni Morrison's Womanist Gospel of Self." *EREA: Revue Electronique D'etudes Sur Le Monde Anglophone,* vol. 8, no. 2, 2011.

Morrison, Toni. *Paradise.* New York: Plume, 1997.

Morrison, Toni. *Song of Solomon.* New York: Plume, 1987.

O'Reilly, Andrea. *Toni Morrison and Motherhood: A Politics of the Heart.* State University of New York Press, 2004.

Reames, Kelly. *Toni Morrison's* Paradise: *A Reader's Guide.* Continuum, 2001.

Rich, Adrienne. *Of Woman Born: Motherhood as Experience and Institution.* New York: Norton, 1995. Print.

Sempruch, Justyna. "The Sacred Mothers, the Evil Witches and the Politics of Household in Toni Morrison's *Paradise.*" *Journal of the Association for Research on Mothering* vol. 7, no. 1, 2005, pp. 98-109.

Schomburg, Connie R. *The Significance of Sibling Relationships in Literature*. Popular, 1992.

Tally, Justine. *Paradise Reconsidered: Toni Morrison's (Hi)stories and Truths*. FORECAAST 3, Transaction Press, 1999.

Wagner-Martin, Linda. *Toni Morrison and the Maternal: From* The Bluest Eye *to* Home. Peter Lang, 2014.

Woodward, Kathleen. "Traumatic Shame: Toni Morrison, Televisual Culture, and the Cultural Politics of the Emotions." *Cultural Critique*, vol. 46, 2000, pp. 210-240.

Yates, Kimberley A. "Explosions of 'Maternal Instinct': Images of Motherhood in Selected Novels by Toni Morrison." *Fissions and Fusions*, edited by Lesley Marx, Lesley, University of the Western Cape Press, 1997, pp. 21-32.

From Sweetness to Toya Graham

Intersectionality and the (Im)Possibilities
of Maternal Ethics

JESSE A. GOLDBERG

"That's my son and I don't want him to be a Freddie Gray."
—Toya Graham, explaining why she slapped her son
when she found him among protestors in Baltimore
following the death of Freddie Gray

"But you have to understand. I had to protect her. She
didn't know the world."
—Sweetness, from Toni Morrison's *God Help the Child*

"There is no protection."
—Florens's mother, from Toni Morrison's *A Mercy*

TONI MORRISON'S FICTION PRESENTS readers with dozens
of mother-child relationships, and among these there is no
shortage of mothers who do violence to their children: Eva Peace
in *Sula*, Sethe in *Beloved*, and Sweetness in *God Help the Child*
come readily to mind. Although these characters perform actions
toward their children that readers may quickly see as morally reprehensible—be it killing an adult child, infanticide, or emotional
abuse—Morrison's contextualizations of these characters render
them too complex to be reduced to a single ethical judgment of an
individual. This chapter, then, seeks to think with this complexity,
and argues that in Morrison's fiction, motherhood cannot be raised
to the level of universal experience. Rather it is always experienced
intersectionally, and so what may be called a "maternal ethics"
is rendered both impossible on the level of universal imperative

yet material and necessary in an anti-Black, patriarchal world. The framework of ethics I propose positions motherhood within larger networks of power, which leads to an understanding of maternal ethics not merely in terms of individuals but also in the worlds in which those individuals live. Thinking with Morrison on the question of maternal ethics, I believe, provides vocabulary for thinking the moment in April 2015 when audiences across the U.S. encountered video footage of Toya Graham, a Black mother in Baltimore, striking her son in order to keep him from participating in protests against police violence in reaction to the death of twenty-five-year-old Freddie Gray. Ultimately, if the ethical demand of "motherhood" is to protect children, then Black mothers in the U.S., insofar as they remain beyond the purview of "protection," are always acting to fulfill an impossible ethical demand.

In making this argument, I am both extending and departing from Naomi Morgenstern's 2014 essay, "Maternal Love/Maternal Violence: Inventing Ethics in Toni Morrison's *A Mercy*," in which she argues that "Morrison's mothers, then, might be said to invent ethics or to bring an ethical realm into being because, through performance, they must constitute the right to mother as an absolute responsibility" (23). Like Morgenstern, I find that psychoanalytic theory falls short in attempting to think maternal subjectivity, and so my chapter turns to Black feminist theory, critical race theory, and afro-pessimist theorizing rather than psychoanalysis in order to think motherhood and mothering. I also agree with a number of strands of Morgenstern's reading of *A Mercy*; however, I believe her analysis of the relationship between slavery and mothering in Morrison's fiction misreads the functions of power in the novels and the historical moments they invoke. Morgenstern writes, "The challenge for Morrison's characters and readers is to *disentangle* the difficult experience of mothering and being mothered from the violence of racialized subjection" (13, emphasis added). With this in mind, much of her insightful essay's energy is spent attempting to disarticulate a maternal ethics from the particular context of slavery in order to arrive at an image of the mother and daughter unsullied by the particularities of material racial experience. As a result, some of the essay's greatest moments of analytical momentum are cut short by the limits of what Claudia Rankine and Beth

Loffreda may call "the racial imaginary." For example, Morgenstern notes that "Morrison's mothers also make traumatically isolating choices that they will never be able to explain to their daughters. These mothers will never be recognized by their daughters for their profound acts of love.... Morrison's mothers choose when there are no clear options" (23). Although this attention to choice opens a space for profound and difficult confrontation with the machinations of violent power, such an inquiry is foreclosed in a gesture toward celebrating a kind of heroically resistant agency on the part of these mothers, who Morgenstern reads as able to "forge a choice out of no option" (23).

Such a gesture is exactly the kind that Saidiya Hartman warns against in *Scenes of Subjection: Terror, Slavery, and Self-Making in Nineteenth-Century America* when she asks the following questions: "How is it possible to think 'agency' when the slave's very condition of being or social existence is defined as a state of determinate negation? In other words, what are the constituents of agency when one's social condition is defined by negation and personhood refigured in the fetishized and fungible terms of object of property?" (52). Hartman's argument cautions readers to inter- rogate the impulse to claim victory or agency for enslaved subjects, and at the very least, it complicates the very concept of choice as a knowable discourse. The force of her argument is in moving readers to reckon with the absolutely circumscribed nature of all forms of so-called agency under the condition of slavery, not to look for ways out—the forging of something out of nothing—but rather to do the more difficult work of looking for how life is lived squarely within what she and Frank Wilderson call "the space of death" or "the space of negation."

Hartman's arguments in *Scenes of Subjection* are, among other things, exercises in intersectional analysis, and it is precisely this analytical framework born out of Black feminist thought and critical race theory that pushes against Morgenstern's impulse to "disentangle" motherhood and racial subjection in Morrison's novels. Indeed, as we shall see, it is impossible to disentangle intersectional forces.

Although Black women writers in the U.S. since the nineteenth century (at least) have written about the ways in which racial and sexual oppression intersect in the experiences of Black women, it is contemporary legal scholar Kimberle Crenshaw who is credited with introducing the term "intersectionality" into (Black) feminist lexicon. Thus, it is to her I turn in briefly accounting for how this analytical frame pushes against the impulse to disentangle and moves toward an analysis of motherhood in Morrison's fiction—most specifically for my chapter her latest novel, *God Help the Child*—that opens space for thinking the simultaneous universal impossibility and material necessity of maternal ethics under the conditions of racial subjection.

Not merely a theory of identity, intersectionality describes the coming together of multiple forces of oppression within the experiences of individuals whose identities fall along multiple axes of difference—for example, race and sex. Although the term has positively moved into nonacademic feminist spaces, it is sometimes employed without grounding in the legal theorizing that spawned it, and so it is often used to signify simply additive principles of identity, for instance, to make sure one lists all of one's identities to account for one's position in society. One result of this casual "list-like" mobilization of intersectionality as a tool for feminist analysis, besides the calls to move beyond what some see as a now obsolete concept, is the political conclusion that to be intersectional one must merely account for each identity intersecting within an individual subject. This reductive conclusion misses a key point of intersectionality, namely, that the principle is not a "totalizing theory of identity" (Crenshaw, "Mapping the Margins" 358). Rather, it is a theorization of the functions of power, oppression, and antioppressive action.

Intersectionality does not merely demand listing identifications; it demands interrogating the *forces* that structure those identifications and then acting to quell the oppressions enacted by those forces. To quote Crenshaw: "These problems of exclusion cannot be solved simply by including Black women within an already established analytical structure. *Because the intersectional experience is greater than the sum of racism and sexism,* any analysis that does not take intersectionality into account cannot sufficiently address the particular manner in which Black women are subordinated" (58, emphasis added). This means that to understand the abstract concepts of "motherhood," "mothering," or "maternal ethics" through an analysis of the Black mothers in Morrison's novels, one's analysis must be intersectional or risk not merely "leaving something out," but getting the entire picture wrong in the first place. In other words, despite attempts by reviewers and critics to thrust Morrison out of the "box" of her racial particularity and into the realm of universal humanism (an impulse Rankine and Loffreda identify in their introduction to *The Racial Imaginary*), the result of an investigation into motherhood in Morrison's fiction will not yield insights about a universal concept of motherhood but about motherhood as an always already raced and racial practice. (To say it differently one more time, there are no mere mothers in Morrison's fiction, but there are Black mothers, white mothers, poor mothers, disabled mothers, and so on.)[1]

Similarly, to witness the video of Graham hitting her son as *only* an event of mothering without attending to the force of race within Black motherhood is to misrecognize the event completely, as became evident in the numerous divergent statements of praise for Graham's heroism or criticisms of her use of violence. I will have more to say about this discourse at the end of this chapter, but at the very least, the footage of Graham striking her son forced a national confrontation with the possibility of maternal violence, although the conversation ensuing from this confrontation was often reduced to the binary debate between whether or not she was right to do what she did. Such a question resonates with Morrison's most well-known and most frequently written about novel, *Beloved*, in which her protagonist Sethe, in a fictional performance of an act committed by the real enslaved woman Margaret Garner, infamously kills her own daughter rather than let her be taken back into slavery. In a 1987 *New York Times* interview, Morrison herself says of Sethe's killing of Beloved, "It was absolutely the right thing to do, but she had no right to do it" (qtd. in Rothstein). Morgenstern offers an insightful reading of this comment: "The first 'right' is the right that precedes civil society—the natural or divine right that does not need to wait for the law. The invocation of 'no right' belongs, instead, to the civil state of constituted laws and the violation of a social contract. The slippage between these two senses of 'right' opens up a space of wild indeterminacy that is the space of the ethical" (22). This is an important point, but it misses something crucial. Not only is the space between the "right" that precedes law and the "rights" of civil society and social contracts the space in which one may find ethics, but it is also precisely the space in which one will find Blackness as a political ontological category.

One of Hartman's central arguments in *Scenes of Subjection* is that Black subjects in the U.S. are positioned simultaneously inside and outside of the law, thus leaving them in the space between the "right" that precedes law and the "rights" codified in law. This argument is most precisely delineated in Hartman's discussion of the 1855 court case *State of Missouri v. Celia, a slave*, in which she demonstrates how enslaved Africans were outside the law's boundaries of protection from injury—thus left to nothing but "rights" that precede law, which without law offers no protection from violation—while simultaneously inside the law's boundaries of punishment for crime. Celia was not protected from rape, but she was punishable for killing her rapist. This space within the slip between the rights that precede law and the rights written in law thus becomes the space of (legal) Black subjectivity, and although slavery ends as a legal institution, Blackness continues to occupy this space within a condition of what Salamishah Tillet calls "civic estrangement." In searching for an articulation of maternal ethics in Morrison's fiction, then, by turning to Black mother characters, one dwells not only in the space of ethics but, perhaps not as contradictorily as it may seem at first, also in the space of Blackness as that racialized subjectivity carved by the force of slavery—a legal institution that was nothing if not a violent obliteration of the rights that precede law.

It is in this space that readers encounter Sethe in *Beloved*. Sethe's decision to kill her daughter is inextricable both from the demands of motherhood and the violence of slavery, and it is impossible to disentangle the two in thinking the difficulty of her act. This does not place Sethe beyond the reach of ethical analysis but rather places ethical analysis beyond the reach of universalism, grounding it squarely in the particularities of racial subjection. We can then return to Morrison's evaluation of her character's action: since neither Sethe nor her daughter, nor the two of them as a mother-child unit, has access to any rights within the domain of law, we can read Morrison as not slipping between two "rights" but as consistently invoking the rights that precede law. Even though Sethe had no "right" to kill her daughter, because the first ethical demand of motherhood is to protect one's own children, she was in that moment of her decision absolutely right and absolutely ethically correct to kill her child to keep her from slavery. The demand to protect her child from a fate worse than death forced her to commit a moral act of yet ethically unforgivable violence. Though the reader, like Paul D, may want to come to an easy ethical evaluation of her, Sethe knows that the demands of Black motherhood are too complex for such individual judgment. As she says to Paul D, "It ain't my job to know what's worse. It's my job to know what is and to keep them away from what I know is terrible. I did that" (165).

Set a century and a half after *Beloved*, Morrison's latest novel, *God Help the Child*, begins with a character who apparently needs to defend herself from ethical judgment: "It's not my fault. So you can't blame me" (3). Although the major mother character in this novel is not living under the conditions of legal chattel slavery and the violence she commits is neither as spectacular nor as ethically reprehensible as infanticide, Sweetness, like Sethe, appears before readers having committed maternal violence in attempting to exercise maternal ethics. As readers progress through the novel and read the first-person narrations of different characters, we learn that Sweetness was, at least, an emotionally abusive parent to Lula Ann, her daughter who calls herself Bride. Early in the novel, Bride recalls the intense pleasure she got when Sweetness finally held her hand for the first time after she testified in court against an accused child rapist, saying, "She never did that before and it surprised me as much as it pleased me because I always knew she didn't like touching me.... I used to pray she would slap my face or spank me just to feel her touch" (36). Not only does Bride feel deprived of physical and emotional affection to the point where she actively tries to get her mother to strike her so that she can feel her touch, but we eventually learn that in an attempt to do exactly as her mother wanted she lied on the witness stand to help convict Sofia Huxley of child rape:

"You lied? What the hell for?"
"So my mother would hold my hand!"
"What?"
"And look at me with proud eyes, for once."
"So, did she?"
"Yes. She even liked me." (181)

At this point in Bride's fight with her lover Booker, both characters learn that the violence they had turned toward each other was motivated by wounds inflicted on them as children.

Sweetness does not kill Bride, but the harm of her neglect is certainly a form of maternal violence. And she knows it. It is after all Sweetness who says, "What you do to children matters. And they might never forget" (50). At the same time, though, she insists that she cannot be judged, and the novel—especially by giving the mother the last word—challenges readers to confront Sweetness in the space of Blackness and the space of ethics in which we confront Sethe. After all, Sweetness does not let the reader forget the stakes of racial subjection in accounting for her own mothering of Bride.

For a novel written and set in the so-called postracial moment of the early twenty-first century that offers a character who insists that race isn't real and only makes one feel inferior if one lets it, God Help the Child opens with a character's testimony that reveals how materially present race and racial subjection are in the lives of its characters and the world in which they live. Right after asserting that she cannot be blamed, Sweetness recalls her daughter's birth, saying, "She was so black she scared me" (3). Although this can certainly be read as colourism—indeed, Bride reads it this way when she remarks that "[Sweetness] had ways of punishing me without touching the skin she hated" (36)—it can also be read as fear, since what follows is Sweetness's testimony of the myriad ways in which dark skin can lock a Black person outside of access to not only the rights of civil society but the civility of civil society as well. Indeed, she notes both that "the law was against discriminating in who you could rent to, but not many landlords paid attention to it" (7) and that being visibly black meant "walking in the gutter to let whites have the whole sidewalk" (4). So while Sweetness enacts frightful violence in the moment when she presses a pillow over her baby's face, even though she only does it once and pulls it away before she can kill the child, the hatred she harbours toward Bride's dark black skin comes both from a place of fear and a clinging to a perverse conception of "dignity." This colourism is violent, yes, but its complexity demands something beyond simple condemnation.

Sweetness's colourism emerges from an internalized hierarchy of skin colour, in which the lighter one's skin is, the more dignified one is compared to those with darker skin. She admits early on that her child's dark skin "embarrassed" her from the moment she saw her in the maternity ward of the hospital. Yet even as some readers (though not all—just as there are no universal mothers, there are no universal readers) may bristle at the thought of a mother being "embarrassed" by her own child's skin colour, the text briefly reveals that Sweetness is not the only one to harbour such feelings towards Bride. Sweetness's husband, Louis, is repulsed by the child. Sweetness recalls, "We argued and argued until I told him her blackness must be from his own family—not mine. That's when it got worse, so bad he just up and left and I had to look for another, cheaper place to live" (6). After being abandoned by her husband, Sweetness finds cheap housing and temporarily receives welfare to support herself and her daughter. It is in this cheap apartment that Bride experiences one of her first traumatic and formative moments of her childhood: she witnesses their landlord raping a young boy. The landlord sees her and calls her a "nigger cunt"; she tells her mother, and her mother screams at her to never repeat what she has said (63-64). In a grossly reductive and linear fashion, but in a way that nonetheless *matters*, in terms of the novel's narrative economy of cause and effect, if Sweetness's husband does not abandon her and her child, then Sweetness does not seek different, cheaper housing. And if Sweetness does not seek cheaper housing, then she and Bride do not wind up in Mr. Leigh's apartment building, the location in which this traumatic experience takes place. Although it is reductive and dishonest to say that her father's abandonment *caused* Bride's trauma, it is imperative to understand that her trauma is embedded in a network of material conditions— including structural racism in the form of housing discrimination as well as in poverty and employment as they are experienced by a Black mother raising a child without a second income supporting her household. To be absolutely clear, the novel is not presenting the "absent Black father" trope as the ultimate cause of Black people's problems, and it certainly does not suggest that some kind of normative, nuclear, and patriarchal family structure is the solution to trauma in Black communities or individual Black people's lives, as the counter-example of Booker's family makes abundantly clear. What the novel does is forces readers to reckon with Sweetness's actions and decisions within the material contexts in which they occur, which means there is no analysis of Sweetness that can escape or disentangle the character's ethics from the realities of racism. To reduce Sweetness's colourism to a personal failing is to fail to account for the structuring forces of that colourism. It is not Sweetness that must be the ultimate subject of ethical critique; it is the anti-Black world, in which her violence makes a kind of sense, that must be deconstructed.

In her narration, Sweetness further clarifies that her colourism is embedded within the material conditions of structural racism, and it is in fact these material conditions that, therefore, structure her intentional parenting style that Bride experiences as emotional neglect, which may indeed be strong enough to qualify as emotional abuse. Sweetness leaves no ambiguity about her intentions; at the end of her first narration, she says, "I had to be strict, very strict. Lula Ann needed to learn how to behave, how to keep her head down and not to make trouble" (8). Bride remembers her mother as withholding affection, enough to push her to the point of desiring even a violent touch, just to feel any touch at all, and enough to lie in a court of law just to have her mother hold her hand. On the other hand, Sweetness remembers her parenting as a strictness meant to teach her daughter not to make trouble, knowing that making trouble could mean being put out of one's home by a white landlord against whom black skin was an unquestionable disadvantage. The novel asks us to examine what would it mean, ethically, if maternal emotional abuse is embedded in the violence of both anti-Black racism and sexism. What ethics are possible in the face of such inextricable entanglement?

Sweetness recalls her own mother, Lula Mae, in contextualizing her mothering of Lula Ann, or Bride, at the very beginning of her narration. Sweetness remembers how her mother was light skinned enough to pass for white but chose not to and paid a price for that decision. She narrates that when her parents were married, they swore by placing their hands on a Bible reserved for "Negroes," as if black hands could not touch the same Bible that white hands touched. "My mother was a housekeeper for a rich white couple," Sweetness recalls. "They ate every meal she cooked and insisted she scrub their backs while they sat in the tub and God knows what other intimate things they made her do, but no touching of the same Bible" (4). Drawing on her mother's experience, Sweetness knows that being a Black woman means experiencing the inter-section of the forces of anti-Black racism and sexual subjection. Her mother's work as a domestic labourer is embedded both in racial hierarchy and sexist misogynoir. On the one hand, anti-Black racism relegates Black workers to jobs as quasi-servants who may work but never live in intimate proximity to wealthy white people. On the other hand is the specific misogynoir that renders the Black female body vulnerable to violation but never redress because of the assumption of the always already willing sexual promiscuity imagined to be inherent in Black women. As a witness to this, Sweetness then enacts a maternal ethics herself that is embedded in this anti-Black racism and misogynoir. Thus, although as a mother she is charged with protecting her child, as a Black woman she is left in the position of being required to do so while under a condition in which, as Florens's mother repeats three times in Morrison's 2008 novel *A Mercy*, "There is no protection" (195).

A reason is not an excuse, but Sweetness's second narration in the novel thoroughly explains why her mothering took the shape it did—and it is because of the threat of racism. She opens this narration the following way:

> Oh, yeah, I feel bad sometimes about how I treated Lula Ann when she was little. But you have to understand: I had to protect her. She didn't know the world. There was no point in being tough or sassy when you were right. Not in a world where you could be sent to a juvenile lockup for talking back or fighting in school, a world where you'd be the last one hired and the first one fired. She couldn't

know any of that or how her black skin would scare white
people or make them laugh or trick her.... See if I hadn't
trained Lula Ann properly she wouldn't know to always
cross the street and avoid white boys. (47-48)

At this juncture in the novel, mothering clearly cannot be disen-
tangled from race. It is also the moment wherein maternal ethics is
most clearly articulated as always already an attempt at fulfilling
an impossible imperative for Black mothers. Sweetness was not
thoughtlessly neglectful of Bride; her emotional distance was both
a manifestation of her own colourism and an intentional tactic of
teaching her daughter to be safe in a world designed to destroy
her. And Sweetness eventually believes that she sees evidence in
her success, when a young Bride, still called Lula Ann, helps to
prosecute a group of teachers who were accused of sexually abus-
ing children. Sweetness reads her daughter's testimony as an act
of "courage" and is enormously proud of her because "it's not
often you see a little black girl take down some evil whites" (49).

   In yet another instance of mother-child misreading in Morrison's
fiction, Sweetness is of course wrong in witnessing Bride's testimony
as courage; it is in fact born out of fear and longing. Bride herself
gives "when fear rules, obedience is the only survival choice" as
an explanation for her "good behavior" at the trial for the accused
teachers (36), and at the end of the novel, she reveals to Booker
that she lied and put a woman in jail precisely because she longed
for her mother's affection. Sweetness believes that she successfully
protected her child from the violence of racism (that she fulfilled
the universal obligation of maternal ethics). Yet it is in this very
effort to protect her daughter that her daughter experiences most
powerfully the violence of racism as that force which structures
the mother-daughter relationship and constricts the possibilities of
maternal ethics for Sweetness to squarely within the intersection
of anti-Blackness and misogyny.

   This is, of course, the lesson that Sethe and Florens's mother
learn during slavery in Morrison's earlier novels. To repeat again,
"There is no protection"—in their very gestures of protection, these
Black mothers do violence to their children, so their ultimately most
admirable ethical actions are also their most violent. What *God*

Help the Child does is not merely a repetition with a difference of these two enslaved characters' simultaneously protective and violent actions, but also a figuration of Black motherhood that takes seriously the legacy of slavery after the moment of emancipation. In a country where, as Hartman writes, "motherhood, specifically, and parenting, in general, were social relations without legal recognition in terms of either positive or negative entitlements" for Black people (98), maternal ethics is rendered (im)possible, such that in the twenty-first century, a Black mother like Sweetness is called upon to protect her child from violence while living under the condition of always already being susceptible to the violence of anti-Black racism and misogynoir.

Toya Graham knows this story well, and we can hear it in her statement that she didn't want her son to become another Freddie Gray as an explanation for why she physically struck him in public in order to bring him home from a protest against police brutality. In an article in the *Baltimore Sun* written after video of Graham slapping her son went viral on traditional and social media outlets, Graham is interviewed and explains that the issues that came to light in the case of Freddie Gray (a twenty-five-year-old Black man arrested by officers in the Baltimore Police Department who died of spinal cord injuries sustained while riding in a police van following his arrest) are things she sees "on a daily basis" (Williams IV). It is with this knowledge that she thus inflicts violence against her son as means to protect him from police violence. Many white commenters, such as *Boston Globe*'s columnist Michael Cohen, condemned her use of violence out of an inability to confront the intersectionality of racial oppression and the gendered demands of motherhood. Cohen, for example, alludes to understanding that Graham was trying to protect her son, but he utterly fails to name the forces against which her son needs protecting, probably because those are the very forces (which indeed have names like racial capitalism and white supremacy) that protect his own white daughters while they fail to protect Graham's Black son. Yet what is more interesting is the divergent praise for Graham.

On the one hand, there was the praise mounted on her by venues such as the conservative morning news show *Fox & Friends* that framed her disciplining her young Black son as an action worthy of praise because it somehow denounced the rioting in Baltimore. Never mind that Graham herself has said that people "need to understand that we are fed up," and so the riots are expressions of that (Williams IV). In an article on *The Huffington Post* titled "Dear White America: Toya Graham Is Not Your Hero," Julia Craven quotes Baltimore resident Danielle Williams, and reasons from Williams's insights that Graham was receiving the praise she was from white Americans precisely because she had used violence to intervene in a disruption of white supremacy. Unlike Cohen who condemns Graham outright for failing to live up to the universal standards of motherhood or white commenters such as the talking heads on *Fox & Friends* and Black male authority figures such Baltimore Police Department commissioner Anthony Blatts who praised her for intervening in the violent disruption to restore respectability and order, Craven recognizes that Graham was not condemning the riots or teaching her son a lesson about being a version of the "respectable Negro." Rather, she was protecting him from the forces of anti-Blackness. She did not want him to become another Freddie Gray, arrested and killed by police, thus leaving her as a mother of another dead Black child.

Each slap Graham landed on her son's head fell with the weight of the intersectionality of Black motherhood. It is in the sounds of those slaps (the feeling of violence that causes pain to protect against possible annihilation) that one hears the (im)possibilities of maternal ethics. Those sounds may echo the chilling vibrations of Sethe slitting Beloved's throat, the pained tones of Florens's mother begging a white man to take her daughter away, or the ferocity of Sweetness screaming at Lula Ann to never, ever testify to the violence she has witnessed—all in the hope that their children are shielded from the violence of a world conditioned upon their destruction. Yes, Beloved dies. But Florens lives—albeit traumatized and never able to learn her mother's truth, but she nevertheless lives. Bride also lives, although she does not yet understand her mother's neglect. By living, she prepares to bring into the world another Black child, although she still lives under the condition that Christina Sharpe describes as "disfigure[d] black maternity," which "turn[s] the womb into a factory (producing blackness as abjection much like the slave ship's hold and the prison), and turning the birth canal into another domestic middle passage with black mothers, after the end of legal hypodescent, still ushering their children into her condition; her non-status, her non-being-ness" (63). Under the sign of social death imposed upon Blackness by the political ontology of slavery, maternal ethics demands protecting the child for its future—a future whose very impossibility is the condition of possibility for the futurity of whiteness and the figure of the white child, even if that means doing violence in the present.[2] Sweetness reflects, "I may have done some hurtful things to my only child because I had to protect her. Had to. All because of skin privileges" (49).

Toya Graham did the same. It is easy to condemn maternal violence on the level of individuals, and it is a misjudgment to see maternal violence as a way of escaping other forms of violence. It is difficult and necessary, though, to face the impossibility of disentangling maternal ethics from racism so that the possibilities of an ethics forged not as an escape from or as an alternative to, but squarely within the terror of racial subjection may be given language. Toni Morrison's Black mother characters teach that it is possible to articulate that which is impossible, because as Florens' mother knows, although there is no protection, there is difference. Such a language may make it possible to witness such moments as Graham's striking of her son and ask questions of maternal ethics that open not toward the possibilities of the ethical judgments of oppressed individuals (an all-to-easy and obfuscating game) but rather toward the possibilities of doing the impossible, of overturning the discursive world itself.[3]

ENDNOTES

[1]Hartman writes incisively about not only the need to call the universalism of the subject into question but more particularly the need to call the universalism of the theoretical "woman" of feminism or women's studies into question in a way that both extends and refigures Crenshaw's framework of intersectionality by returning analysis of power to questions of identity through attending to the violence packed into the truism of gender's "social construction." See chapter 3, "Seduction and the Ruses of Power,"

especially pages 94-101, in *Scenes of Subjection*. Christina Sharpe also engages this thread of analysis by thinking with both Hartman and Hortense Spillers in her own essay, "Black Studies: In the Wake." More broadly, scholars working in the field of Black queer studies continue to build on Crenshaw, Hartman, and Spillers in theorizing gender and race as co-constitutive.

[2]See Robin Bernstein's *Racial Innocence: Performing American Childhood from Slavery to Civil Rights* as well as Katherine Capshaw and Anna Mae Duane's co-edited volume *Who Writes for Black Children: African American Children's Literature Before 1900* (especially Brigitte Fielder's essay, "No Rights That Any Body Is Bound To Respect") for an extended discussion of the racialization of childhood and the exclusion of Black children from the discursive category of the child.

[3]Although I end with a gesture toward overturning the discursive world, my intention is not to land on a utopian appeal to a future in which the history (of slavery) that hurts is healed. Such an appeal would be the kind of move Hartman, Wilderson, and others rail against and which I find unpersuasive in Morgenstern's analysis. Rather, what I hope to signal in this final sentence is the way in which Morrison's novels give readers a language for a conceptual impossibility within the discursive limits set by white supremacy as it structures the world in which we live. This final note, then, does not signal an unmitigated belief in the revolutionary power of literature, or a romanticization of reading a novel as an inherently radical political act, so much as a belief in the potential for literature to articulate the seemingly impossible by reaching for language beyond the terms set by dominant discourse.

WORKS CITED

Bernstein, Robin. *Racial Innocence: Performing American Childhood from Slavery to the Civil War*. New York University Press, 2011.

Capshaw, Katherine and Anna Mae Duane. *Who Writes for Black Children?: African American Children's Literature Before 1900*. University of Minnesota Press, 2017.

Cohen, Michael A. "Baltimore Mother Toya Graham is No

Hero." *The Boston Globe*, 30 April 2015, https://www.bostonglobe.com/opinion/2015/04/30/baltimore-mother-toya-graham-hero/80sxXZEBSWZ156H8GFLXMI/story.html. Accessed 20 May 2017.

Craven, Julia. "Dear White America: Toya Graham Is Not Your Hero." *The Huffington Post.* 20 April 29, 2015, http://www.huffingtonpost.com/2015/04/29/toya-graham-hero-mom_n_7175754.html. Accessed 20 May 2017.

Crenshaw, Kimberle Williams. "Demarginalizing the Intersection of Race and Sex: A Black Feminist Critique of Antidiscrimination Doctrine, Feminist Theory, and Antiracist Politics." *Feminist Legal Theory: Readings in Law and Gender*, edited by Katherine T. Bartlett and Rosanne Kennedy, Westview Press, 1991, pp. 57-80.

Crenshaw, Kimberle Williams. "Mapping the Margins: Intersectionality, Identity Politics, and Violence Against Women of Color." *Critical Race Theory: The Critical Writings that Formed the Movement*, edited by Kimberle Crenshaw et al., The New Press, 1995, pp. 357-383.

Hartman, Saidiya. *Scenes of Subjection: Terror, Slavery, and Self-Making in Nineteenth-Century America.* Oxford University Press, 1997.

Hartman, Saidiya and Frank Wilderson. "The Position of the Unthought." *Qui Parle*, vol. 13, no. 2, Spring/Summer 2003, pp. 183-201.

Morgenstern, Naomi. "Maternal Love/Maternal Violence: Inventing Ethics in Toni Morrison's *A Mercy.*" *MELUS: The Society for the Study of Multi-Ethnic Literature of the United States*, vol. 39, no. 1, Spring 2014, pp. 7-29.

Morrison, Toni. *A Mercy.* Vintage Books, 2008.

Morrison, Toni. *Beloved.* Plume, 1987.

Morrison, Toni. *God Help the Child.* Random House Large Print, 2015.

Rankine, Claudia, Beth Loffreda. *The Racial Imaginary.* Fence Books, 2015.

Rothstein, Mervyn. "Toni Morrison, in her New Novel, Defends Women." *The New York Times.* 26 Aug. 26 1987, http://www.nytimes.com/1987/08/26/books/toni-morrison-in-her-new-novel-defends-women.html. Accessed 20 May 2017.

Sharpe, Christina. "Black Studies: In the Wake." *The Black Scholar*, vol. 44, no. 2, 2014, pp. 59-69.

Tillet, Salamishah. *Sites of Slavery: Citizenship and Racial Democracy in the Post-Civil Rights Imagination*. Duke University Press, 2012.

Wilderson, Frank B. *Red, White, and Black: The Structures of U.S. Antagonisms*. Duke University Press, 2010.

Williams IV, John-John. "For Baltimore 'Hero Mom,' Video Captures Only Part of Her Life'sStruggle." *The Baltimore Sun*, 12 May 2015, http://www.baltimoresun.com/features/bs-ae-toya-graham-20150512-story.html. Accessed 20 May 2017.

Racialized Intimacies and Alternative Kinship Relations

Toni Morrison's *Home*

ROSANNE KENNEDY

IN TONI MORRISON'S *Beloved* PAUL D complains that Sethe's maternal love is "too thick" (164). In *Home*, maternal love, rather than "too thick" is much too thin—absent or even hateful. *Home* returns us to the preoccupations of Morrison's first novel, *The Bluest Eye*. Specifically, Morrison again tracks the costs, especially to young black girls, of growing up in households infected by, or attempting to replicate, the dominant aesthetic, cultural, and economic values of white society. The households in both novels are sites of neglect and even hostility because of economic exigencies, internalized racist notions of good and worthy subjects and failed attempts at "respectability." Instead of a refuge, the household and family replicate the dominant culture's implicit insistence on the unloveability of children, such as Pecola Breedlove (*The Bluest Eye*) and Cee and Frank Money (*Home*). However, *Home*, unlike *The Bluest Eye*, is a story about not only loss and disintegration—both psychic and communal—but also survival, healing, and the (re) founding of a counter community.

The difference or gap between the endings of *The Bluest Eye* and *Home* is instructive and generative. What are the conditions that allow Cee and Frank to survive, even flourish, in the absence of conventional (Oedipalized) maternal love and attention, even in the face of maternal resentment and hatred? How does the ending of *Home* provoke us to expand and rethink ideas of the maternal, mothering, home, and sociality? In other words, how does *Home* generate a more expansive view of the maternal away from the Oedipal nuclear family toward one that Fred Moten has called a "general socialisation of the maternal" (*The Undercommons* 154)? How may this "maternal ecology"[1] contest and enlarge normative frames of not only biologically determined familial belonging but also communal belonging beyond (white) individualized notions of property, ownership, and appropriation? If we think of mothering, as Alexis Pauline Gumbs suggests, as an activity rather than a status or gendered identity can we then detach it from the biologically determined to a "technology of transformation" ("M/other Ourselves" 23)? *Home*, I believe, compels us to rethink practices of mothering, sociality, and living together outside (and against) normative white models of the family, heteropatriarchy, gendered identity, and individualization. The novel both critiques dominant white models of family and society, and enacts an alternative way of living and being together premised on the socialization of the maternal.

The trajectory of the novel follows the flight of the brother and sister, Frank and Cee, from their hometown, Lotus, Georgia. Neglected by overworked parents and abused by a "mean grandmother," Frank and Cee first flee Lotus, Georgia, according to overdetermined (white) nationalist and gendered scripts: Frank enlists in the army and Cee marries. This first impulse of escape from the negative domestic space toward the "adventure" of the battlefield or the promises of the city (Atlanta) and married life serves as a disastrous wrong turn for both Frank and Cee. It is only when they return together to their childhood home (notably absent of parental relations) in Lotus, Georgia, that Frank and Cee can feel "at home." This sense of being at home is dependent on the community of maternal women—who were always there but disregarded by Cee and Frank—who heal, welcome, teach, and mother the returning brother and sister (especially Cee). The maternal community of Lotus, which is predicated on "ancient" ways of caring, living, and producing, models an alternative form of belonging and kinship outside of normative frameworks of the white, heteropatriarchal nuclear family and "patriarchilized gender."[2] It is a place of nonbiological, even nongenerational, mothering and noncapitalist reproduction and consumption—a black counter community on the edges of patriarchal and racist America. As an alternative site of living, working, and making in common, Lotus becomes for Cee and Frank a space of healing and freedom, what Stefano Harney and Moten may call a "contrapuntal island" (*The Undercommons* 94) or Morrison a "race specific yet nonracist home" (Morrison, "Home" 5).

In invoking the phrase a "race specific yet nonracist home" I am of course referring to Morrison's 1997 essay, also titled "Home," in which she makes a distinction between the "house" and "home" to describe her own writing, the work she intends it to do as well as the hopes, limits, and risks involved in such a project. The distinction between house and home functions to distinguish between the "racial house," which is the signifying economy of the "master's voice and its assumptions of the all-knowing white father" (4) and home which is the creation of a literary space of "racial specificity minus racist hierarchy" (8). In creating a racially specific literary space, Morrison cites refusal: refusal to join (assimilate) or counter the master's voice (playing according to the "house rules"). Instead, she sees her task as carving out a "home," a sovereign space of freedom in which the master's signifying economy no longer matters. Yet Morrison also recognizes the impossibility of this search for absolute freedom and sovereignty from the master's voice, the impossibility of remaining completely untouched or outside the dominant discourse. If the dream of absolute sovereignty and freedom from the racial house (a postracial utopia) is impossible, her narratives instead work to concretize a space on the "boundaries of the racial imaginary" (4)—what she also terms an "inscape" or "home" rather than utopia or "nonexistent Eden" (11). In describing what this inscape looks like Morrison says, "I want to inhabit, walk around, a site clear of racist detritus; a place where race both matters and is rendered impotent....I want to imagine not the threat of freedom, or its tentative panting fragility but the concrete thrill of borderlessness—a kind of out of doors safety" (9).

If the metaphoric distinction between house and home describes her narrative, aesthetic, and political aims, it is not surprisingly, as she suggests, the literal subject of much of her fiction. Almost every novel speaks to this divide—the conflict between the two, the pull and difficulty of eluding the racial house, and the risks and difficulties of creating and maintaining a home. *Home* documents Cee's and Frank's respective efforts to find a home but more so their continuous misrecognition of home and family—whether missing the home right in front of them or seeing a home where none exists. Each of their journeys is a repeated encounter with the racial house and a mistaking of the racial house for home until their final return to Lotus.

The novel opens epigraphically, with Morrison's lyrics from the song "Whose House Is This?" immediately signaling to the reader the unhomeliness of some houses and the uncanny defamiliarization of the familiar: "Whose house is this? Whose night keeps out the light in here? Say who owns this house? It is not mine. I had another sweeter, brighter with a view of lakes crossed painted boats; of fields wide as arms open for me. This house is strange. Its shadows lie. Say, tell me, why does its lock fit my key?" (2). Morrison's use of "house" rather than "home," signals immediately to the reader that one is in the racial house. On a general level, this uncanny sense of not being at home in one's own house speaks to what it is like to be black in America, in which homelessness, dispossession, and unfamiliarity are the defining ontological position. But we may also interpret these lyrics as applying specifically to Morrison's stated intention to "rip off the veil and fluff" of the "aggressively happy" dominant narrative of 1950s America (Morrison, *Interview*). In ripping the veil off the dominant white narrative of America in the 1950s, Morrison shows us another America through the lens of black life. In his 1919 essay "The Uncanny," Freud describes the uncanny as that which marks the return of the repressed in which what was most familiar and homelike becomes unhomelike. "The uncanny (the unhomely) is what was once familiar ('homely' 'homey'). The negative prefix *un-* is the indicator of repression" (151). Morrison foregrounds what has been repressed and left out of happier white images of this era: forced migration and relocations, war, segregationist policies and practices—in the North and not just the South—McCarthyism, racialized medical experiments and forced sterilizations, and overt racialized police violence.

Yet *Home*, unlike the movement of the uncanny, does not travel from the familiar to unfamiliar, rather in the opposite direction: from the unfamiliar to the familiar. In a series of flashbacks, we learn that Frank and Cee, as children, never felt at home in Lotus. Indeed, the siblings feel disconnected from the place and history of their childhood home. As they sense that they belong nowhere and only having affective ties to each other (Frank also has his friends, Mike and Stuff), the siblings drift and play aimlessly on the fringes of the community. It is only after separate and perilous migratory journeys that they rediscover and recognize their childhood home as, well, home. Perhaps it is also a queer home. Queer meaning a non-normative home—neither the patriarchal nuclear familial home vaunted by the dominant white culture nor the ostensible matriarchy of the black family pathologized in sociological studies: a brother and sister living together with a community of singular, often eccentric, healing women versed in the ancient properties, and living on rented, sharecropper land (but making it their own).

In documenting their respective journey away and then back to Lotus, Morrison gives us various examples of familial relationships (black and white) that the siblings individually encounter—some positive, but mostly negative. These examples describe not only the difference between the house and the home but what Morrison in a 1981 interview calls the "confrontation between the old values of the tribes and new urban values" (qtd. in Taylor-Guthrie 121). In her essay "Rootedness: The Ancestor as Foundation," Morrison elaborates on this confrontation and the importance of the "ancestor" in negotiating the new urban spaces. Ancestors "are not just parents [although they are more often grandparents and particularly grandmothers], they are sort of timeless people whose relationships to the characters are benevolent, instructive, and protective, and they provide a certain kind of wisdom" (62). The ancestor provides an anchoring presence, a connection to the past, and serves as a guide to the present. "When you kill the ancestor you kill yourself.... Nice things don't always happen to the totally self-reliant if there is no conscious historical connection" (64). Although Cee and Frank may be archetypically described as "peasants," they have not learned the tribal values. They lack "rootedness" because the ancestor has been absent. And it is this absence and disconnection that lead to their bafflement and misrecognition of various relations and situations on their respective journeys. Disavowing their own history and past in their efforts to follow the mythical American dream in which they were never in any case the addressees, Frank and Cee inevitably encounter "not nice things."

The initial sense of rootlessness and disconnection that structure Cee and Frank's story begins before Cee is born. The Money family—Luther, Ida pregnant with Cee, and four-year old Frank—us forcibly removed from its home in Texas. As the unnamed narrator tells us: "You could be living inside, living in your house for years, and still, men with or without badges but always with guns could force you, your family, your neighbors to pack up and move.... Twenty years ago ... residents of fifteen houses had been ordered to leave their little neighborhood on the edge of town. Twenty-four hours, they were told, or else. 'Else' meaning 'die'" (9-10). The family leaves, walking and hitching rides, until they reach Lotus; Cee is born along the way in a church basement.

The sudden forced dispossession and migration take them to their grandfather and step-grandmother's home in Lotus, Georgia, where they fortunately find temporary shelter but unfortunately not a home. Lenore, the grandmother, in fact, resents their presence. Lenore considers herself superior to the rest of the community because she owned her house, had savings, and owned, not one, but two of the cars in Lotus. Money and property give Lenore her sense of respectability and superiority to the rest of the inhabitants of Lotus. Cee, the girl born on the road (or in Lenore's words, "the gutter"), becomes the specific object of Lenore's hatred and disdain:

> Lenore, who believed herself superior to everybody else in Lotus, chose to focus her resentment on the little girl born "in the street." A frown creased her every glance when the girl entered, her lips turned down at every drop of a spoon, rip on the door saddle, a loosening braid. Most of all was the murmur of "gutter child" as she walked away from a failing that was always on display form her step-granddaughter. (45)

Lenore has everything that the dominant white culture considers valuable and a marker of success: a husband, property, and money (91). The only thing lacking from this normative framework is, presumably, children (and grandchildren). But this is precisely what she rejects. Lenore refuses to adopt the maternal position or, in Morrison's words, the role of the "ancestor." However, we may interpret Lenore's refusal to be entirely consistent with normative injunctions, specifically the emphasis on biological rather than cultural connection and on reproduction rather than construction: Cee and Frank are not her "real" grandchildren.

With Ida and Luther too busy working "from sunrise until dark" (43) and so tired that "any affection they showed was like a razor—sharp, short, and thin" (53), they are essentially absent and affective relations with their children are almost nonexistent. The parents' absence in their children's lives is stated intermittently, but what strikes the reader is their almost complete lack of presence in the novel. The novel replicates the attenuation of affective ties as Ida and Luther disappear from the narrative soon after their appearance. Indeed, their deaths are noted and recorded as a factual event, rather than lingered on and mourned: both die in quick succession from illnesses related to hard work, and the funerals are attended or not by the children according to convenience. Initially, Frank becomes a maternal figure for Cee filling in the maternal space vacated by their mother and grandmother. Four-year-old Frank becomes the "real mother to the infant [Cee]" (88). For Frank, Cee functions as "his original caring-for, a selfishness without gain or emotional profit" (35). It is Frank who performs maternal duties in the absence of a maternal figure: he protects her from the grandmother and from the outside world, watches over and cares for her, tends her bruises and cuts, and even performs such pedestrian, ritual maternal acts as saving her baby teeth.

Frank, his two best friends, Stuff and Mike (significantly he calls them his "homeys"), and Cee are "tight." Their affective ties are seen as modeling "the way a family ought to be" (52). When Frank, along with Stuff and Mike, enlist in the army to escape what they see as the futureless Lotus, Cee, at fourteen, becomes in a sense without family. Adrift, Cee falls for the first man, Principal, who pays attention to her. Attracted by his "city clothes" (his "thin-soled shoes") and urban manners ("big-city accent"), Cee marries the "Prince" (48). Although the novel explicitly casts itself as a reworking of the Hansel and Gretel fairy tale, the novel here references a truncated version of Cinderella. This reference immediately signals to the reader a disastrous rather than happy ending. As Morrison warns in "Unspeakable Things Unspoken," "whenever characters are cloaked in Western fable, they are in deep trouble" (157). Following the white gender script of Western fantasy, Cee indeed ends up in deep trouble. The Prince borrows Lenore's Ford to drive them to Atlanta and then quickly abandons Cee. Prince, it becomes evident, married her for the car. On her own for the first time and too fearful of Lenore's wrath over the stolen car to return home, even for her father's funeral, Cee must quickly find a way to support herself.

Taking a live-in position in the white suburbs as an assistant to Dr. Beauregard Scott, a doctor and self-described scientist, Cee is enthralled with the beautiful house, the white uniform, and her clean room. She is especially impressed by Dr. Beau's ostensible erudition and book-filled shelves. The reader though is quickly aware of the threat. A cursory glance at the titles on the bookshelf (*The Passing of the Great Race*; *Heredity, Race, and Society*) signals to the reader the types of experiments that Dr. Beau is engaged in. Cee, not understanding what "eugenics" means, is convinced that she has found a home: "This was a good, safe place, she knew, and Sarah [the other caretaker/domestic] had become her family, her friend, and her confidante" (65). Cee misrecognizes the danger she is in and instead sees the opposite: safety and family. The chapter ends with a final ominous foreshadowing of Cee's fate. Looking over some Honeydew melons to enjoy on a hot summer day, Cee and Sarah search for a "female" melon—"always the sweetest," "always the juiciest." When they find one, Sarah slides "a long, sharp knife from the drawer," and cuts "the girl in two" (66).

When it becomes clear that Cee is being killed by Dr. Beau's reproductive experiments, Sarah sends a cryptic but effective note to Frank who has been discharged and living in Seattle: "Come fast. She be dead if you tarry" (8). The bulk of the novel charts Frank's journey to rescue Cee from the Scott household. From Central City, Washington, to Atlanta, Frank's voyage is cast as a twentieth-century trip along a reverse underground railroad. But it also documents possible familial models and kinship relationships. Positive models are those that in some way hold onto the ancestor, history, and values of the tribes, which are welcoming and hospitable. Positive models are also those that are predicated on equality, and on non-normative and nonhierarchical gender roles—kinship and familial relations that do not replicate the dominant values of patriarchy and patriarchialized gender. Negative models are those that replicate hierarchical and exploitative gender roles.

When Frank receives Sarah's note, he is living with his newfound love, Lily. Frank describes meeting Lily as a homecoming, "I'd felt like I'd come home. Finally. I'd been wandering" (68). But on Lily's part, what is missing is a house to call her own. Racial exclusionary policies preclude Lily from purchasing her own home, despite her having the means to do so. Lily's anger and humiliation in the face of housing discrimination coupled with what she views as Frank's lack of ambition (and his repeated episodes of withdrawal and flight because of trauma from his wartime experiences) counters the initial good feelings. Thus when Frank tells her he must leave to save Cee, Lily feels only a moment of regret. On Frank's part, in retrospect, he realizes that his life with Lily was a displacement of his "disorder, his rage, and his shame" (108), a temporary respite rather than a lasting home. Frank, in short, has misrecognized a brief layover as home. Unable to assume the paternal function and the normative masculine role and refusing the injunctions of white ambition and desires (home ownership), Frank is relieved to be called away.

During his journey to Atlanta, Frank meets different families and kinship relations: the kindly Reverend John Locke and his wife, Jean; the suspicious Reverend Maynard, who makes Frank sleep on the porch under the watchful, smiling grill of a Rocket 98 Oldsmobile because his "daughters are inside the house"(22); the battered couple on the train to Chicago—the man kicked and beaten for trying to buy coffee at the train stop, with his wife whose nose was bloodied and broken by a thrown rock for trying to help her husband; Billy who invites Frank to stay with him and meet his family, wife Arlene, and their son Thomas, who was shot by the police; the pimp, Sonny, with his brand new Cadillac and the two prostitutes fighting over him; a gang of boys who rob him and the white hippie that helps him by giving him a few dollars and telling him to "stay in the light" (107); the suburban upper-middle-class white household of the deranged Dr. Beauregard Scott, his laudanum-addicted and equally racist wife, and the absent encephalitic children; and finally Miss Ethel and the women of Lotus who heal Cee.

These encounters illustrate the Morrisonian difference between peasant-village values and urban values, and the clash or accommodation between the two. The family of Billie, Arlene, and the boy Thomas is a paradigmatic example of maintaining some connection with the tribe or peasant values in the context of the urban environment of Chicago. After meeting Frank in a diner—itself described as "welcoming" where "Laborers and the idle, mothers and street women, all ate and drank with the ease of family in their won kitchens" (27)—Billy invites him to meet his family and stay the night. He even makes Frank breakfast and takes him shopping for new clothes and shoes the next day before sending him on the next leg of his journey. These quotidian chores—making breakfast, sending children to school, shopping—are interrupted when Billy and Frank are robbed by the police. Billy and Frank shrug this encounter off as so banal and expected it "was not worth comment" (37). But if this encounter is too banal to elicit commentary, an everyday occurrence, the dangers of police violence and arbitrary power are not underestimated. The son, Thomas, was shot at eight years old by a "drive-by cop." As Billy tells Frank, "Cops shoot anything they want. This here's a mob city" (31).

What is noteworthy about this family, beyond their generosity and hospitality, is that they are able to survive despite economic difficulties and amid the terrorism of arbitrary police violence by means of familial and communal solidarity. The partnership of Arlene and Billy is particularly notable and can be described as what Morrison calls a relationship of "comrades." Comrade relationships, Morrison says in an interview, are those in which there is no "imbalance or unevenness ... or struggle for dominance" based on gender (qtd. in Taylor-Guthrie 141).These types of comrade partnerships, as the word comrade suggests, are those relationships of the past based on equality within the marriage and directed at surviving amid inequalities and dangers from without. Modeling this type of comrade relationship, Arlene and Billy simply do what needs to be done, without reference to gender roles. Arlene works the night shift while Billy, on strike, takes whatever day jobs available. The task of the daily caretaking duties—making breakfast, walking their son to school—falls to him. Certainly this could be an idealization of marriages of the past, but it points to Morrison's foregrounding of race or how race always inflects understandings of gender. As James Bliss has argued "Blackness is ontologically *prior to* and *productive* of the back-slashed pairing 'gender/sexuality.' This is not to produce an argument about the political *priority* of 'race' over and against gender and sexuality, but to argue that to attempt an analytic of Blackness must always also be to attempt to account for the categories made possible as the shadow of Blackness" (88).

Following Bliss's argument then, we can read Morrison's ostensibly idealized account of the married couple and its comradeship as not the idealized Oedipal relationship and normative nuclear family, but rather as an equal partnership in the face of racial inequality. Gender equality within the family is thus an effect of racial inequality—the couple is turned outward in a common struggle of survival rather than inward, precisely because race, according to the dominant culture, precedes the categorization of gender and sexuality. In this comrade relationship, although it may appear to replicate that of the dominant culture, the dynamics are quite different. Frank himself is intrigued by this "normal" family, not only because it differs from his own upbringing but precisely because he has no idea how other families work. Yet this family is not one he envies or desires to replicate: "The rules and accommodations normal families made were a fascination that did not rise to the level of envy" (35). This lack of envy is telling. Certainly, the family of Billy, Arlene, and Thomas suggests a positive model of familial belonging, black sociality, and survival within and against the context of racial terror. But it also implies accommodation and the limits of surviving within the context of the racial house (resonating with perhaps the accommodations that Frank would have had to make to stay with Lily), which leave Frank nonplussed.

If Billy, Arlene, and Thomas model one way of familial belonging, most of Frank's other encounters model alternative masculine roles that mimic or exacerbate white masculine domination and patriarchy. Morrison quite often invokes objects, most frequently the American car, as masculine tropes. In *Home*, the American car is an ominous sign of either patriarchal control or masculine domination: the Oldsmobile of the inhospitable Reverend protecting his daughters, the pimp's brand-new Cadillac, and of course, the Ford that Principal stole after marrying Cee. (We should also consider the prominence of the car in Morrison's other novels: the prized Cadillac that Mavis steals from her husband in *Paradise* or Bride's Jaguar in *God Help the Child*.) The American car signifies not only big city values but also dominant American values, which signify masculine dreams of upper mobility or flight.

Frank himself is intermittently drawn to the freedom and escape that is promised by owning a car. He casts an admiring glance on the pimp's Cadillac before realizing who owns it and, of course, how it was paid for. He has an occasional dream of owning one himself. But this dream is a fleeting one of masculine glamour, style, and danger. At first glance, it may also be likened to the zoot-suited ghost that keeps interrupting Frank's dreams, both waking and sleeping. But the ghost has little appeal or attraction for Frank; its sartorial style is too outrageous. Frank prefers a more primitive and traditional masculine garb: "If they were the signals of manhood, he would have preferred a loincloth and some white paint artfully smeared on forehead and cheeks. Holding a spear, of course" (34). The enigma of the zoot-suited ghost and what it signifies is particularly confounding in the novel. Juda Bennett is certainly correct in asserting that this Morrison ghost is especially ambivalent; it is not a familiar ghost or a family ghost, nor it is a known haunting. Rather it is an outrageous stranger ghost (148).[3] Frank, though, dismisses this alternative performance of masculinity and indeed finds its appearance comic. Frank is certainly aware of the political significance of the zoot suit and that it makes enough of a fashion statement to "interest riot cops on each coast" (34). But this type of outrageous form of (black) masculine performance does not captivate Frank, perhaps because it is not easily decipherable and is indeed "strange."[4] Frank instead seems to prefer the most obvious signifiers of traditional, African masculinity—loincloth, body paint, and spears—over the black subculture's adoption of the zoot suit. Indeed, Frank seems to prefer or at least recognize other modern signifiers of masculinity: not just the American automobile but the service medal he holds onto; the found Bulova watch; police badges; work boots; and the "reefer and gasoline smell, the rapid sneaker tread ... the gang breath" of the teenage hoodlums who beat him up and rob him (106). He recognizes and either embraces or repels these signs of masculinity, but the zoot-suited interloper remains too exorbitant for Frank to see as either an alternative or as oppositional.

Once Frank rescues Cee and returns to Lotus, the zoot-suited ghost takes leave of Frank. Perhaps since Frank no longer sees Lotus as the dead end futureless place he yearns to escape, other alternatives (no matter how exorbitant) become particularly beside the point: dreams of masculine flight and autonomy no longer hold sway. Consider how Frank first describes Lotus:

> the worst place in the world, worse than any battlefield. At least on the field there is a goal, excitement, daring, and some chance of winning along with many chances of losing. Death is a sure thing but life is just as certain. Problem is you can't know in advance. In Lotus you did know in advance since there was *no future*, just long stretches of killing time. There was no goal other than breathing, nothing to win and, save for somebody else's quiet death, nothing to survive or worth surviving for.... Nobody in Lotus knew anything or wanted to learn anything. It sure didn't look like anyplace you'd want to be. Maybe a hundred or so people living in some fifty spread-out rickety houses. (83, emphasis added)

When Frank returns with Cee, this place that seemed to him to be a place with "no future"[5] now seems entirely different, vividly coloured and fully alive with brightly hued flowers and deep green leaved trees, a place of "safety and goodwill" (119). In place of the drab, broken down hamlet, Lotus now appears to Frank both "fresh and ancient, safe and demanding" (132).

Cee is also transformed by her return to Lotus. Near death after Dr. Beau's medical experimentation, Cee is taken by Frank to Miss Ethel Fordham's house, where the women of Lotus work together furiously for months to heal her, employing ancient recipes and a final "sun smacking" (124). At times, they scold her and berate her, and at other times, they are more sympathetic and comforting. As she heals, they also teach her to garden, cook, and quilt. In other words, they mother her. But unlike the "othermothering" described by Patricia Hill Collins,[6] this mothering is directed at a grown woman rather than a child. Stepping in to fill the absent mother figure in Cee's life, the women of Lotus communally and belatedly take on this role.

When Cee reflects on why and how she ends up abandoned in Atlanta, she first traces it back to the lack of maternal presence as a girl; she has neither the caring, doting attention of a grandmother nor the guidance of a mother: "A mean grandmother is one of the worst things a girl could have. Mamas are supposed to spank and rule you so you grow up knowing right from wrong. Grandmothers, even when they've been hard on their own children, are forgiving and generous to the grandchildren. Ain't that so" (43)? Certainly, a mean grandmother such as Lenore is a terrible thing, but Cee also lacked the attention of her mother. Cee wonders why her mother never countered Lenore's meanness. But Cee did have Frank, but although "his devotion shielded her, it did not strengthen her" (129). Frank's mothering was, oxymoronically, too "paternalistic" in that he overly protected her so that she failed to develop her own survival skills. He also unwittingly shielded her not just from the anger and violence of the grandmother but from the women of Lotus. As a girl, Cee finds their watchfulness intrusive and dismisses them out of hand as "ignorant" (47). It is only when she is surrounded by them during her healing that Cee pays them the attention that she never did before (122). Cee discovers that far from ignorant, the women of Lotus are highly skilled and artful despite (or because of) their lack of education or even literacy. Indeed, they have "perfect memory, photographic minds, keen senses of smell and hearing." And they can repair what an "educated bandit doctor ... plundered" (128).

Cee also discovers that the women of Lotus—although each is singular, and each has endured her own tragedies (a child's death, disabling work accidents, illnesses)—share a similar approach to living:

> Although each of her nurses was markedly different from
> the others in looks, dress, manner of speech, food and med-
> ical preferences, their similarities were glaring. There was
> no excess in their gardens because they shared everything.
> There was no trash or garbage in their homes because they
> had a use for everything. They took responsibility for their
> lives and for whatever, whoever else needed them. (123)

What is notable are not the differences among the women, but
their shared responsibility to each other and to the community.
Lotus is the paradigm of a sharing community and economy, rather
than one of individual acquisitive accumulation prevalent in the
dominant society.

But in order for Cee to be part of this sharing community, she
must first figure out her role and what she herself has to give or
share. Ethel gives her the following advice:

> look to yourself. You free. Nothing and nobody is obliged
> to save you but you. Seed your own land. You young and
> a woman and there's serious limitations in both, but you
> a person too. Don't let Lenore, or some trifling boyfriend
> and certainly no devil doctor decide who you are. That's
> slavery. Somewhere inside you is that free person I'm
> talking about. Locate her and let her do some good in the
> world. (126)

Interestingly, Ethel mentions Cee's youth and gender as limitations
but not race. That is, although the words "slavery" and "free
person" reference the history of black life in America, Ethel also
suggests that in the black community of Lotus (an example of a
race-specific but non-racist place), one can live freely.

Ethel's advice and injunction stick, and Cee thinks about what
it would mean to live "freely:"

> So it was just herself. In this world with these people she
> wanted to be the person would never again need rescue …
> she wanted to be the one who rescued her own self. Did
> she have a mind, or not? Wishing would not make it so,

nor would blame, but thinking might. If she did not respect
herself, why should anybody else? (129)

At first glance, it may seem as if Cee (and Ethel) models her
self-becoming on that of the liberal, autonomous subject particularly entrenched in white American ideology. But that would be
to ignore the reality that independence and freedom happen *with*
others ("in this world *with* these people"), rather than apart from.
Responsibility encompasses not just people's individual lives but
also the lives of others around them. But before this responsibility
and care can be extended to others, one must, as Audre Lorde
insists, learn to mother oneself. Lorde writes the following:

> Mothering. Claiming some power over who we choose
> to be, and knowing that such power is relative within the
> realities of our lives. Yet knowing that only through the
> use of that power can we effectively change those realities
> Mothering means the laying to rest of what is weak, tim-
> id, and damaged—without despisal—the protection and
> support of what is useful for survival and change, and our
> joint explorations of the difference. (173-174)

This mothering of self, Lorde insists, is necessary for the survival
of the self so that self can be "in the service of ourselves and each
other" (174). This injunction then is far from the (white) liberal
self predicated on autonomy and individualism; it is a means of
learning how to care for others or, in other words, learning how
to mother.

Perhaps the single extraordinary example of the women's responsibility to others is that the women care for Lenore after she
suffers a stroke. Lenore, they knew, despised them and had kept
herself apart: "It was a testimony to the goodwill of churchgoing
and God-fearing women that they brought her plates of food,
swept the floors, washed her linen and would have bathed her
too, except her pride and their sensitivity forbade it" (92). The
caring for, or mothering, practised by the women of Lotus is en-
compassing; it extends to whomever needs it and despite whether
they are liked by the community. Their presence in the community

is sufficient. Morrisonian maternal communities (the women in *Paradise* and the Bottom in *Sula* are also examples) are not predicated on sameness but expansive; they accept the divergent, the outlier, even the hateful.

In their parent's house, Cee and Frank recreate a home. Indeed, it is an unusual home, even a queer home: an adult brother and sister living together without parents and without children. In other words, it is a non-nuclear family outside of reproductive generativity but is nonetheless tied together and to the community by strong affection. The most devastating effect of Dr. Beau's experiments is that Cee will never have children. Cee becomes haunted by the image of her unborn daughter, and, significantly, she does imagine a daughter: "I didn't feel anything at first when Miss Ethel told me, but now I think about it all the time. It's like there's a baby girl down here waiting to be born. She's somewhere close by in the air, in this house, and she picked me to be born to. And now she has to find some other mother" (131). If at first the reader fears another baby haunting reminiscent of *Beloved* and the house of 124, we are soon relieved. Cee's haunting is more akin to mourning than melancholy. When Frank attempts to soothe her by telling her not to cry, she replies: "Why not? I can be miserable if I want to. You don't need to try and make it go away. It shouldn't go away. It's just as sad as it ought to be and I'm not going to hide from what's true just because it hurts" (131). Because Cee avows her loss and holds onto it, she can work through it, as painful and difficult as it may be. We might also think of Cee's grieving as finding a reparative outlet: quilting. After Cee declares her grief, she begins "sorting and re-sorting quilt pieces" (132). As a means of "sorting" through her feelings, quilting becomes a process of reparation, a piecing together and thinking through—a symbolic stitching together of her psychic and physical wounding.

Cee's confession, though, provokes Frank to finally confront his own repressed memory. Frank has attributed his nightmares to witnessing Mike's and Stuff's horrific deaths in Korea, but now he is confronted with the true memory of his haunting: his murder of the Korean girl who tempted him to take him "down to a place [he] didn't know was in [him]... to that place where [he] unzip[s] [his] fly and let her taste [him] right then and there" (134). Cee's visions of the "toothless smiles" forces Frank to "sort out" what has been really troubling him and to confront the shame that his "thick" mourning for his friends displaced (132-q33). The toothless smile of the baby ghost forces Frank to remember the toothless, starving Korean girl, who offered herself to him in exchange for food with the phrase "yum yum." Frank's shame in being aroused signals not only his own dehumanization but the dehumanization of others.

How to fix the unfixable? How to repair the unrepairable? How to dislodge the hook "deep inside his chest" (135)? Frank's despair takes him back to a memory from childhood (which opens the novel) when Cee and Frank happened upon horses fighting in a field: "they stood like men" (5). The pronoun refers to the horses though and not men, a confusion of the animal and the human. This confusion, though, is further stressed by what follows. Cee and Frank witness the hurried burial of a man, who is dumped upside down into an open grave by a group of (white) men. A "black foot" sticking up over the edge of the grave is quickly "whacked" back in (4). Back in Lotus, Frank finally learns what happened. A father and son, grandfather Salem tells Frank, were abducted and forced to fight to the death for sport, "[t]urning men into dogs" (139). The father refusing to kill his own son ordered his son to commit patricide. At the close of the novel, Frank seeks to give a proper burial to the father. Eliciting the help of Cee, and specifically her newly made quilt, Frank and Cee return to the field. Digging up the "small" bones and the "clean and smiling" skull, Frank reassembles and wraps them in the "lilac, crimson, yellow, and dark navy blue" quilt, and carries them down to the river (143). Digging a perpendicular grave under the "sweet bay tree—split down the middle, beheaded, undead spreading its arms one to the right, one to the left," Frank places the "crayon-colored coffin" (144). Once buried, Frank attaches a wooden marker with the words: "Here Stands A Man."

The reader can read the scene in multiple ways. The reburial of the father killed in a cruel and dehumanizing game is provided a decent, if somewhat unusual, burial. Because they buried him standing up, Cee and Frank have symbolically returned him to his position as a man and not a "dog" killed for sport. However, the details of the burial—the "crayon-colored quilt," "small bones," "smiling skull," and the "four or five feet" grave (144)—suggest that Frank and Cee are symbolically burying both the Korean girl and Cee's unborn girl baby. The marker, "Here Stands A Man," is thus ambiguous. Does it refer to the buried bones or to Frank himself? Does it signify that Frank has regained his own sense of humanity? And how do we read the placing of the bones underneath the bay tree— "split in the middle" but also "alive and well" (147)? If we are to understand the tree as a feminine presence as Morrison tells us we should—"with all due respect to the dream landscape of Freud, trees have always seemed feminine to me" ("Unspeakable Things Unspoken" 153)—are we then to understand the tree to represent Cee? The tree and Cee, both "split down the middle," make this seem likely. Or can we understand the acephalic tree—split, wounded, and divided but still "alive" and "well"—as referencing the community and especially the women of Lotus? In contrast to the "scientific" and "rational" practices of the evil doctor who gutted Cee, the healing practices of the women of Lotus are based on the maternal, and on tradition, love, and respect. Or are we perhaps to view the tree more generally as the tree of (black) life in America: "strong," "beautiful," "hurt right down the middle, but alive and well" (147)?

All of these interpretations seem possible, since all reference the possibility of survival and even thriving, despite the wounding of the racial house. However, the ending also leaves us with a mystery. Just before the "ghosts" (the lynched, the unborn child, and the murdered girl) have been laid to rest, the zoot-suited ghost makes one final appearance. Confounding the mystery further, the ghost appears to Cee and not Frank. On the opposite bank of the river, Cee spots "a small man in a funny suit swinging a watch chain. And grinning" (144). Is the grin a malevolent mocking smile or one that is conspiratorial or approving? Or both? And why does the ghost haunt Cee now rather than Frank?

If the ghost is trying to tell Cee something—something that Frank could not decipher though he did for an instant consider the ghost was a "sign trying to tell him something" (34)—what is the message? The emphasis on the "swinging watch chain" suggests that the ghost is calling attention to the passing of time or perhaps the threat of time. Lotus is described as existing outside linear time: a place of "no future" but also one in which time was "pure and subject to anybody's interpretation" like the broken, Bulova watch Frank found with "no stem, no hands" (120). If the ghost is a sign of the intrusion of history on the community of Lotus, or more threateningly that of Father Time and impending death (of the community), are we then left without hope for the sustainability and preservation of alternative communities and counter-narratives?

One way to read this warning (if indeed it is a warning) is to reference the battle waged by Miss Ethel in the care of her garden:

> An aggressive gardener, Miss Ethel blocked or destroyed enemies and nurtured plants. Slugs curled and died under vinegar-seasoned water. Bold, confidant raccoons cried and ran away when their tender feet touched crushed newspaper or chicken wire placed around plants. Cornstalks safe from skunks slept in peace under paper bags. Under her care pole beans curved, then straightened to advertise their readiness. Strawberry tendrils wandered, their royal-scarlet berries shining in the morning rain. Honeybees gathered to salute *Illicium* and drink the juice. Her garden was not Eden; it was so much more than that. For her the whole predatory world threatened her garden, competing with its nourishment, its beauty, its benefits, and its demands. And she loved it. (130)

Like Miss Ethel's garden, Lotus is "not Eden" or a utopia but an "inscape," a race specific yet nonracist home. But this garden (beautiful, nourishing, and demanding) is under constant threat and requires aggressive vigilance against "predators" (i.e., dominant white narratives and injunctions). May we then consider Miss Ethel's garden, and indeed Lotus, not as a specific geographical location but the literary enactment of possible alternative modes of sociality and responsibility based on the generalization of the maternal? Could it represent an alternative maternal model to the white hetereopatriarchal culture in which kinship is constructed

177

and extended rather than biologically given and reproduced, a place of temporal asynchronicity, of perhaps "no future" but a place worth living in and protecting (if only in the imaginary)?

ENDNOTES

[1] "Maternal ecology" is Stefano Harney and Fred Moten's term to describe a sociality based on the maternal or radical interdependency. See Harney and Moten, "Michael Brown" (87).

[2] "Patriarchilized gender" is the term Hortense Spillers employs in "Mama's Baby, Papa's Maybe: An American Grammar Book" to describe white female gender "which, from one point of view, is the *only* female gender there is" (73). That is, the black female, has been essentially de-gendered since she has been rendered mere "flesh" decoupled from traditional notions (and protections) of 'womanhood' propagated by the white patriarchy. This condition of not belonging to the white women's community has also a radical potentiality: "This problematizing of gender places her [the black female], in my view, *out* of the traditional symbolics of female gender, and it is our task to make a place for this different social subject. In doing so, we are less interested in joining the ranks of gendered femaleness than gaining the *insurgent* ground of a female social subject" (80).

[3] Bennett makes an intriguing argument that the zoot-suited ghost is a transgender figure in *Toni Morrison and the Queer Pleasure of Ghosts* (157-158).

[4] Ralph Ellison famously describes the zoot suit as a powerful, unsolved political signifier. "Much in Negro life remains a mystery; perhaps the zoot suit conceals profound political meaning; perhaps the symmetrical frenzy of the Lindy Hop conceals clues to great potential power – if only Negro leaders would solve this riddle" (qtd, in Kelly 161).

[5] The phrase "no future" puts the reader in mind of Lee Edelman's *No Future: Queer Theory and the Death Drive*. Although Edelman's book does not focus on race, other theorists have begun to explore the connections and disagreements between queer theory and black feminism. See for example, Sharon Holland, *The Erotic Life of Racism*; Alexis Pauline Gumbs, "Speculative Poetics: Audre Lorde

as Prologue for Queer Black Feminism" in *The Black Imagination*, eds. Sandra Jackson and Julie E. Moody-Freeman (Peter Lang, 2011); and James Bliss, " Hope against Hope," among others.
⁶See Collins's *Black Feminist Thought* for an empirical account of the practices of othermothering (192-198).

WORKS CITED

Bennett, Juda. *Toni Morrison and the Queer Pleasure of Ghosts*. State University of New York Press, 2014.

Bliss, James. "Hope Against Hope: Queer Negativity, Black Feminist Theorizing, and Reproduction without Futurity." *Mosaic: A Journal for the Interdisciplinary Study of Literature*, vol. 48, no. 1, 2015, pp. 83-98. *Project Muse*, doi: 10.1353/mos.2015.0007.

Collins, Patricia Hill. *Black Feminist Thought: Knowledge, Consciousness, and the Politics of Empowerment*. Routledge, 2000.

Edelman, Lee. *No Future: Queer Theory and the Death Drive*. Duke University Press, 2004.

Freud, Sigmund. *The Uncanny*. Translated by David McLintock. London: Penguin, 2003. 123-162.

Gumbs, Alexis Pauline. "M/other Ourselves: a Black Queer Feminist Genealogy for Radical Mothering." *Revolutionary Mothering: Love on the Front Lines*, edited by Alexis Pauline Gumbs, et al., PM Press, 2016, pp. 19-31.

Gumbs, Alexis Pauline. "Speculative Poetics: Audre Lorde as Prologue for Queer Black Futurism." *The Black Imagination, Science Fiction, Futurism, and the Speculative*, edited by Sandra Jackson and Julie E. Moody Freeman, Peter Lang, 2011, pp. 130-146.

Harney, Stefano, and Fred Moten. "Michael Brown." *boundary 2*, vol. 42, no. 4, 2015, pp.81-87. doi:10.1215/01903659-3156141.

Harney, Stefano, and Fred Moten. *The Undercommons: Fugitive Planning and Black Study*. Minor Compositions, 2013.

Holland, Sharon. *The Erotic Life of Racism*. Duke University Press, 2012.

Kelly, Robin D. G. *Race Rebels: Culture Politics and the Black Working Class*. The Free Press, 1994.

Lorde, Audre. "Eye to Eye: Black Women, Hatred, and Anger."

Sister Outsider: Essays and Speeches. Crossing Press, 2007, pp. 124-133.

Morrison, Toni. *Beloved*. Knopf, 1987.

Morrison, Toni. "Home." *The House That Race Built*, edited by Wahneema Lubiano, Vintage, 1998, pp. 3-12.

Morrison, Toni. *Home*. Vintage, 2012.

Morrison, Toni. Interview with by Christopher Bollen. *Interview Magazine*, 5 July 2012, http://www.interviewmagazine.com/culture/toni-morrison. Accessed 18 May 2017.

Morrison, Toni. "Rootedness: The Ancestor as Foundation." *What Moves at the Margin*, edited by Carolyn C. Denard, University Press of Mississippi, 2008, pp. 56-63.

Morrison, Toni. "Unspeakable Things Unspoken: The Afro-American Presence in American Literature." *Michigan Quarterly Review*, vol. 28, no. 1, 1989, pp. 1-34.

Spillers, Hortense. "Mama's Baby, Papa's Maybe: An American Grammar Book." *Diacritics*, vol. 17, no. 2, 1987, pp. 64-81. *JSTOR*, doi: 10.2307/464747.

Taylor-Guthrie, Danille, editor. *Conversations with Toni Morrison*. University Press of Mississippi, 1994.

III.
Lack of Mothering

Failed Mothers and the Black Girl-Child Victim of Incestuous Rape in *The Bluest Eye* and *Push*

CANDICE PIPES

IN 1970, SHORTLY BEFORE Toni Morrison's *The Bluest Eye* appeared and within weeks of Toni Cade Bambara's *The Black Woman: An Anthology*, Maya Angelou published her memoir, *I Know Why the Caged Bird Sings*. In it, Angelou reveals her sexual abuse as a young girl. Raped by her mother's live-in boyfriend at the age of eight, Angelou describes in horrific detail the escalation of the abuse from her abuser, Mr. Freeman. The unwanted attention began with seemingly benign rubbing and progressed to rape: "Then there was the pain. A breaking and entering when even the senses are torn apart. The act of rape on an eight-year-old body is a matter of the needle giving because the camel can't. The child gives, because the body can, and the mind of the violator cannot" (Angelou 65). Angelou's choice to voice her experience of girl-child rape stands as a historical confession of the abuses many young black girls suffer in what is supposed to be the safety of their private, domestic space. Distressing as a true account of child sexual abuse, Angelou's experience validates what novels such as Ralph Ellison's *Invisible Man*, Toni Morrison's *The Bluest Eye*, Alice Walker's *The Color Purple*, and Sapphire's *Push* fictitiously represent. These fictional imaginings of child incestuous rape work to accomplish what Angelou began with her testimony: to resist the myth of the seductive daughter, to expose the brutality of child sexual abuse and the horrific reality of the black girl-child's body in pain, and to offer strategies (whether successful or not) for resistance and survivorship. As part of the project of reclaiming the black girl-child's body from its abuse, an examination of the role of mothering becomes critical. Reading *Push* as, ostensibly, a rewriting of *The Bluest Eye*, I examine the sociologically determined and gendered roles of incest in the novels: the abused black girl-child and her violated body, the Rule of the Father, and the role of the bad mother. Ultimately, I argue that these novels suggest that a reordering of the black community is necessary to save black girl-children from incest. Specifically, this reordering requires exposing the myth of a false patriarchy, a dangerous dynamic that threatens the existence of mothers, even as these novels advocate for the necessity of mothering if black girls are to survive.

One cannot overstate the role that patriarchy plays in the perpetuation of incestuous rape,[1] specifically those instances in which the father is the offender and the daughter the victim. In *Father-Daughter Incest*, Judith Herman argues that "without an understanding of male supremacy and female oppression, it is impossible to explain why the vast majority of incest perpetrators (uncles, older brothers, stepfathers, and fathers) are male, and why the majority of victims (nieces, younger sisters and daughters) are female" (3). Sociologists Elizabeth Ward and Sandra Butler[2] add to Herman's claim, each arguing that the patriarchal structure of our society and its Rule of/by the Father works to undermine the incest taboo,[3] using its silencing power to the Father's full advantage. In patriarchal culture, the daughter is understood to be the possession of the Father. By promoting the incest taboo in public spaces and undercutting it in private spaces, patriarchal cultures entrap their daughters in a culture that simultaneously silences and denies its most powerless victims. Incestuous child-rape, like adult rape, becomes a method by which "girl-children are controlled in a male supremacist society" (Ward 95).

Acknowledging that incestuous rape, like all rape, is about power—and more accurately, the acquisition of power by one who seemingly lacks power but who society claims is deserving of power—presents a specific challenge to our understanding of incestuous rape in the black community. As Calvin Hernton argues in *Sex and Racism*, "we are forced to realize that the centuries of slavery and racism, and the struggle to overcome them, have not informed the humanity of black men when it comes to black women," including their own daughters (7). My position is not that all black men are predisposed to incestuous rape, or even as Butler suggests that society predisposes men, in general, to incestuous rape.[4] I argue, rather, that these novels depict incestuous rape as a definite reality in the black community but also consequential of racist and sexist socioeconomic systems and institutions—the stress of which manifests in the weakest of men when they commit the crime of incestuous rape.

THE RULE OF THE FATHER

The patriarchal structure of the black family and the larger social dynamic it mirrors allows incestuous rape to occur in an environment that denies the act because of the Rule of the Father. The emasculated black father following the Rule of the Father determines the oppression of women and injects the fear of rape as a form of domination. As Butler articulates, "perhaps the most insidious aspect of incestuous assault is that in the same way men have been societally permitted to be sexual predators, their daughters have been trained into the role of victim by virtue of their femaleness" (82-83). The Rule of the Father includes father-daughter incest as one of many "manifestations of despotic rule," a rule established with violent means for power-creating ends (Herman 63). Morrison aggressively documents the Rule of the Father through Pecola's father-rapist, Cholly, and seeks to understand his tyranny, whereas Sapphire leaves her father-rapist at the margins of the text. Both texts name the ruler-father as abuser-rapist in an effort to recover the raped black girl-child body, but both authors find it difficult to fully escape patriarchal control by problematically attempting to understand the father at the expense of the child-daughter's raped body and abused self and at the expense of the child-daughter's mother.

Morrison states in her afterword to *The Bluest Eye* that she "did not want to dehumanize the characters who trashed Pecola and contributed to her collapse," and this includes Pecola's rapist-father, Cholly Breedlove (211). For this reason, Morrison goes to great lengths to give the reader a complete understanding of the kind of black man who would rape his own daughter. We know that at "four days old his mother wrapped him in two blankets and one newspaper and placed him on a junk heap by the railroad" (133). Discarded like the garbage through which his daughter rifles at the end of the novel, Cholly is rescued by his Great Aunt and lives incident-free until her death. At his Great Aunt's funeral reception, Cholly attempts to acquire his manhood, experiencing his first sexual intercourse with a girl, Darlene. Two white men with "long guns" abruptly interrupt this scene of romantic innocence and negate the possibility for Cholly to "shoot his long gun" into Darlene, "paralyzing" the two youths in fear (147, 148). The white men force a now limp Cholly to continue having sexual intercourse with Darlene, and Cholly performs his masculinity "with violence born of total helplessness" (148).

Emasculated and embarrassed, Cholly's reaction is not violence against the white men but against the black women he, just moments before, touched and "kissed" gently—a scene that foreshadows the dichotomous feeling Cholly later senses as he desires to "fuck" his daughter "tenderly." Cholly "hated [Darlene]. He almost wished he could do it—hard, long and painfully, he hated her so much" (148). Cholly's violent anger is acknowledged by the text to be misdirected. Cholly first scapegoats Darlene before doing the same to Pecola decades later: "Sullen, irritable, he cultivated his hatred of Darlene. Never did he once consider directing his hatred toward the hunters. Such an emotion would have destroyed him. They were big, white, and armed. He was small, black, and helpless" (150). Unable to protect Darlene and himself from the racialized violence of the white men, Cholly assumes the only position of power he owns and asserts his patriarchal privilege over Darlene, "the one who bore witness to his failure, his impotence" (151). Already, Cholly recognizes that the black girl-child can be sacrificed for his own survival.

Morrison describes Cholly as a murderer, a physical abuser of women, and a possessor of things not meant to be possessed. Significantly, she identifies Cholly's violent acquisition of self as freedom: "he had already killed three white men. Free to take a woman's insults for his body had already conquered hers. Free to even knock her in the head, for he had already cradled that head in his arms. Free to be gentle when she was sick or mop her floor, for she knew what and where his maleness was" (159). The text ironically suggests Cholly's understanding of freedom is the ide-al—"Cholly was truly free" (160)—even as the reader understands this ideal assumes a perverted value system. As such, Cholly's "freed" state blindly excuses the murders, physical violence and unwanted possession, and instead celebrates Cholly's triumph over his own figurative rape and societal dismissals by his violent assertion of self. Because Cholly is, as J. Brooks Bouson writes, "deeply traumatized and shamed at the disgraceful exposure of himself as weak and contemptible ... [he] invokes the inherited stereotype of the 'bad nigger'—the defiant, but also unrestrained and potentially dangerous, male" (35). But this "bad" is both "bad" as in not good, and "bad" as in the slang sense of "cool" or "bad-ass." In this way, Cholly's documented violent nature is problematically romanticized and idealized. In fact, Cholly's choice to marry and the resulting family are both offered as instances of Cholly's hamartia, which Morrison describes as "the constantness, varietylessness, the sheer weight of sameness," that drives "him to despair and froze his imagination" (160). Marriage and family enslave Cholly, causing him to use alcohol as an escape—"only in drink was there some break, some floodlight, and when that closed, there was oblivion (160). And so it is in one such alcohol-fueled moment Cholly that "stagger[s] home reeling drunk," and rapes his daughter (161).

Morrison's characterization of Cholly ultimately works, in many ways, to justify Cholly's crime of incestuous rape, and many crit-ics use the text's narrative construction as a means of accepting Cholly's act of rape. Mark Ledbetter reasons that Cholly's raping of Pecola is because of "failed communities," adding that "in a world where men define their power in terms of sexuality, to be powerless is to resort to sexual extremes," and so Cholly rapes "in order to regain some sense of control in his life" (31). Paula Eckard suggests that Cholly is mentally ill and connects his mind-state to his daughter's madness: "Cholly's sense of self, particularly his manhood, has been similarly warped through white influence." But Eckard does not properly name Cholly as the "influence" causing his daughter's schizophrenia (39).

For her part, Morrison tries to subvert these analyses by claim-ing the rape, "this most masculine act of aggression becomes feminized in my language, 'passive' and, I think more accurately repellent when deprived of the male 'glamour of shame' rape is (or once was) routinely given" ("Unspeakable Things" 388). I disagree. Instead of "fucking" Pecola, Morrison depicts Cholly as "tenderly fucking" Pecola in a rhetorical move that displaces the assumed violence of the act of "fucking" with an unexpected softness. Thus, "feminization" of the rape by definition makes it less repellent, softens the violent act of sexual violation, and discounts the "masculine" aggressiveness of the brutalization that Pecola's girl-child body experiences.

Explaining how "Pecola's rape therefore seems to be perpetuated by the encounter in the woods in which Cholly was forced by whites to perform what became, under scrutiny, a contrived sex act," Minrose Gwin rightly comments on the shifting of responsibility that occurs when Cholly's backstory is more closely examined (321). Gwin claims that it is precisely the knowledge of Cholly's personal victimization that allows Pecola to be seen "more as a perpetrator of incest rather than a rape victim" (321) by the black community. Pecola stands as yet another manifestation of Cholly's failure: "How dare she love him? Hadn't she any sense at all? What was he supposed to do about that? ...What could his heavy arms and befuddled brain accomplish that would earn him his own respect, that would in turn allow him to accept her love?" (Morrison 161-162). Pecola is, in effect, blamed for victimizing Cholly, and her punishment for her violation of him (both her existence as his daughter and her stifling oppression act as a reflection of his inadequacy) is rape.

Sapphire offers significantly less characterization of Carl Kenwood Jones, Precious's father-rapist, in *Push*. As Jones is largely absent from the novel as he is largely absent from Precious's life, the text reveals few details about the man who not only rapes his daughter but also infects her with HIV. The only explanation given for Carl's raping of his daughter is the aforementioned influence of white supremacy: "Crackers is the cause of everything bad. It why my father ack like he do" (Sapphire 34). This difference between the two narratives is noteworthy. Whereas Morrison's thorough explanation serves, in ways, as a justification, Sapphire resists developing Carl at all, thereby reducing his authority over the text. Sapphire's narrative construction pushes the father-rapist to the margins and centralizes the raped black girl-child body. In this sense, Morrison misjudges her project in *The Bluest Eye* when the narrator states, "since why is difficult to handle, one must take refuge in how" (6). The concentration on Cholly's backstory is precisely the "why," while Sapphire attempts to understand the "how."

In leaving Carl all but undefined, the father-rapist becomes everyman, or at least every black man. The tragedies suffered by Cholly help to explain his post-traumatic stress, which, in part, justifies his cruelty, and the reader is comforted, in the end, that only a black man having suffered such destructive abandonment, emasculation, and rejection is capable of raping his daughter with such brutality.[5] Sapphire also comforts the reader by representing Carl as a nonfather, almost excusing him from the role of father all together, thus removing the incestuous component from the rape. If the greatest sin associated with incestuous rape is the betrayal of trust and love nurtured in a traditional father-daughter relationship, then this element is absent from Precious's rapes. Precious—after remembering Alice Walker's twist in *The Color Purple* when Celie finds out her father-rapist is really only her stepfather—asks her mother, "you huzbn, Carl, my real daddy?" (86). Her mother responds, "he your daddy, couldn't no one else be your daddy. I was with him since I was sixteen. I never been with nobody else. We not married though, he got a wife though, purty light-skin woman he got two kids by" (86). Precious manifests her confusion between the person who is named her father and her idea of what a father should be by alternatively calling her father "daddy" and "Carl." Carl's figuration as a nonfather detaches the reader from the traumatic reality of incestuous rape, even as the reader accepts the disturbing nature of the biological relationship that Carl and Precious share.

What my analysis of the father-rapist in these two novels reveals is the difficulty these black women writers faced in attempting to represent black incestuous rape and the complexity of telling it. For this reason, the texts are full of contradictions regarding the black girl-child victim of incestuous rape. As both novelists attempt to recover the raped black girl-child body, this effort is, at times, undermined by the larger cultural environment—an environment still very much rooted in racial uplift and entrenched in the denial of the possibility of incestuous rape. The Rule of the Father inconspicuously governs the texts, making Morrison believe that Cholly's backstory is necessary, whereas Pecola's version of the rape is not. In contrast, the fear of the Rule of the Father pressures Sapphire into virtually eliminating the father-rapist from the text, a strategic choice that ultimately backfires. Both novelists retreat in different ways from the incestuous, and most egregious nature of the rape and, in doing so, leave the black girl-child body *un*covered but not *re*covered. The horror of incestuous rape and its father-rapists are revealed but are not convicted, either in the narrative or by the reader. Instead, in both novels, the mother accepts much of the blame for her daughter's victimization.

THE BAD MOTHER

Judith Herman submits that the mothers of incestuous rape victims are traditionally blamed in three significant ways for their daughters' abuse: "first, she failed to perform her marital duties; second, she, not the father, forced the daughter to take her rightful place; and third, she knew about, tolerated, or in some cases actively enjoyed the incest" (42). Many sociologists cite the mother's unnatural co-dependency on the father-rapist as essential to the mother's complicity in her child's rape. Herman reasons that loyalty to the husband plays a critical role in these "unusually oppressed" mothers' involvement in incestuous rape; she states, "if the price of maintaining the marriage includes the sexual sacrifice of her daughter, she will raise no effective objections. Her first loyalty is to her husband, regardless of his behavior. She sees no other choice. Maternal collusion in incest, when it occurs, is a measure of maternal powerlessness" (49). Ward argues that the mother's forced collusion is its own kind of rape: "In keeping silent about the Father, the Mother betrays herself: herself as female, reflected in her Daughter. To that extent, the Mother too, is being raped" (164). What works at the core of the tendency to blame the mother is the inability for outsiders who are not "unusually oppressed" to comprehend the magnitude of dependency and powerlessness that would allow a mother to either collude in her daughter's rape or abandon her daughter in pain.[6]

What must be understood is that the issue here is not that mothers collude and abandon their raped girl-children but that the mothers are blamed for the incestuous rape of their daughters because of these roles in their abuse. "Blamed principally for *causing* it," these mothers are more often figured as rapists than victims of rape (Ward 163). Both *The Bluest Eye* and *Push* blame the mother in each of the three ways that Herman offers, and *Push*'s addition of mother-daughter incestuous rape further demonizes the mother.

In *The Bluest Eye*, Pauline Breedlove describes making love to Cholly in the early years of their marriage: "I know he wants me to come first. But I can't. Not until he does. Not until I know that my flesh is all that be on his mind. That he couldn't stop if he had to. That he would die rather than take his thing out of me. Of me. Not until he has let go of all he has, and give it to me. To me. To me. When he does, I feel a power. I be strong, I be pretty, I be young" (130). Not only is the sex mutually fulfilling, it is also empowering and self-validating. But Pauline quickly informs us that these episodes of lovemaking are short lived and are replaced by passionless, violent sex: "but it ain't like that anymore. Most times he's thrashing away inside me before I'm woke, and through when I am. The rest of the time I can't even be next to his stinking drunk self" (131). This detailing of the progressive sexlessness of the Breedlove marriage works to provide cause for Cholly's need to satisfy a sexual longing using his own daughter. Pauline's recalling of a time when sex was welcomed connects to Cholly's remembering of her in her youth as he begins to "nibble" the calf of his daughter. Cholly, yearning for the sexual relationship of his early marriage, transposes his child-wife onto his child-daughter and attempts to reenact the lovemaking of a previous time.

The scene of incestuous rape cast in this light blames Pauline for failing to fulfill her marital duties—she lacks sexual desire for her husband. Her desire for romantic love only overcome by her desire for physical beauty, Pauline's naïve and simple understanding of love is disrupted as love and beauty become obsessions: "both originated in envy, thrived in insecurity, and ended in disillusion. In equating physical beauty with virtue she stripped her mind, bound it, and collected self-contempt by the heap" (122). After losing more than one tooth and resigning herself to ugliness, Pauline gives up, assuming that she is unworthy of her ideal of romantic love: "she stopped trying to keep her house. The things she could afford to buy did not last, had no beauty or style, and were absorbed by the dingy storefront. More and more she neglected her house, her children, her man—they were like afterthoughts one has just before sleep" (127). Considering Cholly as an "afterthought," pushed to the margins of his wife's existence, left "outdoors," emasculated and embarrassed, Cholly's rape of Pecola is figured as the desperate act of a lonely man, well intentioned and pitiable. Pauline as the "bad mother" and her failure to serve as the "good wife" are upheld as the catalyst for Cholly's stumbling into his daughter's virgin vagina.

Sapphire, signifying on *The Bluest Eye*, similarly connects the notion of blackness to ugliness and an inability to satisfy masculine sexual desire. In *Push*, the morbid obesity of Precious's mother, Mary, is offered as the reason why she, as "wife," can no longer satisfy Carl sexually. Precious repeatedly mentions her mother's "big woman smell," and makes clear that she "don't smell like [her] muver" (36). The textual inference is that although Mary's "husband"/Precious's father enjoys big women (as his nickname for Precious, "Butter Ball Big Mama Two Ton of Fun," describes), Mary has let herself go beyond sexual desirability (37). Whereas Pauline no longer wants her husband sexually, Mary still desires Carl, and Precious hints that part of the reason for her continued sexual abuse is an agreement between her mother and father: "she bring him to me. I ain't crazy, that stinky hoe give me to him. Probably thas' what he require to fuck her, some of me" (24). Mary, as Precious's pimp, incites the incestuous rape of her daughter in order to maintain a sexual relationship with Carl herself.

In *Push*, the impetus for Precious's mother's sexual violence against her daughter stems from what Beverly Ogilvie[7] ascertains is the "hostility and self-hatred" at the root of mother-daughter incestuous rape. Ogilvie identifies mother-daughter incestuous rape as a form of slavery; the children "feel imprisoned because the captor has total control over their existence and unlimited access to their bodies" (49). Precious's victimization by her father is exponentially compounded by her mother's sexual abuse, which, like Carl's, is a demonstration of a need for power and control. As Ogilvie explains, "perpetrators of mother-daughter incest controlled their victims methodically and repetitively by inflicting psychological trauma. Through words, they disempowered and disconnected their victims. They instilled terror and helplessness and destroyed the victims' sense of self in relation to others" (90). Precious is never allowed to construct a self that is absent from sexual abuse. Mary's incestuous rape of Precious imparts on Precious the responsibility to fulfill the "marital duties" for both parents. For Carl, who is no longer sexually attracted to his obese partner, Precious serves as a substitute, and for Mary, rejected and displaced, Precious becomes the source of her sexual fulfillment. In all of this self-serving behaviour, Precious's humanity is lost.

Symbolic of Pecola's and Precious's lost humanity as victims of incestuous rape, the mothers in these texts fail to recognize their daughters as daughters; rather, they see them as wife substitutes who carry out the terms of Herman's second indictment of the blamed mother: forcing or permitting "the daughter to take her rightful place" (42). By all accounts, both girl-children effectively take on the role of their mothers as wives. As Pauline "neglects" her role as wife, Pecola is placed in the position of her mother in order to maintain the home. Pecola is washing dishes when Cholly sees her in the kitchen and is reminded of his wife. Likewise, Precious makes clear that "Mama never do anything" (22). Mary tells Precious "that what you here for" (22)—to cook, clean, and financially support the household with welfare cheques garnered as the result of her incestuously begotten children. Both fathers, conditioned to view a woman's existence only in relation to themselves and their needs, accept their daughters' new role as wives. The false patriarchy is further solidified as the girl-children are removed by their mothers as daughters in order to act as wives. In both cases, the mothers fail to nurture their children and perform as wives, which place Pecola and Precious in a heightened state of vulnerability. They become scapegoats in their own homes; they act as scapegoats for a larger community. Claudia identifies this reality in *The Bluest Eye*: "all of our waste which we dumped on her and which she absorbed. And all of our beauty, which was hers first and which she gave to us. All of us—all who knew her—felt so wholesome after we cleaned ourselves on her. We were so beautiful when we stood astride her ugliness" (205). These raped girl-children become the sacrificial lambs allowing these mothers (and communities) to attain their own sense of power and control.

Lastly, *The Bluest Eye* and *Push* both blame the mother for the incestuous rape of her child because of her knowledge and toleration of the abuse. Both mothers not only disbelieve their daughters' abuse, but they also punish their daughters for voicing their rape. Pecola, when speaking to her alternative self, says "she didn't even believe me when I told her" about the first time (200). Pauline's response is instead a violent betrayal of Pecola's trust: "they say the way her mama beat her she lucky to be alive herself" (189). Pauline's denial of Pecola's incestuous rape, beyond even the trauma of the rape itself, is what silences Pecola, a silencing that inevitably leads to Pecola's self-destruction. Her alternative self asks, "so that's why you didn't tell her about the second time?" to which Pecola responds, "she wouldn't have believed me then either" (200). The implication remains: had her mother believed her the first time, her body would have been saved from the second violation. Pauline is further condemned in that she is the one who witnesses Pecola's raped child-body and fails to comfort her. In fact, she harms her further. Pauline finds her daughter, still unconscious, "lying on the kitchen floor, under a heavy quilt, trying to connect the pain between her legs with the face of her mother looming over her" (163). In this sequence, Pecola equates her body in pain to her mother's face, and identifies her mother as pain—an initial assessment validated through Pauline's subsequent physical violence enacted upon a body already in pain. Pauline not only fails to stop the sexual abuse of her daughter but she participates as an inflictor of additional pain.

Precious's mother does not disbelieve the incestuous sexual relationship between Carl and Precious, but she does not consider the sex rape. She screams, "Thank you Miz Claireece Precious Jones for fucking mu husband you nasty slut" (19). Figuring Precious as the seductress and blaming her for her victimization, Mary absolves Carl of all responsibility for raping his daughter. Mary testifies to knowing about Precious's abuse from its inception, but what spurs her violent outburst—"I should KILL you!" (19)—is Precious's birthing of Carl's children (19). In the beginning of the novel, Precious is seen giving birth on the kitchen floor, screaming out for "Mommy," needing a nurturing, caregiving presence to guide her body through the pain of child birth. Mary violently rejects Precious's pleading: as Precious reports, "she KICK me side of my face! 'Whore! Whore!' she screamin" (9). Precious continues to yell, "Mommy," as the beating continues. The circumstances surrounding the birth of Precious's second child are no different. Returning from the hospital with Abdul, Precious is forced to leave her house and sleep in a homeless shelter after her mother viciously attacks her: "I got new baby boy in my arms 'n she callin me bitch hoe slut say she gonna kill me 'cause I ruin her life" (79).

Sapphire's depiction of Mary, a Mommy Dearest–kind of horror villain, as an antimother presents her as more of a monster than Carl. By demonizing Mary and further corroborating her evilness as a rapist, Carl is removed from the text as the villain just as he is removed from the text with his death from AIDS. Mary is left to shoulder the full culpability of Precious's abuse. These novels relieve the father-rapists of their responsibility for violating the girl-child bodies of their daughters; while the daughters are silenced, both Cholly and Carl disappear from the texts without consequence, and the mothers are left to blame.

Both novels suggest that even as Pecola's and Precious's mothers fail them, the presence of a maternal figure is critical to their survival. In the absence of adult empathy, Pecola's girlfriends Claudia and Frieda try, as children, to act as mother surrogates. Claudia remembers, "I believe our sorrow was the more intense because nobody else seemed to share it" (190). Unable to adequately mother Pecola, the girls take on the role symbolically and plant marigold seeds,[8] promising to "watch over them. And when they come up, we'll know everything is all right" (192). The flowers never bloom, and Pecola is not all right. The critique Morrison makes is that in a community where no one but two little girls "want the black baby to live," the black baby dies (190). Sapphire revises this and provides Miss Rain, Precious's teacher, as an example of an effective surrogate mother. Janet Montelaro in an essay about *The Color Purple* offers that the novel "foregrounds women whose maternal subjectivities emerge through a number of discourses, which often problematize conventional notions of motherhood," which both challenge the status quo and allow for an expanded understanding of motherhood (72). Similarly, Miss Rain opposes conventional notions of motherhood as an unconventional teacher and lesbian. Unlike Pauline and Mary, Miss Rain believes Precious and listens to her story. She offers unconditional love and an environment of mutual respect. Just as Celie responds to Shug's nurturance, Precious flourishes under the maternal care of Miss Rain, and she can imagine for the first time the clear idea of a future. bell hooks argues that "displacing motherhood as a central signifier for female being, and emphasizing sisterhood, Walker posits a relational basis for self-definition that valorizes and affirms woman bonding" (294). *The Bluest Eye* and *Push* also work within Walker's womanist framework, suggesting that healing is possible through maternal surrogates if mature and capable. Morrison, by critiquing the lack of a communal maternal presence, calls for what Sapphire presents in Miss Rain as an example of the power of maternal nurturance on the acquisition of the abused black girl-child's self.

Unfortunately, we must recognize the limit of Sapphire's pseudo happy ending. For the same reasons bell hooks critiques *The Color Purple* for the "fantasy of change without effort," *The Bluest Eye* and *Push* promote endings "wherein an oppressed black woman can experience self-recovery without a dialectical process; without collective political effort; without radical change in society" (hooks 295). Herman further validates this critique and points out that effort must accompany change, reasoning that "if incestuous abuse is indeed an inevitable result of patriarchal family structure, then preventing sexual abuse will ultimately require a radical transformation of the family" (202). I would add that such radical transformation is also necessary within the larger community. Perhaps reordering the black community is too large a task for one novel to accomplish, but what the novels do suggest is that the raped black girl-child body cannot be fully recovered unless men stop performing masculinity and power on the bodies of their girl-children and at the expense of these girl-children's mothers. Finally, the raped black girl-child body cannot be fully recovered unless capable mothers intervene with impossible strength and indescribable courage to love and save their daughters. This a high order indeed. As *The Bluest Eye* teaches us, "love is never any better than the lover" (204).

ENDNOTES

[1]Definitions of incest include a wide range of sexually indiscriminate behaviour from adult consensual "sexual relations" to what we commonly consider incest—the abuse of a child by a family member. Because of the word's rather innocuous definition, it is necessary for me to be explicit in my conception of the term "incest." For this reason, I will use the terminology "incestuous rape" when referring to the sexual abuse portrayed in the novels. This two-part phrasing is important to my project in that it properly addresses the improper familial sexual acts divulged within the texts while also properly naming the sexual violence as rape. Adding the word "rape" to "incestuous" serves to constantly remind myself and the reading audience of what Tony Martens explains as core to the character of incest: "acts of incest and child sexual abuse themselves define violence. These are acts of aggression, domination, coercion, manipulation and self-seeking with no regard for the damage done to the victim" (6). Elizabeth Ward makes a similar choice by using the term "father-daughter rape" instead of incest in her work.

[2]Elizabeth Ward asserts that "the rape of girl-children by a Father is an integral product of our society, based on its male supremacist attitudes and organization, reinforced by the fundamental social structure of the family" (77). Sandra Butler adds the following: "although incestuous assault happens within a family context, the family has incorporated the values and standards of our traditional patriarchy. Therefore, as important as it is to understand the personal psychodynamics of the male sexual aggressor, it is equally as important to understand male sexual aggression as an outgrowth of the patriarchal nature of male/female relationships in every aspect of our lives" (6).

[3]Although "incest" is defined differently depending on the civilization, there seems to be a nearly universal taboo against incest, which often aids in silencing the victims of incest by creating a

culture that both disbelieves its victims and shames them, making it a perpetually and grossly underreported crime. Anthropologists such as Claude Levi-Strauss and Arthur P. Wolf suggest that incest was used to promote exogamy, or the mating of two nonrelated beings.

[4]Sandra Butler argues, "it is not these men who are monstrous; rather, it is society that has defined them and taught them to define themselves as a consequence of their gender. When all else in their lives fails, they have been led to believe that the exercise of power of their genitals will assure them of their ultimate competence and power" (65).

[5]Morrison's characterization of Cholly is also problematic. The reader is comforted by Cholly as victim, Cholly as poor, Cholly as overtly oppressed and emasculated, and so we can limit her definition of a father-rapist to this kind of black man. The problem is that perpetrators of incestuous rape do not necessarily fit this profile and come from every kind of racial, economic, and social background. Without this, the black male pathology is offered as the reason for black men raping their daughters, and Carl exists as representative of this distorted sense of black masculinity, as symbolic of the stereotype, as the dangerous, predatory black male. What Sapphire does not do is offer another alternative. The black man exists only as father-rapist. Morrison, on the other hand, does offer an alternative. Claudia describes her father's strength and tough love, figuring him as a kind of superhero fighting snow and cold: "winter moves into [his face] and presides there ... wolf killer turned hawk fighter, he worked night and day to keep one from the door and the other from under the windowsills" (61). Morrison submits Claudia's father as an example that the hard existence of the black man does not have to translate into violent abuse of the woman connected to him, whether it be physical or sexual.

[6]Ward further explains that "the internalization of passivity by women differs in degree along a spectrum: it is a direct result of a male supremacist cultural system that indoctrinates women to exist only as the playthings or nurturers of men. Female sex-role conditioning, fostered within the rape ideology which inculcates fear of men as a way of living has inevitably led women to respond 'inadequately' in the face of father-daughter rape" (171).

[7]Beverly Ogilvie's 2004 work, *Mother-Daughter Incest: A Guide for Helping Professionals*, is the first major sociological study on the subject. In Ogilvie's assessment, "mother-daughter incest is not rare; it is underestimated and underreported because its occurrence involves the breaking of two taboos, incest and homosexuality" (4). [8]Claudia and Frieda's failure to grow flowers is even more disconcerting when we understand that marigolds "bloom better and more profusely in poor soil" (The Old Farmer's Almanac). The soil (the family, the community, our society) is so ruined and corrupted that even the most resilient of plants refuse to bloom.

WORKS CITED

Angelou, Maya. *I Know Why the Caged Bird Sings*. Bantam Books, 1970.

Bouson, J. Brooks. *Quiet as It's Kept: Shame, Trauma, and Race in the Novels of Toni Morrison*. State University of New York Press, 1999.

Butler, Sandra. *Conspiracy of Silence: The Trauma of Incest*. New Glide Publications, 1978.

Eckard, Paula Gallant. *Maternal Body and Voice in Toni Morrison, Bobbie Ann Mason, and Lee Smith*. University of Missouri Press, 2002.

Gwin, Minrose C. "'Hereisthehouse:' Cultural Spaces of Incest in *The Bluest Eye*." *Incest and the Literary Imagination*, edited by Elizabeth Barnes, University Press of Florida, 2002, pp.316-328.

Herman, Judith. *Father-Daughter Incest*. 1981. Harvard University Press, 2000.

Hernton, Calvin. *Sex and Racism in America*. Doubleday, 1965.

hooks, bell. "Reading and Resistance: *The Color Purple*." *Alice Walker Critical Perspectives Past and Present*, edited by Henry Louis Gates, Jr. and K.A. Appiah, Amistad, 1993, pp. 284-295.

Ledbetter, Mark. *Victims and Postmodern Narrative, or Doing Violence to the Body: An Ethic of Reading and Writing*. St. Martin's Press, 1996.

"Marigolds." *The Old Farmer's Almanac*, 2017, http://www.almanac.com/topics/gardening/plants/flowers/annuals/marigolds. Accessed 15 May 2017.

Martens, Tony. *The Spirit Weeps: Characteristics and Dynamics of Incest and Child Sexual Abuse*. Nichi Institute, 1988.

Montelaro, Janet. *Producing a Womanist Text: The Maternal as Signifier in Alice Walker's* The Color Purple. University of Victoria Press, 1996.

Morrison, Toni. *The Bluest Eye*. 1970. NY: Knopf, 2000.

Morrison, Toni. "Unspeakable Things Unspoken: The Afro-American Presence in American Literature." *Within the Circle: An Anthology of African American Literary Criticism from the Harlem Renaissance to Present*, edited by Angelyn Mitchell, Duke University Press, 1994, pp. 368-398.

Ogilvie, Beverly A. *Mother-Daughter Incest: A Guide for Helping Professionals*. The Haworth Maltreatment and Trauma Press, 2004.

Sapphire. *Push*. Vintage Books, 1996.

Ward, Elizabeth. *Father-Daughter Rape*. The Woman's Press, 1984.

Mothering Oneself in *Sula*

MARTHA SATZ

*S*ULA CALLS AND EVEN MANDATES its readers to do the radical epistemological work of inversion, to question conventional schemata and to reinterpret them—most notably the concept that the most significant emotional relationship of intimacy is that between spouses, between husband and wife. Indeed, in the last lines of the novel, one of the two major characters, Nel, reveals that her most intimate bedrock, loving relationship has been that with her friend, Sula, rather than that with her husband, Jude. And this insight liberates her to vent her feelings for the first time in both her authentic, idiosyncratic language and in her languageless voice, which enables her to mourn the essential gap in her life:

> "We was girls together," she said as though explaining something. "O Lord, Sula," she cried, "girl, girl, girlgirlgirl."
> It was a fine cry—loud and long—but it had not bottom and it had not top, just circles and circles of sorrow. (174)

Margaret Homans tellingly notes about this utterance, "What finally expresses her woman-identified self is of necessity non-representational" (192).

Thus, in a novel that struggles to portray female experience authentically and, when necessary, linguistically inventively, it is not surprising that although centrally about the friendship of two female characters, Nel and Sula, it is also about motherhood as well—the mothering relationship that occurs sometimes or even often between female friends and the intergenerational effect of

201

positive or negative mothering on the psychological makeup of female beings.

Jay McInerney remarks in his *New York Times* review of *Curious Incident of a Dog in the Nighttime:* "a literary novel requires new reading skills and teaches them within its pages" (1). Accordingly, *Sula* instructs its readers in how to understand the novel from its first pages, calling attention to its narrative work of reversal. As Deborah E. McDowell comments, "Whatever coherence and meaning resides in the narrative, the reader must struggle to create" (69). It begins with a discourse about the name of the setting of the novel, the Bottom: "that part of town where the Negroes lived, the part they called the Bottom in spite of the fact that it was up in the hills" (4). The name arises from a joke, in which a master deceives a slave, and when the slave upon discovering the reality protests, "But it's high up in the hills," the master responds, "High up from us ... but when God looks down it's the bottom. That's why we call it so. It's the bottom of heaven—best land there is" (5). Thus, the beginning of the novel focuses on a reversal: the bottom is in reality the top. And, indeed, the novel emphasizes the aptness of this inversion: "And the farmers who went there sometimes wondered in private if maybe the white farmer was right after all. Maybe it was the bottom of heaven" (6).

To further emphasize inversion as a major strategy of the work, in a work about the friendship between two female characters, the first character the novel introduces proves to be a male character marginal to the plot—Shadrack, an erratic being who suffers from what we would now call post-traumatic stress syndrome. The novel invokes a gruesome image as the genesis of Shadrack's problem: "[he] saw the face of a soldier near him fly off.... But stubbornly, taking no direction from the brain, the body of the headless soldier ran on, with energy and grace, ignoring altogether the drip and slide of brain tissue down its back" (8). The headless body, motion without reason, a dissolution of governing forces, this image presents itself early, which suggests to the reader that the world must be reassembled on new terms. And it is Shadrack who invents his own holiday, which becomes part of the community calendar, "National Suicide Day," an occasion invented to control anxiety and to give permission to all those who want to kill themselves to do so on that very day. Again, near the beginning of the novel, a paradox presents itself: one has the freedom to kill oneself on a designated day in order to stave off the fear of death.

There are larger inversions present as well. The novel transposes the conventions of the canon of Western literature. In *Sula*, men and males are taken to be insignificant accessories to females' lives; they are valuable as a diversion, and on occasion a pleasure, but are not to be taken seriously. Morrison alerts us to this fact by the names that she confers upon her male characters. An early significant character is called BoyBoy, a name with an inner repetition as if to say to the reader: if you do not comprehend the insignificance and immaturity of this character at first, the narration will emphasize it by this reiteration. Other male characters have such names as Chicken Little, and three little boys—indistinguishable from one another to everyone although they are physically very different—are referred to as the Deweys, recalling the numbers of a library catalogue. The only male character that has an auspicious name is Ajax; however, that heroic appellation proves to be a misunderstanding. His real name is the mundane A. Jacks, reminiscent of a girl's plaything. In this novel, men are accorded an inconsequential place, which reminds the reader often that they may be the source of transient pleasure but are not to be taken seriously. Thus, the work reverses ancient, traditional cultural and literary male-female roles.

The story's main characters, Nel and Sula, are introduced in terms of their matrilineal heritage, implying they cannot be understood without this important psychological and biological history. Indeed, they come from complementary inadequate households and histories of mothering, and it may be conjectured that they are attracted to each other in order to seek what is lacking in their own mothering and nurturing. The narrator calls attention to their lack of nurturing by describing them as "daughters of distant mothers" (52).

Helene Wright, Nel's mother, is rigid and fastidious. She is described as "A woman who won all social battles with presence and a conviction of the legitimacy of her authority" (18). Both her last name, a homonym of "right," and her everyday behaviour suggest that her guiding principle is adherence to conventional rules, without questioning their origin or meaning. Helene, raised by her grandmother, has achieved some physical if not psychological distance from her mother. However, her approach to life seems to be a reaction formation to her own mother, whom the book suggests is if not a prostitute at least a "much-handled woman" (27). Sparked by Helene's grandmother's illness, Helene and her daughter, Nel, undertake a train trip from Ohio to New Orleans, a trip that shatters the inflexible construct Helene has manufactured for herself and her daughter and reveals to Nel that Helene's edifice of "right" is a flimsy structure indeed.

Almost as soon as they leave the station, an abusive, racist train conductor confronts prim and proper Helene when she inadvertently boards the wrong car, not the "Coloured Only" car that is their designated destination: "What was you doin' back there? What was you doin' in that coach yonder? … We don't 'low no mistakes on this train. Now git your butt on in there" (21). But puzzling to her daughter, when the train conductor thus verbally invades Helene's bodily dignity, her mother has a bewildering response: "for no earthly reason, at least no reason that anybody could understand, certainly no reason that Nel understood then or later, she smiled … Smiled dazzling and coquettishly at the salmon-colored face of the conductor" (21). A group of black soldiers on the train observing this interchange stare at her mother with hatred. Noting all that transpires, Nel's view of her mother alters. In her daughter's eyes, Helene has been transformed into "custard." Looking at her mother's dress, she undergoes a revelation: "She stared at the hem, wanting to believe in its weight but knowing that custard was all that it hid. If this tall, proud woman, this woman who was very particular about her friends, who slipped into church with unequaled elegance, who could quell a roustabout with a look, if *she* were really custard, then there was a chance that Nel was too" (22). After witnessing all that has happened, on the way home from the trip, Nel inwardly declares her independence from her mother and her mother's worldview: "'I'm me,' she whispered. 'Me.' … 'I'm me. I'm not their daughter. I'm not Nel. I'm me. Me'" (28).

Her realization and her assertion of her independence from her mother and her mother's compliance with a conventional, patriarchal, racist structure prepare her to meet and bond with a clear alternative to her mother and her mother's view of herself—Sula, someone who has been prepared to be ferociously autonomous. Clearly, Nel's mother smiles at the conductor to placate authority, to ward away problems, and to please someone in power. Her mother cedes her strength to conventional authority and, thereby, exposes herself to her daughter as an inauthentic poseur. The mask of dignity that she has assumed in her own community cannot be maintained in the larger world, and, hence, it is a false representation. Nel desires to reject the role model that her mother offers her; she wants to be authentic, unique, and what Carl Rogers calls "congruent," the state when one's ideal self accords with one's actual behaviour. So she melds with Sula, who, like Nel, is introduced in terms of her matrilineal heritage, one that is complementary to Nel's.

Whereas Nel's background is in many ways mundane, Sula's heritage is a mixture of the real and the fantastical mythic. Whereas Nel lives in the house of Wright (Right), Sula lives in the contrasting house of Peace. Whereas Nel's house is governed by rules and conventions, Sula's house is ruled by human, familial, and female relationships. Sula's house is essentially female, as it is presided over by her grandmother, Eva Peace, whose name recalls both the original woman and a lost maternal world of Peace. The narrative terms Eva "the creator and sovereign" of the house. And such words "creator and sovereign" recall descriptions of the deity. Certainly, Eva merits that portrayal. Not only does she have the power of naming, as evidenced in her mystifying labelling of the Deweys, she also controversially takes upon herself the power of life and death over her subjects. As noted, her description is evocative not only of the deity but of the quintessential cultural stereotype of the self-sacrificial mother. For in some mysterious way that the text never makes clear, she trades her leg to gain the money to support her children. Morrison creates Eva as a puzzling mixture of a realistic and mythical figure, either utopian or dystopian, depending on the reader's point of view, and that mixture and the acts that follow from it have generated a great deal of disagreement.

In any case, the contrast between Helene Wright and Eva Peace could not be starker. Helene's strength is a dubious construct, ready to fall when pushed by racist and patriarchal structures;

Eva's strength linguistically declares itself to be metaphysical, and she embraces her female power over all within her domain, particularly her children, with assurance and utter self-confidence. Both girls, Nel and Sula, assume their way of life based on their maternal progenitors. Nel adopts a conventional way of life; Sula, an egocentric and experimental one. However, the narration furnishes a plethora of images to assure the reader that the girls are part of each other and are necessary for each other's existence, each part of a female existence. In an interview with Bill Moyers, Toni Morrison says that Nel and Sula "put together two strands of Black womanhood" ("A Writer's Work").

As noted above, Eva has the power of life. There are notable scenes in which Eva saves or attempts to save one of her children's lives. The novel presents a graphic scene that takes place in an outhouse after Plum, at that time her baby son, becomes severely constipated. She wraps him in blankets and takes him to the outhouse:

> Deep in its darkness and freezing stench she squatted down, turned the baby over on her knees, exposed his buttocks and shoved the last bit of food she had in the world (besides three beets) up his ass. Softening the insertion with the dab of lard, she probed with her middle finger to loosen his bowels. Her fingernail snagged what felt like a pebble; she pulled it out and others followed. Plum stopped crying as the black hard stools ricocheted onto the frozen ground. And now that it was over, Eva squatted there wondering why she had come all the way out there to free his stools, and what was she doing down on her haunches with her beloved baby boy warmed by her body in the almost total darkness, her shins and teeth freezing, her nostrils assailed. (34)

One wonders why Morrison provides us with such an extended, disagreeable, and graphic description of a mother saving her baby in an outhouse. Perhaps here she provides us with another element of mythic motherhood, not sublime, but realistic. Without shying away from anything, she presents the notion that a mother will literally go through shit to save her child.

This scene, like many others in the novel, is one of a linked pair. Thus, it is fitting that as Eva saves her child Plum from death, eventually she kills him by, as enigmatic as it is to describe, lovingly burning him to death. As she is able to devotedly save her child from death, so she adoringly puts him to death—both with maternal assurance and authority. When Plum becomes addicted to drugs, Eva comes in the middle of night, rocking her now adult son, crying and reminiscing and eventually setting him on fire. And the reader is treated to the scene from Plum's point of view:

> Now there seemed to be some kind of wet light traveling over his legs and stomach with a deeply attractive smell. It wound itself—this wet light—all about him, splashing and running into his skin. He opened his eyes and saw what he imagined was the great wing of an eagle pouring a wet lightness over him. Some kind of baptism, some kind of blessing, he thought. Everything is going to be all right, it said. Knowing that it was so he closed his eyes and sank back into the bright hole of sleep. (47)

How is the reader to regard this scene? Can Eva's burning of her son be accepted as warranted? Does this moment in the text provide an ultimate test for the strategy of inversion? Does it demonstrate that what is so ostensibly wrong may in fact be right? Clearly, burning someone to death is not an act that can be justified by any principle. But perhaps it can be seen as an act of maternal caring. Here we may say that Eva's act can be justified by a care ethic, one that feminist philosophers have in the last decades brought to the foreground. A bit of poetry may introduce this view. An interesting moment, perhaps unnoticed by most listeners, occurred in the poem recited at Barack Obama's inauguration, when Elizabeth Alexander reciting, "Praise Song for the Day," entered an ethical debate:

> Some live by *love thy neighbor as thyself,*others by *first do no harm* or *take no more than you need.* What if the mightiest word is love?
> Love beyond marital, filial, national, love that casts a

widening pool of light,
love with no need to pre-empt grievance.

With these stanzas of her poem, Alexander casts her lot with
a care-based system of ethics. From this viewpoint, ethical acts
should be based on those feelings that one has in primary care-
based relationships, such as mothering and friendship, and they
extend outward when the person making decisions chooses to act
in a way that recoups the feelings and attitudes of those care-based
relationships (Noddings). At the base of this view is a concept
called "attentive love." For example, Sara Ruddick maintains in
"Maternal Thinking" that maternal practice and thought culminate
in the virtue of "attentive love," which contains both a cognitive
capacity and the virtue of love, in the case of maternal love—seeing
the world from the perspective of the child, without the mediation
and intervention of maternal desires. Ruddick, incorporating and
interpolating the thought of Iris Murdoch, writes, "The difficulty
is to keep the attention fixed on the real situation or as I would say
on the real children. Attention to real children, children seen by
the patient eye of love ... teaches us how real things [real children]
can be looked at and loved without being seized and used, without
being appropriated in the greedy organism of the self" (122-123).

Thus, in accordance with care ethics, we would interpret Eva's
killing of Plum as an act that sees and feels Plum, and concludes
that what is best for Plum is to be ushered lovingly out of this
world. Much later, Eva explains to her daughter Hannah why she
ended Plum's life:

> he wanted to crawl back in my womb and well I ain't got
> the room no more even if he could do it.... Being helpless
> and thinking baby thoughts and dreaming baby dreams
> and messing up his pants again and smiling all the time. I
> had room enough in my heart, but not in my womb, not
> no more.... I had to keep him out so I just thought of a
> way he could die like a man not all scrunched up inside
> my womb, but like a man. (71-72)

Eva explains her killing of Plum, as illogical as it seems, in terms of

Plum's benefit and his autonomy. It is her maternal care, her seeing things from his position and wanting to preserve his dignity, as she sees it, that leads her to kill him. Axel Nissen comments, "Through the manipulation of speed, voice, perspective, and order, Morrison has given a lead-up to Eva's killing of her son that will not make it easy to dismiss her and that will guarantee, if not the reader's sympathy, at least his or her attempt at understanding" (270). It is in the reader's view, and perhaps in Eva's own, an unprincipled decision, but it is, as she believes, a caring one. Certainly, it is a presumptuous one. Terry Otten confirms the view that Eva's decision is one of caring, " Eva, who could commit the 'crime' of burning to death her only son in a profound act of love ... experiences good and evil in human rather than moralistic terms" (43).

Eva discusses maternal love stripped of conventionality within the text. Hannah asks her mother about her maternal feelings during Hannah's childhood:

> "Mama, did you ever loves us? ... I mean, did you? You know. When we was little"
> "No, I don't reckon I did. Not the way you thinkin"
> "Did you ever, you know play with us?"
> "You want me to tinkle you under the jaw and forget 'bout them sores in your mouth? Pearl was shittin' worms and I was supposed to play rang-around-the rosie?.... what you talkin' 'bout did I love you girl I stayed alive for you can't you get that through your thick head or what is that between your ears, heifer?" (67-69)

Clearly, the two are talking at cross purposes. Hannah seeks a narrative of conventional, storybook maternal love. Eva attempts to convey the reality of her maternal experience to her daughter. In some ways, the conversation is a miniaturization of the conceptual thrust throughout the book: conventional concepts overthrown by actual lived experience. Just a short time after this conversation, Hannah catches on fire and Eva, her one-legged mother, throws herself from a third-floor window in what proves to be a vain effort to cover her daughter's body with her own. It is a story of maternal love written in flesh. But the story of the Peace family, much like that of the Wright family, is one of alternation and re-action formation. The powerful and mythic Eva Peace produces, as the earlier recorded conversation attests, a rather conventional daughter, detached from her own daughter, Sula. In fact, at some point Sula overhears her mother Hannah saying that she does not really like her daughter.

As a result of their maternal history, both girls find in each other what they would have wanted in a mother, Nel finding someone who is not custard, who is uncowed by anything, who meets all assaults and vicissitudes with courage. Correspondingly, Sula finds in Nel attachment and devotion. When they are still girls and at-tacked by a group of Irish boys, Sula takes out a knife:

> Holding the knife in her right hand, she pulled the slate toward her and pressed her left forefinger down hard on its edge. Her aim was determined but inaccurate. She slashed off only the tip of her finger. The four boys stared open-mouthed at the wound and the scrap of flesh, like a button mushroom, curling in the cherry blood that ran into the corners of the slate.... Her voice was quiet. "If I can do that to myself, what you suppose I'll do to you?" (54-55)

This is a scene that resonates with a multitude of female and mater-nal themes. Sula echoes her grandmother's maternal self-sacrifice, acting as mother toward Nel. She sacrifices part of her bodily self, her finger tip, for Nel, as her grandmother surrendered her leg for her children. And seemingly in an illustrative case of what Jean Baker Miller describes as "female psychology," she turns her anger from its apparent outer cause on herself. And most importantly, as indicated by such phrases as "button mushroom" and "cherry blood," she symbolically performs a sexual act upon herself to avoid any violation from males. In contrast to Helene, she does not yield to anything external. She is not custard and hence Nel, attached to her, cannot be custard either. In a complementary fashion, Sula also finds in Nel what she seeks in a maternal figure: someone who is devoted to her.

It is soon after this encounter with the boys that Nel and Sula symbolically merge in a grass play scene, in which each digs a hole in the grass with sticks unambiguously phallic in nature: "Nel found a thick twig and, with her thumbnail, pulled away its bark until it was stripped to a smooth, creamy innocence…. But soon she grew impatient and poked her twig rhythmically and intensely into the earth" (58). And on a symbolic level as the sticks are phallic, so are the holes representative of their female selves. As they dig, soon the two separate holes become one. And as Morrison comments in the interview mentioned earlier, "I happen to think they need each other" ("A Writer's Work). She notes that they represent conventionality, dependence, and passivity on the one hand, and imagination, independence, and selfishness on the other. It is soon after this merging that they inadvertently drop a small boy, Chicken Little, into the water, and he drowns. But as the boy's name indicates, his death is deemed insignificant by the narrative, by the world at large, and by the girls themselves.

Nel marries Jude and leads a conventional life. Sula goes off to college and unspecified other places to lead an experimental life, a selfish life. Upon her return, she responds to Eva's telling her that "You need to have some babies. It'll settle you" (92). She declares, "I don't want to make somebody else. I want to make myself" (92). Sula thereby affirms that she will mother herself. Yet, in fact, she will also mother Nel in the sense that she will bring important insight to her, and also she will leave herself open to being mothered by Nel when she lets herself be cared for by her when no one else will do so.

With Sula's return, she intrudes upon the conventional life Nel is living. Her disruptive quality is perhaps best illustrated by a conversation that Jude is having with Nel, a conversation the reader imagines is part of a perpetual dialogue. Jude complains to Nel about the terrible way black men are treated in the world: "He ended it with the observation that a Negro man had a hard row to hoe in this world. He expected his story to dovetail into milkwarm commiseration, but before Nel could excrete it, Sula said she didn't know about that" (103). Morrison suggests in the narrative phrasing "milkwarm" and "excrete" that the interaction between Jude and Nel echoes that between infant and child and has done so perpetually. Sula disturbs this pattern by launching on a refuting speech, which appeals to Jude's intellect rather than his childlike needs. As he reflects, "she stirred a man's mind maybe, but not his body" (104). Sula refuses to mother Jude and does not allow Nel to do so either.

Sula sleeps with Jude and that action severs the friendship between Nel and Sula for a long time. She is perceived as a villain in the community, and that very perception makes those within it more conventionally maternal. Sula becomes isolated, but Nel reconciles with her on Sula's deathbed. And Sula's last thoughts are those of Nel. Nel eventually comes to understand the importance of Sula in her life. Both are in some way midwifed to self-actualization and maturity by the other. Calling upon their own maternal history, they mother each other and mother themselves. The maternal traditions they invoke are deep, authentic, mythical, and cultural; they undo the conventional. The custard that Nel fears becoming instead gels into something so solid that it is the foundation of the world on which Eva sits atop.

WORKS CITED

"A Writer's Work with Toni Morrison." *A World of Ideas with Bill Moyers* Public Affairs Television, directed by Gail Pellett, 1990. Videocassette.

Alexander, Elizabeth. "Praise Song for the Day." *The New York Times,* 20 Jan. 2009, http://www.nytimes.com/2009/01/20/us/politics/20text-poem.html. Accessed 24 May 2017.

Homans, Margaret. "'Her Very Own Howl': The Ambiguities of Representation in Recent Women's Fiction." *Signs,* vol. 9, no. 2, 1983, pp. 186-205.

McDowell, Deborah E. "Boundaries: Or Distant Relations and Close Kin." *Afro-American Literary Study in the 1990s,* edited by Houston A. Baker, Jr. and Patricia Redmond, University of Chicago Press, 1989, pp. 51-70.

McInerney, Jay. "The Remains of the Dog." *New York Times,* 15 June 2003, http://www.nytimes.com/2003/06/15/books/the-remains-of-the-dog.html. Accessed 24 May 2017.

Miller, Jean Baker. *Toward a New Psychology of Women.* Beacon Press, 1987.

Morrison, Toni. *Sula.* Knopf, 1973.

Murdoch, Iris. *The Sovereignty of Good*. Schocken Books, 1971.

Nissen, Axel. "Form Matters: Toni Morrison's *Sula* and the Ethics of Narrative." *Contemporary Literature, vol. xl, no. 2,* 1999, pp. 263-285.

Noddings, Nel. *A Feminine Approach to Ethics and Moral Education*. University of California Press, 1984.

Otten, Terry. *The Crime of Innocence in the Fiction of Toni Morrison*. University of Missouri Press, 1989.

Ruddick, Sara. "Maternal Thinking." *Feminist Studies*, vol. 6, no. 2, 1980, pp. 342-367.

Black Motherhood, Beauty and
Soul ~~Murder~~ Wound

ALTHEA TAIT

Your daughter is ugly.
She knows loss intimately....
    —Warsan Shire "Ugly"

My father had a turning place
Mamma
We had a turning place
Mamma
White folks had a turning place
All of us
There was nobody for Mama to turn to
She was it.
   —Bernice Reagon "My Black Mothers and Sisters"

"YOUR DAUGHTER IS UGLY"

IN HER POEM, "UGLY," Black British female poet Warsan Shire presents a diasporic vision of a Black mother who transfers her survival skills to her daughter.[1] These survival skills are based on a cultural literacy bound to internalized oppression, which has, as Shire writes, its roots in a body mapped by continents, colonies, islands, and borders (Shire 10). Shire's poetic description of the Black female body and its seeming lack of beauty places the discussion of Black motherhood in a transnational space; more importantly, for this analysis, it links the Black female body to ageless suffering. M. Jackie Alexander describes this transnational space as the Crossing where Black bodies were transported within and to suffering and where an ongoing metaphysical exchange of grief occurs, and that grief travels in part through song (Alexander 289). This corporeal agony is not contained to a static space of time; instead, as I explain later in this work, it sings a sorrow song in harmony with the unspeakable, unspoken echoes resounding through generations.

In the introduction to Toni Morrison's *The Bluest Eye*, Claudia (whose name derives from Claudius—lame or crippled one) utters the crippling existential conundrum of the pain wreaked by intersectional forces of oppression that take root in injurious beauty norms: "There is really nothing more to say—except why. But since why is difficult to handle, one must take refuge in how" (6). The typographical positioning of Claudia's refuge in understanding the mechanics of trauma, if not the causative, is just as important as the words themselves; they are placed just before the opening of one of the novel's four major sections, which are based on the seasons of the year, beginning with autumn—when Demeter mourns Hades' ravaging capture of her beloved Persephone. Although Morrison's arrangement aptly speaks to the nature of pernicious loss and death, I would argue it also provides a frame for understanding the cyclical nature of grief involved with racialized beauty norms imposed through slavery. The intangible grief that haunted the bodies and souls of mothers before is alive in the bodies of the daughters, the mothers, the daughters, the mothers, and the daughters beyond: an endless cycle calls to be disrupted.

Just as bodies are altered by geography and grief, so too are souls. Black women's struggles with injurious Eurocentric beauty norms have produced an inheritance passed down between mothers and daughters as faithfully as a treasure of pearls or fine china. As Evelyn Jaffe Schreiber explains, children absorb their parents' wounds through learned behaviour (87). Sociologists such as Joy DeGruy in *the Post Traumatic Slave Syndrome* and other literary scholars such as J. M. Bouson in *Quiet as It's Kept: Shame, Trauma, and Race in the Novels of Toni Morrison* have argued convincingly that the effects of trauma are lasting and multigenerational for Black Americans because of the legacy of slavery. Brian Diaz posits a similar argument in relation to narrative medicine and the impact of individual and familial biography on the body across generations. Diaz's collaborative work suggests that when an individual experiences intangible or tangible trauma, it alters that individual's DNA to the point that there is a bodily transferal of that trauma to the following generations. The descendants are marked by the trauma indelibly to the point that they experience neurological and physiological responses to the trauma, in varying degrees, as if they had experienced the anguish first hand.[2]

Building on the work of Janelle Hobson and others regarding the disciplining of Black female bodies through Eurocentric beauty norms such as colourism,[3] this project explores the body as the walking depiction of a soul wound historic in scope. In African and African American contexts, the "soul," possesses an integral place in our self-conception and in our understanding of this complex heritage. As writers like Morrison show, when the soul is neglected, the wound deepens. Because of the perpetual oppression linked to institutional racism, Black women, inadvertently and intentionally, have become keepers of the wounds, which they pass down, as Morrison asserts, to the most vulnerable members of society—their daughters.[4] Drawing on Morrison's earliest and most recent books, *The Bluest Eye* (1970) and *God Help the Child* (2015), this essay analyzes instances of soul wounding in relation to transgenerational beauty oppression between Black mothers and daughters in Black girls studies and visual studies spaces as well as in a third Morrison novel, *Home* (2012).

THE SOUL

In her deft study of beauty in Morrison's oeuvre, Katherine Stern employs an Aristotelian reading of the roles of touch and imagination in perceiving beauty (79); this approach endorses a holistic perspective on human bodies, one that does not rely on the controlling ocular realm alone. To Stern's argument, I would add the importance of "soul" in understanding the injuries left by racialized beauty. Arguing that Aristotle's choice of the metaphor of a man who is "wounded through his shield" is inexact in *De Anima* or *On the Soul*, Stern exhibits Aristotle's slippery language (79). For Aristotle the soul is analogous to the description of the "man wounded through his shield ... it is not the stricken shield that struck him, but both he and the shield were struck simultaneously.... From this it is clear that that which is perceptive of what is touched is *within*" (Aristotle 133, emphasis added). Aristotle describes the soul *within* as the unseen form of a person sheltered by the body; the body is anchored by this intangible form that guides it. As Stern observes, Aristotle resists reductive readings. There is no soul/body or body/soul hierarchy; or as Walt Whitman poetically espoused, "the soul is not more than the body, and ... the body is not more than the soul" (248).

Through a theoretical blackening of the soul, Toni Morrison's portrayal of Black mothers' and daughters' struggles with colonizing, injurious beauty norms complicates Aristotle's position on the soul and body interdependent dynamic. The soul, as many African people groups and descendants believe, transcends death, and, thus, also the bodily markers that are transferred through the generations, as Diaz's research supports. As Morrison's *Beloved* attests to, it may become a manifold-burdened mule for generations of wounds. Similar to Robert Farris Thompson,[5] W. E. B. Du Bois views the soul as indestructible in *The Souls of Black Folk*; albeit his argument addresses the descendants of African slaves who adapted to America under colonization. Du Bois demarcates "the tragic soul-life of the slave" (120). The tragedies of trans-Atlantic trafficking and of the institution of slavery were embedded in Black bodies and souls; ultimately they were expressed in sorrow songs.

One of the bitter dividends of this tragic soul life was the soul's splitting into double consciousness (15). In this dual state, one was "torn asunder" (11). Du Bois' answer to this torn state was veil-splitting truth. Du Bois viewed himself as an inheritor, meanwhile, not only of this tragedy but also of Western culture, and so developed a philosophy that crossed this divide: "I sit with Shakespeare ... I move arm in arm with Balzac and Dumas ... I summon Aristotle and Aurelius and what soul I will ... wed with Truth, I dwell above the Veil" (74). Still, Du Bois' work remains bound to White patriarchal values that dismiss the worth and existence of Black women. Left behind the veils of the cultural rites of motherhood and marriage (the latter especially after slavery) Black women's souls were triply injured.

Nearly eighty-five years later in her manifesto "Poetry Is Not a Luxury," Audre Lorde returns to the site of the mother. Despite its unfortunate ties to blind spots in literary imperialism and patriarchal concepts of Africa, the figure of the mother, in Lorde's hands, is rewritten and revalued. She revalues feeling over knowing: "The White fathers told us, I think therefore I am; and the Black mothers in each of us-the poet-whispers in our dreams: I feel therefore I can be free" (149-150). Lorde's position also revises Descartes's declaration of intellect over all other facets of an individual's existence in order to create space for consideration of the wounded Black mother's soul in a way that *The Souls of Black Folk* cannot. A return both to feeling and to the mother is necessary to end what we currently identify as soul murder.

SOUL ~~MURDER~~-WOUND

Leonard Shengold describes soul murder as traumatically "killing the joy in life and interfering with the sense of identity of another human being" (5). This study, however, expands this discourse. If, as observed, the soul is the form of the individual *within* that cannot be vanquished or killed, then the term more accurate to describe the violent destruction of a part of a Black woman's or girl's soul is soul wound, which I will use henceforth in this text. To wound bespeaks injury to living tissue, but the wound is not fatal unto death. It lives on, even in the flesh of the next generation, as Diaz and others have explored. And if not addressed, the wound sustains itself through what Nell Irving Painter describes as the aggregated effects of the condition: "depression, lowered self-esteem, and anger" (16). Added to this list is shame, as J. M. Bouson's indispensable study of shame and trauma in Morrison's oeuvre illuminates. Inevitably, soul wounding is sustained by a wary negotiation of feeling.

Contrary to Lorde's position, because of soul wounds, Black mothers have been culturally bound to what bell hooks conveys as the history of "Strategic detachment [which] was one of the healthy psychological tools used by Black folks so that they could endure the suffering of slavery with their humanity intact" (120). In 1899, the Black female interventionist Lucy Craft Laney encouraged Black mothers to confront strategic detachment by wielding a "gentle sway" of influence on their children (636). The scar tissue of slavery nearly occluded Black mothers' feelings, as Morrison reveals in her second novel, *Sula*. Within the plot, she bridges the living narratives found in Black mothers' lives with the written narrative. When the novel's matriarch Eva is confronted by her daughter Hannah, who asks, "Mamma, did you ever love us? ... Did you ever, you know, play with us?," she responds, "Wasn't nobody playin' in 1895 ... 1895 was a killer, girl. Things was bad" (68). After Eva's husband Boy Boy abandons her and her three children, she subverts the institution of slavery that once used bodies similar to hers by using her body against the legal system that once failed her; she is suspected of purposefully losing her leg in a train accident so as to secure insurance funds to support her children. Eva emphasizes the negotiation with her racial, gender, political, and socioeconomic location as she rebukes Hannah (whose biblical name evokes the nature of desperation) and her love inquiry—"what you talkin' 'bout did I love you girl I stayed alive for you" (69). Her loving survival confirms Andrea O'Reilly's research positing the ways "Morrison deconstructs normative ideologies of motherhood" (124).

Eva's response also allows us to further interrogate the critical inattention to Black mothers' love and the complex ways it has been shown as well as challenged. Early in her indispensible study of Black mothers, O'Reilly aptly posits that Black mothers who are separated from the motherline are more vulnerable to the harm of racism; the motherline, as O'Reilly describes, is the physical and narrative linkage between the Black female ancestors and their descendants (12). In the case of some Black mothers within Morrison's oeuvre, these mothers are "more susceptible to the seductions of the beauty myth because they do not have a mother's love or motherline to shield them" (78). Conceptually, this is accurate, but it is not contextually accurate. If we make such claims—claims that negate the fictional Black mothers and those breathing off the page who "suffered from internal conflict and stress" and spent "proportionately less time caring for their own" families because they were economically forced to care for White families—we reify the conditions for the break in the line

(Jones 111).[6] We can never undo the soul wound cycle. As Eva delineates, while struggling to resist the systematic destruction of their love, many Black mothers love in very different ways. Attention to Morrison's unusual depiction of Black mothers' love interrogates the system that fosters an unforgiving social imposition upon Black mothers—in order to survive, feeling must be contained.

"WHAT THE DEVIL DOES *ANYBODY* NEED WITH *THREE* QUARTS OF MILK?"

One of the spaces in which Black mothers' feeling was contained, and ironically unbound, was the kitchen. The kitchen "recapitulated," as Jacqueline Jones argues "the mistress-slave relationship" (110). In their own homes, Psyche Forsythe Williams argues in *Building Houses Out of Chicken Legs: Black Women, Food, and Power*, Black women "used their kitchens to engage in cultural transmission. By practiing certain rituals, customs, and habits, they exhibited a measure of self-definition and instilled in their children and community aspects of socialization" (112-113). Unfortunately, in response to trauma, some Black mothers' kitchens became, and continue to be, a space for harmful socialization. In her "Kitchen Table" series, Carrie Mae Weems presents a series of images of a courtship, from its beginning to its end. Midway, Weems presents the Black female bonding ritual in which a woman soothes the scalp of another with oil after difficulty or weariness threatens the soul, and in this case after a lover has left. The next slide shows Weems sitting before a mirror and sensually adorning herself with lipstick before her daughter who mimics her in her own smaller mirror; Weems invites her to what Peg Zeglin Brand has described as "a ceremonial sharing of information, an induction into the secrets and codes of *beautification*, a transference of power" (1). When coupled with an analysis of race, we can recognize the loss of power also entailed. The mother socializes the daughter with standards of Eurocentric beauty norms, presumably as a performative act necessary to attract love. That the mother intends this as a lesson is reinforced by the next image where Weems sits at the kitchen table reading an imposingly large Bible, and the daughter stands in its shadow. In the following image the daughter alone is seated before the Bible.

In Morrison's oeuvre, the kitchen serves a similar purpose for Black mothers. In a memorable moment in *The Bluest Eye*, the kitchen is the setting for Mrs. MacTeer's scolding her daughters and her ward Pecola for the rapid disappearance of three quarts of milk. Many critics have noted this moment as signaling Pecola's obsession with consuming White values, but I am invested in Mrs. MacTeer's choice of words and the location she speaks them. Arguably, an ordinary evil resides in her kitchen: the *products* endorsing White normative beauty values. Frieda, Pecola, and eventually Claudia consume the milk from Shirley Temple mugs. Although Mrs. MacTeer is a model mother in this novel, as O'Reilly persuasively argues, agents of harm are nonetheless housed in her kitchen (23). The kitchen paradoxically also represents Black mothers' potential escape, since just by possessing the forbidden fruit in that space, their tragic soul life acquires some power. But these products' cultural tutorial in White aesthetic forms of respectability explains why, as Ara Osterweil has noted, the Black community endorsed the image of Shirley Temple, wounding the children with that "cuteness" (30). Cuteness through White normative beauty values seemed to offer salvation from a lifetime of restriction to the political location of Blackness.

Unfortunately, such indoctrination did more harm than good. Early in the novel, Claudia reveals the adults' internalized oppression of race, causing them to exclaim, "Awwwww," in adoration of Shirley Temple-like White girls (22). Claudia and Frieda are loved, but cuteness and adoration are never bestowed upon them or on Pecola. Meanwhile, as O'Reilly explains, mother's milk should be for the daughters (56). Mrs. MacTeer unwittingly wounds her daughters and Pecola when she chides them for consuming too much milk.

This wounding moment pales in comparison to what happens near the novel's end when Mrs. Breedlove strikes down her daughter Pecola after she unintentionally pulls down something sweet from the counter (which she longs for just as much as the nine lovely Mary Jane candies she orgasmically ingests after internalizing the disgust for her Blackness from the White male shopkeeper,

Yacobowski). Mrs. Breedlove responds, "Crazy fool ... my floor, mess ... look what you ... *work* ... get on out ... now that ... crazy ...my floor, my floor ... my floor" (109, emphasis added). Scholars have given significant attention to Mrs. Breedlove's dread and trauma inducing response, but a more nuanced examination reveals that Mrs. Breedlove's focus is not on the pink, blonde Fisher child solely, but on the work. Although her responses suggest an allegiance to White ideals of beauty and/or their associations with power, work matters more to her because it is the one thing she has been able to control after poverty, addiction, and abuse undermined her. Anything less than an intersectional reading of this narrative is incomplete. When Mrs. Breedlove combs the soft hair of the Fisher child, her actions reflect the importance of class as much as that of harmful Eurocentric beauty norms; so too when she imbibes Eurocentric beauty norms in movie theatres through films that celebrate "White men taking such good care of their women. And they all dressed up in big houses with bathtubs right in the room same room as the toilet" (123). Poverty is as much a factor in Mrs. Breedlove's internalization of harmful Eurocentric beauty norms as race is.

A more nuanced reading requires a Black girls studies approach, which reveals Pauline's identity being shaped in the domestic realm and the kitchen, prior to becoming Mrs. Breedlove. In the first period of her life, Morrison explores Pauline Williams's vulnerability to racialized beauty norms and her tutorials, as a Black female child and as a budding fifteen-year-old girl when she meets and marries Cholly Breedlove. Later during Pauline's metamorphosis into Mrs. Breedlove, she faces challenges as a Black woman with a visible disability, as a wife, as a domestic worker for White female employers, and as a mother. In the course of these challenges, Mrs. Breedlove is infected by Hollywood and its false images of beauty. Thereafter, it becomes impossible for Mrs. Breedlove to breed love because she has been so seduced by the beauty industry. Mrs. Breedlove ultimately chooses the soul wound over her daughter; the mother's physical response to her own soul wound is to revisit it upon her daughter, marking the daughter's body and soul.

In the beginning of the novel, Pauline suffers from an injury to her foot that permanently disables her at a young age, rendering her stereotypically "ugly." Disability pierces her life just as the nail had punctured her foot (110). Because of the able versus disabled body caste system, Pauline becomes a pariah, physically and emotionally disfigured by conventional standards in body and soul. In an analysis of Morrison's disabled characters, Rosemary Garland Thompson emphasizes their ability to subvert their marginalization and to create worlds in which they have authority. However, according to Garland Thompson, Pauline fails to convert her dejected state into empowerment. She falls prey to internalized oppression, and as a result, "Morrison denies Pauline one of her chief rhetorical emblems of empowerment: the inclusive woman-centered home where she might have reigned as the priestess of the flesh" (Garland Thompson 123). Though persuasive about this lost possibility, this analysis overlooks Pauline's development into Mrs. Breedlove in the following ways: 1) Pauline was "no more than a girl," a Black girl vulnerable to cultural tutorials and sordid racial oppression once she entered an integrated society, with Pauline specifically noting, "I weren't so used to so much white folks ... Up north they was everywhere ... and colored folks few and far between" (117);[7] and 2) the roots of Pauline's self-hatred derives from experiencing her disability within the domestic space, making the home part of the problem rather than an obvious source of a solution. Although she is an atypical Black mother in Morrison's fiction, she is also anomalous as one of Morrison's disabled Black female characters, who is not strong enough to resist abusive treatment from the Black community as well as the White community. Many living Black women face comparable oppressions in a dominantly able-bodied society.

In addition to moving us beyond mere indictment of Pauline as a failed female outcast, an examination of the possibilities consistent with Pauline's complex position exposes the ways a rejected character may serve as a conscience for readers.[8] Pauline shows how toxic elements in a community's collective unconsciousness, which result in social scapegoating, damage vulnerable members of a community. How does Pauline become the mother who repels most readers? This is the same Pauline who howls her way into visibility when White male doctors dismiss her labour of birthing Pecola as a "horse foaling" (125). Because of class oppression, domestic violence is a regular occurrence in the Breedlove home.[9] "Awwwww" may be the way adults dote on White dolls and child television stars, but an "Awwwwww" is delivered again when Cholly "put his foot in her chest" (close to the heart) after engaging in "muted sound ... flesh on unsurprised flesh" warfare with Pauline (22, 40, 44). It was the pressures of living on the axis of sexism and class oppression, along with racism, that has turned her into the horse that these White patriarchs call her. This conditioning precedes her interaction with her daughter. After losing the berry cobbler (whose purple seems to Pauline as deep as the berries that soaked her dress as a girl) to her daughter's curiosity, "in one gallop [Pauline] [is] on Pecola" and knocks her to the kitchen floor—much as Cholly knocks Pecola to the floor when he sexually violates her because he sees her as a bodily mirage of the day he claimed Pauline in the Kentucky yellow sun (115). She becomes the receptacle for both the mother's and father's troubled souls. These mirroring moments linking past to present, nostalgia to trauma, reoccur within the novel's plot. The impact of these palimpsest moments in Pecola's and Pauline's lives remind us of troubling cycles in black women's lives and the results when rejection turns into self-contempt and takes root in the souls of Black girls, who subsequently become Black women and Black mothers. Any reduction of Pauline to representation, by critics, as an opponent of motherhood constricts this discourse to a binary space that indicts the victim alone while ignoring the system of oppression that molded her.

"THERE WAS NOBODY FOR MAMA TO TURN TO/SHE WAS IT."

In her poem "My Black Mothers and Sisters," Bernice Reagon asks readers to consider the weight Black mothers have shouldered, especially in the era prior to the Civil Rights Movement, the era in which the plot of *The Bluest Eye* is set (300). Although Black and White families could continually turn to her for help, a Black mother had fewer options. At the end of the novel, Claudia reveals that the domestic sphere has become a holding cell for Pauline: Cholly "died in the work house; Mrs. Breedlove still does housework" (205). The interchangeable word pairs of "work" and "house," along with the association of both with prison time, speak directly to Pauline's life of confinement.

There is a starting point to describe this enclosed space that Pauline dwells in—Ada Williams. Driven to become part of the labour force for survival, Ada is consumed with work, whereas Pauline is left to herself and to care for two younger siblings. Nicknamed Chicken and Pie, Pauline's siblings bespeak the kitchen's immanence in Black women's lives. Yet poverty also saves Pauline "from total anonymity" because at the age of two, when a rusty nail pierced her foot, she did not have adequate health care, causing the wound to become a permanent disability—the flopping foot that she pulls up as if "extracting it from little whirlpools that threatened to pull it under" makes her visible to others, who paradoxically may dismiss her existence (110). Although no verbal dialogue is recorded between Ada and Pauline, Ada's influence becomes obvious in Pauline's behaviour. Prior to turning fifteen years of age, Pauline knows how to repair the fence, erect stakes, wire secure them, collect eggs, sweep, cook, wash, "othermother" the twins, and so forth. While Ada Williams is at work, doing all this at a White minister's house, Pauline takes refuge from her mother's absence and the "general feelings of separateness and unworthiness" within the songs sung in the sacred space of the church (111). The transgenerational mother-daughter cycle is at work in the soul even in the appropriated houses of God, both at church and at the minister's home. In spaces that should allow for the soul's freedom, Black mother and daughter are oppressed. The church becomes merely an extension of Pauline's longing for belonging until Cholly appears in a "godlike state" (111).

Although scholars have discussed Pauline's internalized oppression—and, indeed, as Vanessa Dickerson has argued, Pauline cannot see the beauty of others, including her own daughter's because "she cannot bear to see herself" (199)—readers have not given adequate attention to how Pauline has become someone who wounds her daughter in body and soul. Pauline is the product of enforced migration, integration, and domestic subjection, along with injurious Eurocentric beauty norms. Readings that ignore these intersectional forces shaping Black mothers' lives neglect the transgenerational impact on Pecola's soul, damaged in the kitchen where her mother and grandmother were damaged before her.

Although Sweetness, the primary mother figure in Morrison's latest book *God Help the Child*, is not bound to the kitchen as Pauline is, she too is the child of a wounding Black mother. Little is known about Sweetness beyond the fact that she is fairer in complexion and happily married until her daughter Bride's colour suggests Sweetness has committed infidelity. Reviewers and critics view Sweetness as a victim of colourism[10] but have not considered the culture that shaped her. In an analysis of the impact of toxic mothering on children, however, Manuela Lopez Ramirez does provide a relevant account: in Sweetness, the reader encounters a "victim of a race-conscious society" and ultimately an "example of matrilineal transmission of racist ideologies and attitudes due to the rupture in the motherline" (110-111). Because Sweetness is bound also to the prejudices of pigmentocracy and detached from the female values transmitted through oral tradition, no one tells her to prize Blackness (110).

Similarly to Ada Williams's, Sweetness's narrative is limited in the text. We never learn her full name by Morrison's design, and even "Sweetness" is cut short: by the end of the novel she is addressed only as "S." One wonders if Sweetness, similarly to Maureen Peele in *The Bluest Eye*—another fair-complected Black female character who transmits soul wounds—is characterized in such a way as to expose only the brutality of colourism for the souls of Black women and girls.[11] Ironically, Morrison divulges Sweetness's mother's name, Lula Mae, and that constitutes a variation of Bride's real name, Lula Ann. Bride is tied to Sweetness's history through her cultural tutorials on colour; her instruction was meant to teach Bride "how to behave, how to keep her head down" because "Her color is a cross she will always carry" (7). Sweetness is not benevolent in her misguided parenting as is the mother of Marita Golden; in her memoir, *Don't Play in the Sun: One Woman's Journey through the Color Complex*, Golden confesses "My mother had warned me about the power and prestige of lightness because she loved me, not because she didn't" (25). Instead, Sweetness accepts a moral obligation to raise Bride. Because of this, she symbolically suffers with a disease that she describes as the "creeping bone disease," evoking the condition of bone necrosis—a disease induced by injury of the marrow, that soft and tender space where cells are reproduced (176). Arguably, the marrow suggests the soul—or Aristotle's internal "form"—within, the essential matter of the bone where the disease manifests itself. Sweetness suffers from soul disease.

That soul disease is transferred to her daughter, who names herself Bride after conferring with Jeri, a White male image consultant, who convinces her that her Black skin is consumable in relation to white luxuries: "whipped cream and chocolate soufflé ... Bonbons. Hand-dipped" (33). Without the White drop, she is a beast to be dealt with—"all sable.... a panther" with "wolverine eyes" (34). In this White, sanitized, patriarchal space, she becomes Bride, not wife. Despite herself, she remains betrothed through the soul wound to her mother—until, that is, she is othermothered by Queen, the aunt of her lover, Booker. Ironically, earlier Bride falsely accuses Sophia (her schoolteacher) of child molestation to garner Sweetness's affection and attention, even if temporarily. Later, however, she regrets this earlier accusation and attempts to rescue Sophia from destitution upon her release from prison. Symbolically as her teacher, Sophia, whose name bespeaks wisdom, represents one who could have taught Bride to be a different child, thus a different Black woman altogether. What Sweetness has failed to teach her, Queen, however, does, and the lesson begins in the kitchen.

After Bride begins to lose breast tissue, the flesh of her womanhood in conventional senses, and after she has a car accident in this deteriorated state, she is rescued by a White runaway (who recalls Amy Denver, the character who assists Sethe in *Beloved*) and her guardians. Similarly, the runaway and her caretakers nurture Bride to the moment of her departure in search of Booker, the man who undoes her neatly configured life by abandoning the relationship. This search ultimately leads Bride to Queen's kitchen table, where she consumes bowl after bowl of Queen's homemade soup. After receiving nourishment from Queen, a mother (abandoned by her own children), Bride reads the letters Booker has sent to his aunt, and her soul begins to heal, first, through cleansing anger, and then, through comprehension of Booker's soul wounds; his family suffered the loss of his older brother who was kidnapped and murdered by a pedophile. Thus, he is disgusted by Bride's act of retribution for Sophia, a wrongfully convicted pedophile. There in Queen's kitchen surrounded by images of the children who have abandoned her, Bride, an emotionally abandoned daughter, comes to herself and gains courage enough to confront Booker who once spat at her, "you not the woman I want" and her agreement with his sentiment (8).

Bride returns, in other words, to the abandoned Queen, the mother to undo the soul wound. Without reifying colonial perspectives on Africa as a motherland or Black nation-building concepts of Black women as displaced queens, it is useful nonetheless to note the diasporic pull on Black women's souls. We would do well to avoid romanticizing Africa, as, today, many African women in their humanity indulge in colourist practices, such as bleaching their skin. But returning to the mother in Lordean senses does provide a greater possibility to recover. Black women dwelling in any space designed to oppress the soul can eventually confront the intimate loss from being perceived as ugly as Shire describes.

"I MEAN, HOW DO YOU GET SOMEBODY TO LOVE YOU?" CARRY THEM TO ADORATION

When in *The Bluest Eye* Pecola's soul whimpers, "how do you get somebody to love you?" she speaks in the first person for the first time, but it is not in the declarative voice; it is in the interrogatory. The soul wound query holds a further implication—how do you get somebody to adore you? Love, as I have argued, often differs from adoration. It can be as different as the dance of survival is to the gentle sway of the Black mother. As in Morrison's fictional dialogue between mother and daughter in *Sula* and in the historical work of activist Lucy Laney Craft, Black mothers have loved their daughters by surviving for them. Adoration has been a luxury. In order to end soul wounding and to end the transmission of soul wounds, Pecola's question (a question that belongs to many Black women and girls) must be answered early and continuously in Black girls' lives.

In her most recent opening, Haitian American photographer Lawdy Luc elicits a diasporic understanding of Black women and girls' need for adoration. According to Luc, home can be the most dangerous place available to a Black daughter.[12] In the first photograph, the Black mother hands her darker complexioned daughter, who, similar to Bride, is wearing a white lace dress, a makeup compact (see Figure 1). The daughter's Black undergarments, the ridges of which are visible, speak to the potentially dark and intimate nature of the transferal of beauty rituals between Black mothers and daughters. Along with her garments, the daughter carries a designer-brand purse, evoking the consumerist nature of beauty constructs. The second photograph (see Figure 2) confirms that consumerist note when it depicts the daughter stooped on the bottom staircase holding a cell phone; cell phones, as many scholars have argued, are spaces that contain young girls and women, since the access they provide to social media promotes a harmful web culture of invidious beauty norms. In the third photograph (see Figure 3), the younger sister gazes at the mother and older sister at the door between white stair rails; these rails evoke prison bars.

Figure 1

Ironically, the beautiful younger daughter already shows signs of conforming to a beauty culture, as her eyebrows appear arched and possibly thinned. In another photograph (not reproduced above)

229

Figure 2

Figure 3

the older sister appears, dressed in a white lace top, behind parted curtains, with the younger sister posed in front of the curtains; with her gaze, the older sister seems to lure the young girl to pass into her own shadowy space. Luc depicts this space as one of

Figure 4

darkness, which the image above (see Figure 4) reveals with the sister standing behind a darkened window pane—and its distorted reflections of lights—beckoning with a commanding gaze, while the younger sister stands beside the veil-like curtains in a moment seemingly of decision or indecision. Her contrasting innocence is echoed by the daisy design on the front of her top. The last photograph in Luc's arrangement (also not reproduced here) is of the mother once again. She poses much as the wedded daughter did in the first image, recalling not only the link between mother and daughter but also the status of a mother as always a daughter.[13]

In Luc's images, Black fathers and male relatives are absent, in most cases. However, in *Home*, a powerful narrative about Frank Money's moral injury, Morrison offers readers a radical revision of mothering that rewrites the male role. A discussion of how to end the cycle of soul wounds between Black mothers and daughters begins with a revision of the concepts of mothering. Thus, *Home* involves othermothering not only from Black women but from a Black man as well. Although the focus of this essay has been on Black women and mothering, O'Reilly's emphasis on othermothers can be applied, I would argue, to those who cannot physically birth children. The traumas that bind together the Black community, and

231

broader humanity, must be addressed by all members, regardless of sex; this may seem as if it is a radical shift in the argument, but Black feminists have emphasized this point for some time. In *Home*, Frank Money unfolds for the reader his mother Ida Money's involuntary abandonment of her daughter Ycidra to the care of her father-in-law's wife, Ms. Lenore; like Ada Williams and other Black mothers in Morrison's oeuvre, Ida joined the labour force, weaving her hands in and out of the unforgiving thorny shells of cotton bulbs by day as well as cleaning lumber shacks by night (45). Little more is known about Ida, as she develops asthma from her labour in the lumber mill and dies. Under Ms. Lenore's care, Ycidra is neglected. (Ycidra is called Cee by everyone but Ida who adoringly calls her by name, pronouncing all three syllables with the same care that Sethe requests each letter for Beloved's head-stone.) As the narrator observes, "A mean grandmother is one of the worst things a girl could have" (43). Ms. Lenore lives up to this description and does everything she can to transfer her dislike of Ida to a less powerful Ycidra, who will eventually learn to see all this, as her name Cee phonetically indicates. After being subjected to nearly lethal gynecological medical experiments by her White male employer, another Black female domestic worker implores Frank to come rescue Ycidra. He arrives and literally must carry her through the kitchen out of the dwelling space of harm and return her home, where she will fight for her life.

Frank is a carrier. There is much to learn from the concept of a carrier. A mother carries a child for up to forty weeks, but what if we replace mothering with the concept of carrier in our epis-temologies? O'Reilly leans toward seeing mothering in this light in her introduction to *Toni Morrison and Motherhood* when she returns to Karla Holloway's argument that Black women "carry the voice of the mother—they are the progenitors, the assurance of the line," and as O'Reilly highlights in her analysis of Holloway, "they are carriers of the voice" (123). However, a nongendered definition of a carrier would foster space in our cultural reformation to consider the ways in which any human being can carry the soul of a person, especially a Black daughter, into a space of love and adoration. The third time that adoration is voiced in *The Bluest Eye* is when Cholly's surrogate father Blue—much like Baby Suggs in the clearing in *Beloved*—pronounces to the women, men, and children in a field: "Aw-awww." This exclamation of adoration is followed with a moan from the old man who reflects, "dere go da heart" (135). Blue's cry of adoration—even if caused by the splitting of a watermelon (an iconic stereotypical image associated with former slaves and Black Americans) at a community gathering free from the patrol of White supremacists—is a prophetic call to Baby Suggs's response in *Beloved* published seventeen years later: "the beat and beating heart, love that ... love your heart. For this is the prize" (89). We have a better chance of healing when carriers connect Black girls and mothers to the carrier line. It is, after all, Blue who precedes Baby Suggs in the genealogy of Morrison's oeuvre in emphatically admonishing the people to "Aw-awww" over the heart.

ENDNOTES

[1] I want to thank Terrance Hayes for encouraging me to read Shire's poetry, specifically this poem, during the preliminary discussion for the interview sponsored by the NEH Institute, "Don't Deny My Voice: Reading and Teaching Black Poetry."

[2] Using olfactory studies on mice, Diaz and his team made the discoveries related to transgenerational trauma and its impact on DNA. His lecture was delivered at Emory University during the NEH Institute, "Black Aesthetics."

[3] See Hobson's reading of the ways the Black female body is disciplined (10).

[4] See Morrison's Afterword to the 1993 edition of *the Bluest Eye* (210).

[5] See Thompson's pioneering position where he underlines the immortality of the soul, using the Kongo Cosmogram and the Bekongo belief in the soul's undying spirituality (108).

[6] See Jacqueline Jones's *Labor of Love, Labor of Sorrow: Black Women, Work, and the Family From Slavery to the Present* where she describes the dynamics of domestic work and spaces for Black female workers in the 1930s and 40s—the same period reflected in the plot of *The Bluest Eye*—that forcibly separated Black women from their families, especially their children (111).

[7]See Asante's position in Dinesh D'Souza's *The End of Racism: Principles for a Multiracial Society*. D'Souza reiterates Asante's position on the harm of integration: "integration makes us cultural hostages" (171). O' Reilly similarly argues, "For Pauline, disconnection occurs as a result of migration and assimilation" (58).

[8]See Morrison's interview with Claudia Tate in which she describes the Black community as a pariah, and further asserts pariahs can serve as a conscience for a community (168).

[9]Jones asserts this violence was a byproduct of suffering brutal conditions under systemic racism: "If Whites attempted to cut 'the britches off' Black fathers and husbands, then these men would try to assert their authority over their households with even greater determination. At times that determination was manifested in violence and brutality" (96).

[10]See Kara Walker's controversial review of the novel in the *New York Times*. Walker asserts Sweetness is poisoned by the "strain of color and class anxiety still present in Black communities." Similarly, Thrity Umrigar argues that Sweetness is bedeviled by "color consciousness and its twin, internalized oppression."

[11]In her interview with Gloria Naylor, Morrison acknowledges regret over her "execution" of Maureen Peale's characterization. For Morrison, she was a mechanism to move the plot forward as it pertains to colorism, negating a more complex characterization (581).

[12]Luc articulates the dangers of housing injury in the homes of Black mothers and daughters, in "My Print Collection from Work Share," Received by Althea Tait, 16 Dec 2015.

[13]This moment of clarity about the Black mother's dual existence as a daughter, for which I am grateful, crystallized after a discussion with my colleague Sharon Allen at SUNY, the College at Brockport.

WORKS CITED

Alexander, M. Jacqueline. *Pedagogies of Crossing: Meditations on Feminism, Sexual Politics, Memory*. Duke University Press, 2005.

Aristotle. *On the Soul*. Translated by W. S. Hett, Harvard University Press, 2000.

Bouson, J. Brooks. *Quiet as It's Kept: Shame, Trauma, and Race in the Novels of Toni Morrison*. State University of New York, 2000.

Diaz, Brian. "Transgenerational Inheritance of Ancestry Olfactory Experience." NEH Summer Institute "Black Aesthetics and African Centered Cultural Expressions: Sacred Systems in the Nexus between Cultural Studies, Religion, and Philosophy," 29 July 2014, Emory University. Lecture.

Dickerson, Vanessa. "Summoning Somebody: The Flesh Made Word in Toni Morrison's Fiction." *Recovering the Black Female Body: Self-Representations by African American Women*, edited by Michael Bennett and Vanessa D. Dickerson, Rutgers University Press, 2001, pp. 195-216.

D'Souza, Dinesh. *The End of Racism: Principles for a Multiracial Society*. Free Press, 1995.

Du Bois, W. E. B. *The Souls of Black Folks*. 1903. Norton, 1999.

DuGruy, Joy Leary. *Post Traumatic Slave Syndrome: America's Legacy of Enduring Injury and Healing*. Uptone Press, 2005.

Hobson, Janelle. *Venus in the Dark: Blackness and Beauty in Popular Culture*. Routledge, 2005.

hooks, bell. *Communion*. Harper Collins, 2002.

Jones, Jacqueline. *Labor of Love, Labor of Sorrow: Black Women, Work, and the Family from Slavery to the Present*. Basic Books, 2010. Print.

Laney, Lucy Craft. "The Burden of the Educated Colored Woman." *Call & Response: The Riverside Anthology of African American Literary Tradition*, edited by Patricia Liggins Hill, Houghton Mifflin, 1998, pp. 634-638.

Lorde, Audre. "Man Child: A Black Lesbian Feminist's Response." *Sister Outsider: Essays and Speeches*. Ten Speed Press, 2007, pp. 72-80.

Lorde, Audre. "Poetry Is Not a Luxury." *Flat-footed Truths: Telling Black Women's Lives*, edited by Patricia Bell-Scott and Juanita Johnson-Bailey, Henry Holt and Company, 1998, pp. 147-151.

Luc, Lawdy. "Cinderella Series." 2. Visual Studies Workshop, The College at Brockport, 2015. JPEG file.

Luc, Lawdy. "My Print Collection from Work Share." Received by Althea Tait, 16 Dec 2015.

Naylor, Gloria. "A Conversation." *Southern Review*, vol. 21, no.

3, July 1985, pp. 567-693.

O'Reilly, Andrea. *Toni Morrison and Motherhood: a Politics of the Heart.* SUNY Press, 2004.

Osterweil. Ara. "Reconstructing Shirley: Pedophilia and Romance in Hollywood's Age of Innocence." *Camera Obscura*, vol. 24, no. 3, 2009, pp. 1-39.

Morrison, Toni. *Beloved.* 1987. Plume, 1988.

Morrison, Toni. *The Bluest Eye.* 1970. Plume, 1994.

Morrison, Toni. *God Help the Child.* Knopf, 2015.

Morrison, Toni. *Home.* Vintage Books, 2012.

Morrison, Toni. *Sula.* Knopf, 1973.

Painter, Nell Irvin. *Southern History Across the Color Line.* University North Carolina Press, 2013.

Ramírez, Manuela López. "What You Do to Children Matters: Toxic Motherhood in Toni Morrison's *God Help the Child.*" *The Grove Working Papers in English*, vol. 22, 6 Nov. 2015, pp.107-119.

Reagon, Bernice. "My Black Mothers and Sisters: or, On Beginning a Cultural Autobiography." *U. S. Women in Struggle: A Feminist Studies Anthology*, edited by Heidi Hartmann and Claire Moses, University of Illinois Press, 2015, pp. 296-310. Print.

Schreiber, Evelyn Jaffe. "Personal and Cultural Memory in a Mercy." *Toni Morrison: Memory and Meaning*, edited by Adrienne Lanier Seward and Justine Tally, University of Mississippi, 2014, pp. 80-91.

Shengold, Leonard. *Soul Murder Revisited: Thoughts About Therapy, Hate, Love, and Memory.* Yale University Press, 2000.

Shire, Warsan. "Ugly." *Our Men Do Not Belong to Us.* The Hudson Valley Writers' Center, 2014.

Stern, Katherine. "Toni Morrison's Beauty Formula." *The Aesthetics of Toni Morrison: Speaking the Unspeakable*, University Press of Mississippi, 2000, pp. 77-91.

Tate, Claudia. "Toni Morrison." *Conversations with Toni Morrison*, edited by Danille Taylor-Guthrie, University Press of Mississippi, 1994, pp. 156-170.

Thomson, Rosemary Garland. *Extraordinary Bodies: Figuring Physical Disability into American Culture and Literature.* Columbia University Press, 1997.

Thompson, Robert Farris. *Flash of the Spirit: African and Afro-American Art & Philosophy*. New York: Vintage, 1984.

Umrigar, Thrity. "'God Help the Child' by Toni Morrison." *The Boston Globe*, April 18, 2015, https://www.bostonglobe.com/arts/books/2015/04/18/book-review-god-help-child-toni-morrison/MGA5UlhUJ9vG7dseNPnHGO/story.html. Accessed 7 Jan. 2016.

Walker, Kara. "Toni Morrison's *God Help the Child*." *Sunday Book Review*. *The New York Times*, 13 Apr 2015, https://www.nytimes.com/2015/04/19/books/review/toni-morrisons-god-help-the-child.html?_r=0. Accessed 7 Jan. 2016.

Weems, Carrie Mae. "Kitchen Table Series." *Carrie Mae Weems*, Dec 2015, http://carriemaeweems.net/galleries/kitchen-table.html. Accessed 11 May 2017.

Wendell, Susan. *The Rejected Body*. Routledge Books, 1996.

Whitman, Walt. "Song of Myself." *Leaves of Grass*, edited by Karen Karbiener, Barnes & Noble Classics, 2004, pp. 248.

Williams, Psyche Forsythe. *Building Houses Out of Chicken Legs: Black Women, Food, and Power*. University of North Carolina Press, 2006.

"They Took My Milk"

The Multiple Meanings of Breastmilk in Toni Morrison's *Beloved*

BARBARA MATTAR

B REASTFEEDING, PARTICULARLY PUBLIC breastfeeding, highlights the binary between the sexual breast and the nourishing,
maternal breast. This binary makes breastfeeding problematic in
a society not oriented toward maternal understandings of the female body. Despite the differences in history and culture, and the
marked difference between an enslaved motherhood and a free one,
there are parallels between our current cultural attitudes toward
breastfeeding and Morrison's use of breastmilk in *Beloved* as a
contested source of maternal agency. This essay explores the multiple
meanings of breastmilk as a key image in the novel, and seeks to
draw parallels between Sethe's agency as a lactating mother and our
contemporary cultural meanings and interpretations toward this
bodily fluid, which can draw fascination, hunger, and disgust. In
the words of Edith Frampton, in *Beloved* "Morrison emphatically
foregrounds the mother's body and particularly the breastfeeding
subject" (145). I argue that making a cultural critique of literary
works such as Morrison's is a step toward a fuller understanding
of our responses to lactating subjects. A more affirmative cultural
response is needed to reposition the lactating mother as the source
of agency and the informed decision maker about this aspect of
her body and her relationship with her child.

A brief overview of the statistics shows that U.S. breastfeeding
rates in 2014 are at 79.2 percent, with rates of exclusive breastfeeding (no supplementation with formula) for three-month-old
infants at 36 percent, and six-month-old infants at 16.3 percent
(Disease Control and Prevention). Although rates have risen slightly

in previous years, the rates of exclusive breastfeeding at the ages of three and six months are well below the World Health Organization's (WHO) target. WHO's target is for all infants be exclusively breastfed for the first six months, except in the circumstance of certain medical conditions (WHO). Despite a large global public health campaign and many more operating at the local community level, nursing mothers often face confusion regarding how their breastfeeding will be accepted. Although it is encouraged by health professionals for breastfeeding to be seen a normative practice in the public domain, it still remains a contentious issue for some new mothers who are caught between the desire to feed their baby with their own milk and the possible undesirable attention they may receive from others. The practice of breastfeeding in our culture is not simply about infant feeding, but an intersection of cultural meanings regarding the mother-child relationship, agency over the female body, and the sexualization of the breast. As Bernice Hausman argues, "when we ignore the specificity of these embodied activities of maternity we have difficulty seeing how maternity is, for most women, a profoundly embodied experience ... breastfeeding in public has become an activity women must argue is not obscene or exhibitionistic" (276).

The lactating mother is continuously examining the ways in which her breasts make meaning in her society and how that meaning reflects upon her own self and her mothering practice. Although current Western cultural attitudes toward breastfeeding may run across a spectrum of opinions—from the acceptance of breastfeeding as a practice right through to its rejection—most value the choice and resources given to mothers in the twenty-first century about the ways they can provide nourishment to their babies. In *Beloved*, slave women such as Sethe cannot make these same types of choices, as they are severely restricted or nonexistent to them. The ability to survive the conditions of slavery and the opportunity to escape or be freed is paramount in the minds of slave mothers. The option to nurse one's child is taken away from many mothers and their children.

Morrison's novel cannot be read without taking into account its focus on race, history, and slavery as well as her desire to give a voice to the violence and trauma experienced by three generations of slaves. Her novel was inspired by the true story of Margaret Garner, an escaped slave who was captured in Cincinnati in 1856 and who killed her two-year-old daughter with a butcher's knife rather than have her returned to a life of slavery (Casey). This essay does not attempt to simplify the complexities of this novel by drawing neat lines between breastmilk as used in *Beloved* and women's experiences of breastfeeding in a free society. The lactating body of Sethe, though signifying commonalities to the lactating bodies of mothers across cultures and time periods, is also a racialized and historicized body. The argument emphasized in this analysis does not sideline race or history but focuses on the key image of breastmilk and its many meanings both within the context of Sethe's enslaved experience and within our own contemporary culture.

Beloved moves between two time settings: Sethe's present life in the house of her freed mother-in-law, and her "re-memory" (Morrison 43) of her experiences as an escaped slave. The occurrence of breastmilk will be analyzed in the order it appears in the narrative in order to track the development and significance of this image. Born to a slave mother and an unknown father, Sethe endures much loss in her girlhood. Much of Sethe's early sense of loss is centred on the lack of access to her mother and to her mother's milk. Her memories are vague, remembering "only song and dance. Not even her own mother" (37). Sethe's mother was allowed to nurse her only for a few weeks before being sent back to work. She was then nursed by another woman, remembering "Nan had to nurse whitebabies and me too because Ma'am was in the rice. The little whitebabies got it first and I got what was left. Or none. There was no nursing milk to call my own. I know what it is to be without the milk that belongs to you; to have to fight and holler for it, and to have so little left" (236). Sethe cannot forget this hunger for her absent mother—the hunger to know her and be nursed by her, to drink her warm milk until she is satisfied, to drink until she is full and sleepy and safe. This need troubles Sethe, especially when she becomes a mother herself.

Due to her enslavement, Sethe's mother was denied any authority over her nursing relationship with her child. She was denied that ability to choose when and where and for how long she could breastfeed her child. Current contemporary Western culture views nursing beyond early toddlerhood as problematic. It suggests an image of an overindulged child and a mother who will not let the child grow up. Television comedies such as *Little Britain* use crude humour to mock the concept of extended breastfeeding. For instance, *Little Britain* presents a skit where a twenty-five-year-old man keeps pestering his mother for "bitty," or breastmilk. She relents, much to the horror of the people around her. The common view appears to be that once a child no longer needs breastmilk for nourishment and has achieved a degree of independence and separation from the mother, the nursing relationship is superfluous, and extending it may jeopardize both the mother's sexuality and the child's development. The *Little Britain* skit utilizes the conventions of the grotesque to comment on the collision between the sexual and maternal breast. Linda Blum's research explores cultural expectations of breastfeeding, and the assumption that breasts should be returned to male partners after a reasonable period of breastfeeding. A woman's choice over how she uses her breasts, for what purpose and for how long, raises problems in a culture designed to see breasts through the lens of the male sexual gaze (Blum 39-40). In the culture of *Beloved,* the ability to remain with one's child for as long as possible and breastfeed that child for as long as the mother chooses would ensure their safety and health as well as allow for bonding time. It was a luxury and a dream denied to enslaved women.

When Sethe becomes a mother, she finds the conditions of her Kentucky plantation, Sweet Home, slightly more favourable than her own mother had experienced. Sethe is allowed to nurse her children and to have them with her while she works. Her ability to nurse them bonds her fiercely to her children, yet she feels that she has not truly satisfied them until she can guarantee their freedom from a life of slavery. Sethe is eight months pregnant with her fourth child when she and the slaves of Sweet Home plan an escape. Her three children have been sent away days earlier in the care of other runaway slaves. The youngest of the three is a girl not yet two years old, and Sethe sends instructions for the breastfed child not to be nursed by another woman until Sethe meets them in Cincinnati: "I hadn't stopped nursing her when

241

I sent her ahead.... Anybody could smell me long before he saw me. And when he saw me he'd see the drops of it on the front of my dress. Nothing I could do about that. All I knew was I had to get my milk to my baby girl. Nobody was going to nurse her like me" (19). No woman is allowed to replace Sethe's role as mother and source of nourishment, even under temporary yet difficult circumstances. The relationship she has with her daughter is expressed by Sethe in terms of her ability to breastfeed her, and in this nursing relationship, she feels particularly attuned to her child's needs, both physically and emotionally. This is in direct contrast to Sethe's own relationship with her mother, and her own unquenched desire to know her mother's milk in that intimate nursing relationship.

Breasts engorged and belly bulging with another child, Sethe bides her time until she can escape Sweet Home. Her choice to wait causes the most traumatic episode in her young life. Critical material often refers to it as "the milking scene" (Hummann 67) or a "theft" (Gaard 425; Koolish), but Michele Mock articulates the horror and cruelty of the assault by calling it what it is: "rape" (125). Sethe is ambushed by the schoolteacher and his nephews. In her passionate recounting of the story to Paul D, Sethe tells him:

> "After I left you, those boys came in there and took my milk. That's what they came in there for. Held me down and took it...them boys found out I told on 'em. School-teacher made one open up my back, and when it closed it made a tree. It grows there still."
> "They used cowhide on you?"
> "And they took my milk."
> "They beat you and you was pregnant?"
> "And they took my milk!" (19-20)

Paul D's questions precipitates Sethe's ability to verbalize the anger and frustration she has carried within her since the traumatic event. It was not just that they beat her. It was not just that they beat her and she was pregnant and could have lost that baby. It was not just that this ambush could have foiled her escape plan. It was because they stole the milk that she was keeping safe for her daughter, so that her child would recognize that Sethe was her mother and no one else, so that her daughter would not have her hunger satisfied by anyone else. Sethe is also desperate to ensure her own daughter does not experience the pain of being separated from her mother and her mother's milk the way she did as an infant. The schoolteacher takes notes using ink that Sethe has made while he looks on and instructs his two "boys with mossy teeth" (83) to hold her down and suck the milk from her body. For Frampton, breastmilk, among other bodily fluids, works in this novel as a way of "opposing the ink with which the slave masters inscribe their pseudo-scientific truth" (151). But schoolteacher senses a threat in Sethe's embodied maternity and aims to steal from her "in a code of domination" (Liscio 34) what is most precious about her body—her capacity to nourish her children, to know them intimately, and to satiate their hunger for mother love.

In our contemporary society, young nursing mothers are often frustrated and made angry by the persistent cultural view of the breast as a sexual symbol. In 2012, Lucy Holmes began an online petition against British tabloid *The Sun*, calling for editor David Dismore to remove the bottom half of page three, which features topless girls. Holmes felt the paper sent a clear message to British society that breasts exist only to titillate a male audience. Part of her petition read "you shouldn't show the naked breasts of young women in your widely read 'family' newspaper either. Consider this a long overdue outcry. David, stop showing topless pictures of young women in Britain's most widely read newspaper, stop conditioning your readers to view women as sex objects. Enough is enough" (Holmes).

This overemphasis on the sexualized breast makes public breast-feeding problematic and creates tensions between breasts as erotic zones and breasts as food and comfort for a woman's children. In 1994, Bridgid McConville raised concerns about the sexual-maternal binary of the breast and its impact on ordinary women in her book *Mixed Messages: Our Breasts in Our Lives*. She explores male attitudes to breasts and breastfeeding in the UK and the effect of this on breastfeeding and women with breast cancer. She writes of a "male hostility to breastfeeding" and elaborates further: "More than one midwife told me that men's jealousy was the main reason why women in this country give up breastfeeding early. There is a powerful feeling that breasts are for sex and that, therefore, they 'belong' to a woman's husband or partner" (xvi-xvii).

McConville's research is echoed by Linda Blum and Iris Marion Young among others and the topic still prompts contemporary research (Blum; Young; Bartlett). More than twenty years after McConville's book, grass roots campaigns still work to desexualize the breast and normalize public breastfeeding. Lucy Holmes's concerns about the sexualization of the breast became a nationwide campaign called *No More Page 3* with a large group of volunteers spreading the word online and via community groups. Holly McNish, a spoken-word poet and supporter of the campaign, posted a YouTube video about being forced to breastfeed her baby in a public toilet:

> At first
> I thought it was ok
> I could understand their reasons
> They said 'There might be young children or a nervous man seeing'
> this small piece of flesh that they weren't quite expecting
> so I whispered and tiptoed with nervous discretion.
> But after six months of her life sat sitting on lids
> Sipping on her milk nostrils sniffing up piss
> Trying not to bang her head on toilet roll dispensers
> I wonder whether these public loo feeds offend her?
> Cos I'm getting tired of discretion and being "polite" as my baby's first sips are drowned drenched in shite. (McNish)

The rest of McNish's poem seethes with anger at a society that thinks nothing of exposing her and her baby to bacteria and viruses present in public bathrooms, which no reasonable adult would eat in or ask another person to eat in. Breastmilk, and the practice of breastfeeding, is not seen as nourishment for a young child but as something disgusting. Breasts that appear upon first appearance as sexual but are then used to feed a baby causes a fissure in the sexual-maternal boundary. For McNish, British society sees breastmilk as similar to bodily waste and other fluids, which must remain private and away from food or company.

Expanding on Julia Kristeva's work on abjection in *The Powers of Horror*, Rhonda Shaw's exploration of the objects of our abjection includes "blood, sweat, tears, vomit, phlegm, seminal fluids and breastmilk," yet she argues that "not all these bodily fluids are treated the same" (292). Human bodily fluids that signal illness, waste, or contaminants are seen with more abjection than breastmilk, which "itself is highly valued as life-giving nourishment" (292). However, this value was not given to McNish's breastfeeding practice, and she was exiled to public bathrooms. Likewise in *Beloved*, the breastmilk of a slave is also not given this value. Through Sethe's rape by the schoolteacher's nephews and the reaction of Amy Denver to her leaking breastmilk, readers can see a reaction that positions her milk as abject, alongside her enslaved, feminine maternal body.

Sethe's breastmilk is problematic to the schoolteacher because her body is actively producing and leaking milk. Sethe is horrified by the schoolteacher's nephews and their crime, yet she is also disgusted that her body does not refuse their 'milking' of her breasts, an uncontrollable physical reaction. In contemporary breastfeeding practices women such as Hollie McNish are disgusted by having to breastfeed in a toilet because others see their breastfeeding as offensive. McNish feels abjection towards the bodily excretions she can smell "sitting on lids ... sniffing up piss" while her society positions her milk as abject. Her poem offers a clear argument on which she believes is worse. Schoolteacher views Sethe's leaking maternal breasts as in need of his management and control as overseer of the slaves. He sees her as part of his property on Sweet Home and so calls in his staff (his nephews) to manage the situation of her leaking milk.

To deal with the criticism of the *No More Pg 3* campaign, *The Sun*, in March 2014, attempted to manage the issue by using these topless models to promote breast cancer self-checks and cancer awareness (Greenslade). This allowed the tabloid to hold onto the most popular part of its weekly format and to remain in defiance of a growing social campaign against it. By the end of January 2015, however, changing popular opinion and a relentless campaign by *No More Pg 3* caused *The Sun* remove topless models and replace them with models in swimwear and lingerie (Ridley). In *Beloved*, however, Sethe's embodied maternity highlights deeper racial complexities. The punishment by schoolteacher further depicts his ambivalence about exactly what she is. To him, Sethe is a volatile combination of black, female, and maternal property requiring his authority and control. Her body is sexually arousing, disgusting, and fascinating to him all at once. Michelle Mock writes of the power struggle between Sethe and the schoolteacher and how Sethe "views her children as an integral part of herself in an implication of ownership." Mock continues: "Her children rightfully belong to her. Yet this essential maternal instinct is corrupted when viewed in the context of slavery. For a slave cannot 'own.' Not her individuality. Not her children. Not her milk. Nothing is sacred for those enslaved" (118). Not only do the schoolteacher and his nephews take her precious milk and abuse and invade her body, they also undermine any authority she believes that she has over her breasts as a part of herself—to nourish her babies and not to be used as a sexual object.

After escaping from Sweet Home, Sethe is dying from exposure and her beatings by schoolteacher, and her unborn baby is dying too. A white servant girl escaping from her master finds Sethe collapsed in the grass. Although the scene for some scholars highlights a common bond between slavery and servitude (Hummann 97), it must be remembered that when Sethe tells her that she is going into labour, Amy likens Sethe to an animal who is about to foal. Amy attempts to help Sethe, but she does not seem concerned if the outcome is Sethe or the baby (or both) dying. It is only by keeping Amy talking that Sethe can eventually coax her in assisting at the birth.

> "I said I can't get up." Amy drew her arm across her nose and came slowly back to where Sethe lay. "It's a house back yonder," she said ...
> "How far?"
> "Make a difference, does it? You stay the night here snake get you."
> "Well he may as well come on. I can't stand up let alone walk and God help me, miss, I can't crawl." (39-41)

After finding Sethe, Amy closes up the wounds in Seth's back by draining the pus and massaging her swollen feet. Perhaps it could be argued that this is indeed an act of benevolence as Hummann has written, until Amy's reaction to Sethe's maternal fluids is critically examined. Any shared bond as women oppressed by cruel masters evaporates now that Sethe's body has come undone. It is no longer a "clean and proper" (Grosz 71) slave body; it is changing of its own accord.

When Sethe's breastmilk begins leaking down her dress, Amy states, "What's that all over your dress?" To which Sethe replies "milk." Amy is not sympathetic. "You one mess ... How old are you, Lu? I been bleeding for four years but I ain't having nobody's baby. Won't catch me sweating milk" (97-98). Then Sethe's waters break, and her labour starts. Amy's reaction is stronger this time. "What are you doing that for?" asks Amy. "Ain't you got a brain in your head? Stop that right now. I said stop it, Lu. You the dumbest thing on this here earth. Lu! Lu!" (98). Sethe's fluid disrupts Amy's desire to move beyond the servant class. She dreams of a better life, of social mobility, and the velvet that she seeks to find in Boston stands for the finer things in life, soft, and expensive. Yet Sethe's arrival reiterates how Amy's current life is far away from these luxuries and instead deep in human suffering and oppression. Amy is disgusted by the circumstances she finds herself in, with an escaped black slave women giving birth on the bank of the river. Although she stays long enough to see Sethe emerge from her faint and to encourage the baby to breathe, the two women "never expected to see each other again in this world and at the moment couldn't care less.... Twilight came on and Amy said she had to go" (99-100). As with Amy's need to quickly leave the situation, in our culture birth is an event that people do not clamour to witness. Amy's disgust is not just a reaction to slavery but to childbirth as well.

The combination of extreme pain, milk, blood, amniotic fluid, vernix, the wide opening of the otherwise private vagina, and the often loud vocalization of the birthing woman makes birth a socially unacceptable event. Hospitals routinely offer birthing women numbing drugs and not just for pain relief. Naomi Wolf's exploration of contemporary U.S. hospital birthing practices has led her to write that "The labouring woman on an epidural can be counted on not to make noise" (144). Pregnant women at full term fear that their water will break in public, and nursing women fear their breastmilk leaking through their clothes. Cultural discomfort about women's bodily fluids has ensured an array of absorbent products to draw away that fluid from public view, ensuring "clean and proper" (Grosz 71) behaviour.

Social critique of the proper boundaries of the maternal body has been seen in the recent social media trend of the "brelfie," in which women, and most notably celebrities, post breastfeeding selfies in order to promote a more normalized attitude to public feeding. Actress Alyssa Milano has been particularly outspoken on this issue in an attempt to bring about a more positive cultural approach to mothers breastfeeding whenever and wherever their children need to. In an interview for *Entertainment Tonight* in September 2015 about Milano's brelfies, Lauren Zima reports that "Milano noted the 'crazy' difference between how people react to her pictures versus Miley Cyrus showing her nipple on camera at the MTV Video Music Awards. 'Everyone's fine with her nipples being out,' she says. 'I think people are more comfortable sexualizing breasts than relating them to what they were made for, which is feeding another human'" (qtd. in Zima).

Satire is also successful at promoting a change in attitude toward breastfeeding. In her YouTube posting *4 Reasons Women Should Never Breastfeed in Public*, American celebrity cook and parenting blogger/comedian Kristina Kuzmic receives much positive attention from mothers and breastfeeding advocates in her comedic play on Western culture's complete desensitization to the sexualized breast in advertising and the apparent horror the maternal breast evokes in the general public (Kuzmic). When in public, obviously maternal breasts are an affront to a society that holds a narrow and solely erotic view of the breast.

An analysis of Morrison's use of breastmilk in *Beloved* can function to critique contemporary views of the breast despite its main focus as a narrative exploring racial history. The novel asks pertinent questions about the meanings of breastfeeding relationships. The ghost of Beloved eventually tries to starve Sethe and drive everyone in her life away. In the attempt to satisfy her spectral child, Sethe realizes that this is a hunger that will not be satiated; it is a void that will never be filled as there has been too much absence in Beloved's existence. Beloved's shortened earthly life has created an unquenchable hunger in her ghostly state for her mother's attention, attention given to Denver in her ironic statement that "I swallowed her blood right along with my mother's milk" (242). Lynda Koolish sums up Sethe's maternal struggle in light of her breastmilk:

> The extraordinary unquenchable thirst and hunger of Beloved is the mirror of Sethe's obsession with getting milk to her daughter, enough milk, milk she alone could provide.... Sethe's breasts did not-could not-contain milk enough to feed all who hungered.... Yet the central paradox of the novel is that so great is Sethe's own deprivation that she cannot satiate even one person-that ravenous aspect of herself which is Beloved. (425)

The image of the breast in *Beloved* is more complex than a simple binary between sexual and maternal. It is the contested site of emotional hunger, satisfaction, and maternal love, as well as a means of autonomy or oppression.

Beloved's hunger for her mother's milk mirrors Sethe's hunger for her own mother. Yet Beloved's ability to be satiated means danger to Sethe's own life and any power she has begun to reclaim over it. She realizes that she has only one living relationship out of the four children she gave birth to and that is to Denver, a relationship she must save. Sethe experiences an ongoing struggle in the novel to maintain authority over her body. She has a keen hunger to have her body for herself and her children on her own terms. At the same time, she senses her lack of access to her mother's breasts and to her mother's maternal love as deep loss. These two elements open her to possession by Beloved's ghost. Sethe's eventual exorcism of Beloved from her life is her attempt once again to make a claim of autonomy on her own life.

Through her novel, Morrison has engaged not only with a narrative of historical slavery but with the way in which the female lactating body can become layered with various meanings: gendered, racial, and historical ones. Using the framework of a slavery narrative, the novel explores the embodied maternal experience that resonates with contemporary readers and in current breastfeeding discourse. *Beloved* explores how deeply the maternal breast is linked to a mother-child bond. It highlights the hunger of children for the affection of their mother and the extremes to which this loss can be felt. If our current cultural ambivalence about breastfeeding prevails, if the conflict for nursing mothers between their sexuality and their maternity remains, and breastfeeding rates do not increase, then we may start to feel a common cultural hunger for the absent milk of our mothers. It is a loss that would happen gradually, without the violence and trauma inherent in slavery, but it would be a palpable loss nonetheless. This could be the fate of a culture that would render a mother's milk not as a symbol of her love for her child but as a common bodily fluid: one that needs to be hidden, absorbed, and flushed away in private so as not to taint our great need for a rational, clean, and controllable body. New generations of mothers may find their milk taken from them, not by threat or oppression, but by a continuing reduction in the value accorded to their milk.

WORKS CITED

Bartlett, Alison. *Breastwork*. Sydney: University of New South Wales Press, 2005.

Blum, Linda. *At the Breast: Ideologies of Breastfeeding and Motherhood in the Contemporary United States*. Beacon Press, 1999.

Casey, Nicholas. "Margaret Garner Incident (1856)." *BlackPast. org*, 2017 http://www.blackpast.org/aah/margaret-garner-incident-1856. Accessed 14 May 2017.

Centers for Disease Control and Prevention. *Breastfeeding Report Card 2014*. Centers for *Disease Control and Prevention*, United States, 2015, https://www.cdc.gov/breastfeeding/pdf/2014breastfeedingreportcard.pdf. Accessed 14 May 2017.

Frampton, Edith. "'You Can't Just Fly on Off and Leave a Body': The Intercorporeal Breastfeeding Subject of Toni Morrison's Fiction." *Women: A Cultural Review*, vol. 16, 2005, pp. 141-163.

Gaard, Greta. "*Literary Milk: Breastfeeding across Race, Class and Species in Contemporary U.S. Fiction." The Journal of Ecocriticism,* vol. 5, no. 1, 2013, pp. 1-18.

Greenslade, Roy. "The Sun Uses Page 3 Models to Make Women Aware of Breast Cancer." *The Guardian,* 4 March 2014, https://www.theguardian.com/media/greenslade/2014/mar/04/page-3-breast-cancer. Accessed 14 May 2017.

Grosz, Elizabeth A. *Sexual Subversions: Three French Feminists.* Allen & Unwin, 1989.

Hausman, Bernice. "The Feminist Politics of Breastfeeding." *Australian Feminist Studies,* vol. 19, no. 45, 2010, pp. 273-275.

Holmes, Lucy. "David Dismore: Take the Bare Boobs Out of the Sun." *change.org,* Aug 2012, https://www.change.org/p/david-dinsmore-take-the-bare-boobs-out-of-the-sun-nomorepage3. Accessed 14 May 2017.

Hummann, Heather D. "Bigotry, Breast Milk, Bric-a-Brac and a Bit in 'Beloved': Toni Morrison's Portrayal of Racism and Hegemony." *Interdisciplinary Studies,* vol. 6, no. 1, 2004, pp. 60-78.

Koolish, Lynda. "Fictive Strategies and Cinematic Representation in Toni Morrison's Beloved: Postcolonial Theory/Postcolonial Text." *African American Review,* vol. 29, no. 3, 1995, pp. 421-428.

Kristeva, Julia. *Powers of Horror: An Essay on Abjection.* Translated by Leon S. Roudiez, Columbia University Press, 1982.

Kuzmic, Kristina. "4 Reasons Women Should NEVER Breastfeed in Public." *YouTube,* uploaded by Kristina Kuzmic, 24 June 2015, https://www.youtube.com/watch?v=LURZqBig734. Accessed 14 May 2017.

Liscio, Lorraine. "Beloved's Narrative: Writing Mother's Milk." *Tulsa Studies in Women's Literature,* vol. 11, no. 1, 1992, pp. 31-46.

"Little Britain 'Bitty 2.'" *YouTube,* uploaded by Mylasttears, 10 May 2009, https://www.youtube.com/watch?v=tyHm8oqkOB0. Accessed 14 May 2017.

McConville, Brigid. *Mixed Messages: Our Breasts in Our Lives.* Penguin Books, 1994.

McNish, Hollie. "Embarrassed." *YouTube,* uploaded by Random Acts, 4 July 2013, https://www.youtube.com/watch?v=S6nHrqIFTj8. Accessed 14 May 2017.

Mock, Michele. "Spitting out the Seed: Ownership of Mother,

Child, Breasts, Milk and Voice in Toni Morrison's 'Beloved.'" *College Literature*, vol. 23, no. 3, 1996, pp. 117-126.

Morrison, Toni. *Beloved*. Random House, 1987.

Ridley, Louise. "No More Page 3's Lucy-Anne Holmes Talks Activist Burnout, Being Skint And (Probably) Winning Her Fight Against The Sun." *The Huffington Post UK*, 8 March 2015, http://www. huffingtonpost.co.uk/2015/03/08/lucy-ann-holmes-no-more-page-3-the-sun_n_6826762.html. Accessed 14 May 2017.

Shaw, Rhonda. "The Virtues of Cross-Nursing and the 'Yuk Factor.'" *Australian Feminist Studies*, vol. 19, no. 45, 2010, pp. 287-299.

Wolf, Naomi. *Misconceptions*. Vintage, 2002.

World Health Organization. "The World Health Organization's Infant Feeding Recommendation." *World Health Organization*, 16 April 2002, http://www.who.int/nutrition/topics/infantfeeding_recommendation/en/. Accessed 14 May 2017.

Young, Iris Marion. "Breasted Experience: The Look and the Feeling." *The Politics of Women's Bodies*, edited by Rose Weitz, Oxford University Press, 2010, pp. 179-191

Zima, Lauren. "Alyssa Milano is Going to Keep Breastfeeding Daughter: 'Maybe Even Until She's 6!'" Entertainment Tonight, 8 Sept. 2015, http://www.etonline.com/news/171508_alyssa_milano_is_going_to_keep_breastfeeding_daughter_maybe_even_until_she_6/. Accessed 14 May 2017.

Brother-Mother and Othermothers

Healing the Body of Physical, Psychological, and Emotional Trauma in Toni Morrison's *Home*

TOSHA K. SAMPSON-CHOMA

Black women may find lovers on street corners or even in church pews, but brothers are hard to come by, and are as necessary as air and as precious as love.
—Maya Angelou, "My Brother Jimmy Baldwin"

CULTURAL CRITIC AND FEMINIST SCHOLAR bell hooks has argued, "Problematically, for the most part feminist thinkers have never wanted to call attention to the reality that women are often the primary culprits in everyday violence against children simply because they are the primary parental caregivers" (*Feminism* 73). Men are viewed as the ultimate transgressors against women; however, the abuse suffered at the hands of women is bountiful as well. This paradox is one of many that Toni Morrison explores in her tenth novel, *Home* (2012). In the novel, Morrison challenges the standard perception of motherhood as she depicts Frank Money, a brother who mothers his sister and is the only one capable of rescuing her from a life of pain and destruction. Frank and his sister Ycidra (Cee, as she is affectionately called) are reared by their step-grandmother, who demeans, demoralizes, and emotionally abuses them—particularly Cee—rather than displaying maternal warmth and tenderness. Frank's unconditional love and commitment to his sister become his motivation in life and, thereby, shapes his true identity as what I refer to as the "brother-mother," a concept that further extends Patricia Hill Collins's notion of "othermother." Using Frank's narrative as an opportunity to expand critical conversations on motherhood, Morrison reveals the

Philadelphian, or brotherly, dimension of love, as Frank facilitates Cee's healing and simultaneously rewrites his own narrative in the discourse of the brother-mother.

Most of Morrison's texts celebrate the collaboration and nurturing support found in female circles, although she, likewise, unabashedly critiques injustice committed by anyone. Morrison's goal is not to protect the reputation or interests of specific groups or individuals but to uphold and promote an African American aesthetic. Operating within this framework allows her to explore the complexity of family relationships and the sometimes paradoxical dynamics between mother figures and children. Although women traditionally provide children with necessary nurture and care, *Home* depicts a female transgressor and perpetrator whose maladaptive behaviour has grave and destructive consequences for other women. Parallel to the female oppressor, Morrison creates a twenty-four-year-old male protagonist whose life is fraught with its own paradoxes, yet whose commitment to and love for his sister are her only salvation. Frank Money transcends and defies the restrictions imposed on him as a male. Morrison uses his character to reveal the interconnectedness of men and women and to contend that the struggle for individual wholeness is contingent on mutual gender collaboration. This chapter focuses on the ways Toni Morrison illuminates the strength of the brother-sister bond and demonstrates a man's capacity to function as brother-mother and, thereby, participate in the nurture and cultivation of female selfhood.

The concept of the brother-mother originates from and extends Patricia Hill Collins's concept of "othermother." In her seminal text *Black Feminist Thought*, Collins explains her idea, "othermothers—women who assist bloodmothers by sharing mothering responsibilities—traditionally have been central to the institution of Black motherhood" (178). Black mothers have historically relied upon the support of others in their community to aid in the rearing and guidance of their children. Although othermothers are typically women, Collins explains that "men may be physically present or have well-defined and culturally significant roles in the extended family ... [however] the kin unit tends to be woman-centered, [yet] the centrality of mothers is not predicated on male powerlessness" (178). Although Collins does not use the phrase "brother-mother," the theory easily extends to men, whom she believes are likewise present and active in communities led by women. As she points out, "Because they are often left in charge of younger siblings, many young Black men learn how to care for children" (180). In *Home,* Frank and Cee are left in the care of extended family while their parents are working. This scenario results in Frank learning to love, instruct, shield, and protect his sister from harm and become her brother-mother.

The concept of the brother-mother is significant because it problematizes the idea that females universally share an inherent motherly instinct and desire to nurture, which eludes men. In the novel, Morrison demonstrates how motherhood extends beyond the bounds of traditional gender normativity. She reveals that it is possible for a brother to mother his sister, but even more noteworthy, his ability to identify as brother-mother exhibits personal sacrifice and reflects the internal strength to war against patriarchal societal norms. Assuming this role demands the ability to relinquish personal pursuits to act in the best interest of the surrogate child. Furthermore, it requires the ability to adapt to meet the changing needs of the child throughout the various stages of development, which is shown in the novel. Finally, this type of sacrificial maternal love provides the child space and freedom to grow into who she desires to become and a willingness to accept but also support her growth as needed. It means loving another enough to live in harmony without expectation. Morrison crafts a brother-mother who exceeds all of these challenges as a black man in the 1950s, who struggles with his own trauma.

During and beyond their childhood, Frank has always looked after and cared for his sister. From the beginning of its opening pages, *Home* establishes the inextricable connection between Frank and Cee. With only four years between them and a life of emotional hardship to bind them, the siblings cling to and value each other above all else. As Frank declares to the presumed reporter or writer who has come to record his story: "She was the first person I ever took responsibility for. Down deep inside her lived my secret picture of myself—a strong good me.... Guarding her ... not being afraid of anything ... succeeding at that was the buried seed of all the rest...in my little-boy heart I felt heroic" (104). In this moment, he juxtaposes his view of himself with his function as elder brother. Frank articulates the tension he embodies while trying to reconcile his masculine identity with his inner desire to be quintessential brother-mother. He remembers the defining moment when he felt heroic, strong, and good. These sentiments are tied to his role, yet this identity is not externally imposed but self-proclaimed. Consequently, his determination to guard his sister becomes the impetus for his self-definition. Because of Cee he is compelled to be what he had never before imagined for himself, and this interdependence is what induces Frank to come to his sister's rescue when he receives a stranger's postcard stating that she is on her deathbed.

As is often the case, the Money family's dynamics are shaped by external factors, namely poverty and lack of resources: "Mama and Pap worked from before sunrise until dark" (43). The necessity to work keeps these parents away from their children and forces the children to rely upon each phter. When the racist Klan drives the Moneys out of their Texas hometown, they are forced to relocate to Lotus, Georgia, the only place where they have family. Frank's grandfather Salem and his third wife, Lenore, allow their migrant relatives to stay until they can save up for their own rental home. The problem is that Lenore's house is "big enough for two, maybe three, but not for grandparents plus Pap, Mama, Uncle Frank and two children" (44-45). As a result, "Lenore, who believed herself superior to everybody else in Lotus, chose to focus her resentment on the little girl" (45). Cee's life would be determined by the history that came before her entry into the world. The racism enacted against her parents establishes the structures of her life in that she is born into a transient way of life, and, ultimately, her family is forced to depend upon the limited generosity of extended family; thereby, Cee becomes the scapegoat for resentment directed toward the family. From referring to her step-granddaughter Cee as "gutter child" to giving excessive beatings and uttering demoralizing epithets, Lenore is determined to remind Cee of her place and identity. After three years of living with this incessant daily harassment, Cee's sense of self-worth suffers and continues to lessen while she is "watched by every grown-up from sunrise to sunset and ordered about by not only Lenore but every adult in town" (47). In tying Cee's plight and her family's desperation to historical occurrences with the Klan, Morrison is providing important historical context: "not by avoiding problems and contradictions but by examining them ... not even attempt[ing] to solve social problems but ... [to] try to clarify them" ("Memory" 389). Morrison reveals the circumstances that produced the psychological abuse that Cee endures. The outcome of Cee's life is invariably tied to external factors beyond her control, which require her reliance upon her brother-mother and extended community to navigate.

To better calculate the toll exacted on Cee, hooks' theoretical framework regarding abuse is relevant. As hooks explains, "Beyond the realm of sexual abuse, violence against children takes many forms; the most commonplace forms are acts of verbal and psychological abuse" (*Feminism* 75). Lenore's ceaseless emotional and mental attacks may appear as mere sharp words, but the consistency and poignancy of the attacks—directed at all aspects of Cee's personhood—are defined as psychological and verbal abuse. Yet it appears that this torture escapes the attention of all but Frank and Cee—seeing that no one intervenes. Because of their poverty and desperation, the Money parents entrust their children to someone who causes severe psychological damage to their daughter and irrevocably shapes the family's dynamics. The parents are preoccupied with the rudiments of life, which leaves the two children to become each other's refuge.

With no other source of protection and care, Cee needs Frank who looks out for his sister and views her as his responsibility. Unlike many older brothers, he allows her to join him and his friends. He sees Cee and his friends as one unit: "tight, the way family ought to be" (52). He plays the role of nurturer because "their parents were so beat by the time they came home from work, any affection they showed was like a razor—sharp, short and thin" (53). As Collins has articulated, when brothers are left in the care of younger siblings they learn to care for and nurture children, which is what Frank does in his parents' absence as well as in response to their chastisement. To assuage Cee's pain, he would "touch the top of her head with four fingers, or stroke her nape with his thumb. Don't cry, said the fingers; the welts will disappear.

Don't cry; Mama is tired; she didn't mean it. Don't cry, don't cry girl; I'm right here" (53). Assuming the role of the brother-mother, Frank consistently caters to and protects his sister. He gives her guidance and assistance: "She followed Frank's advice always: recognized poisonous berries, shouted when in snake territory, learned the medicinal uses of spider webs. His instructions were specific, his cautions clear" (52). In all the ways a mother would have, Frank surrounds his sister with love, fights back threats to her safety, teaches her what she should know, and works to reassure her confidence.

The relationship between the Money children can be described in terms of what hooks calls "feminist masculinity." As she points out, "When male parental caregivers embody anti-sexist thought and behavior boys and girls have the opportunity to see feminism in action" (*Feminism* 75). Frank can choose to run off and play as a typical boy would, but, instead, he is cognizant and inclusive of his sister. Resisting normative modes of gendered behaviour and choosing inclusive activities reflects feminist masculinity. Hooks goes on to say that there is a "need for men to participate equally in parenting not just to create gender equity but to build better relationships with children" (*Feminism* 75). Frank exemplifies a positive and loving relationship with Cee. He is not afraid to mother his sister; he creates a healthy space in which she may learn and grow. Cee, thereby, has a male example of someone who unconditionally loves her, protects her, and serves as her advocate. Mar Gallego contributes to the conversation regarding male advocacy of women. He contends the following: "alternative masculinities provide a counterdiscourse against patriarchy, by downplaying distinctions between black men and women and rethinking relationships to the others" (165). Gallego's argument mirrors Frank's ability to be a brother-mother. In treating Cee with love and respect, Frank presents an alternative masculinity instead of the dominant masculine discourse, and he ultimately empowers both himself and his sister.

Conversely, the absence of their empowering relationship leaves Cee unprotected, and at this stage in her life, she cannot discern between authentic love and self-serving ambitions. When Frank enlists in the army to escape life in Lotus, fourteen-year-old Cee is abandoned to loneliness while her absent parents work incessantly. The pressures applied by overbearing Lenore cause her to innocently accept a newcomer's marriage proposal shortly after her brother departs for the Korean War. Eventually, her new husband Prince leaves her when the two relocate to the city of Atlanta. Forced to work for the first time, Cee naively takes an unspecified job in which she is subject to medical experimentation. She is blinded by the allure of reasonable pay and favourable living accommodations, which works to her employer's advantage. Dr. Beau, for whom she works, performs experimental research on her womb, resulting in vaginal trauma and irreversible sterility. The building blocks that have led to her victimization are best categorized as what hooks terms "abusive shaming," which "lays the foundation for other forms of abuse" (*Feminism* 75). Because of the shame and humiliation induced by Lenore, Cee has little self-worth and is susceptible to the tactics of the cunning newcomer, Prince. Without her brother-mother, she is unprotected and falls for someone who talks a good game, marries her, relocates her to a big city, borrows, and then steals her grandparents' car and immediately leaves her. Abandoned, "Cee felt her heart breaking. If Frank were there he would once more touch the top of her head.... But he wasn't there or anywhere near" (53). Consequently, Cee makes desperate choices that stem from her experiences with abusive shaming, parental neglect, and lack of empowerment. She is beyond the bounds of her brother-mother, yet Cee is not the only one who is affected by the disconnection between her and Frank.

Despite being shaped by his identity as Cee's brother-mother, Frank bears his own struggles as a man. Early in the novel, readers learn Frank's story as he shares his narrative with an unnamed listener, perhaps a reporter. He admonishes the listener: "since you're set on telling my story, whatever you think and whatever you write down, know this" (5). The implication is that Frank is uncomfortable with having his story told and remains suspicious of the writer's motives and intent to inscribe his black masculine identity. Yet throughout the novel, he wrestles with the dichotomous objective of telling his story while struggling to subvert hegemonic perceptions of masculinity and abate the internalization of such categorization. Although his sister acquiesces to their grandmother's condescension, Frank spends his life resisting a prescribed identity and seeks to assert his own volition. As exemplified in the directive he gives to the writer, Frank is determined not to succumb to someone else's interpretation of his life, and he refuses to be depicted as an objectified "other," who embodies violent patriarchal notions and reckless behaviour. He wields his only sense of agency in the form of narration, endeavouring to dictate his history and interpret his life according to his perceptions. He strives to project a balanced perspective of his identity as both brother-mother and contrived, self-directed man.

As an adult, he wars with and seeks to eradicate prevailing insidious notions of masculinity, which usurp his authentic self-portrait as loving brother-mother. On the one hand, he is eager to depart from Lotus to define himself as a man, and on the other hand, he cannot help but to worry about his sister. Frank has always taken care of her: "Cee suffered no bruise or cut he had not tended. The only thing he could not do for her was wipe the sorrow, or was it panic from her eyes when he enlisted. He tried to tell her the army was the only solution. Lotus was suffocating, killing him and his two best friends ... Frank assured himself Cee would be okay" (35). Even though he strives to do what he believes is best for himself, Frank continues to be mindful of his sister and his role as brother-mother.

He seeks the balance between living life through his relationship to his sister and seeking to define himself outside the confines of that relationship. Ultimately, Frank and his friends join the army to find themselves as men. They pursue new spaces, physical prowess, aggression, and domination; they choose the epitome of manhood—the life of a soldier. Through his military experiences, Frank finds himself engaging in the discourse of hegemonic masculinity. Although he does not mind the frequent moves and he enjoys the camaraderie of his male bonds, he cannot anticipate the effects of watching his friends die in war. To lose the people he esteems as family in a way that emasculates them causes Frank to lose what little grasp he has on his authentic identity. Frank recalls the following: "Mike in his arms again thrashing, jerking ... [as he whispered], 'Smart, Smart Money. Don't tell Mama.'... By the time the medics got there, the urine on Mike's pants had frozen ... [and the experience of Mike's death] changed him. What died in his arms gave a grotesque life to his childhood" (97). Not only is Frank devastated by the loss, but the way in which Mike cries, wets himself, and begs Frank not to tell his mother shows Frank how easily men become little boys when faced with the travesty of war. It illuminates the brevity of life and reveals how one's constructed masculinity is easily threatened. Upon his return, Frank struggles with post-traumatic stress disorder (PTSD) and is far removed from his sister.

More than simply dealing with the consequences of war, Frank is traumatized and the deaths he experiences resuscitate the childhood memory of him and Cee watching, in secret, a dead man get buried, all of which causes him mental breakdown. When Frank begins his narrative, he chooses to start with the memory of men burying that dead body before he shares his experience escaping a psychiatric ward and travelling to the South to rescue his sister. The significance of the narrative's sequencing can be paralleled to recent findings in trauma studies. Psychotherapy as a field of study has long existed in a variety of forms; however, in the late twentieth-century scholars have more fully attended to the psychological effects of trauma. Cultural studies scholar Shoshana Felman and psychoanalyst Dori Laub published *Testimony: Crises of Witnessing in Literature, Psychoanalysis, and History* in 1992. Leading cultural studies scholar Cathy Caruth edited the ground-breaking text *Trauma: Explorations in Memory* in 1995 and later published a monograph, *Unclaimed Experience: Trauma, Narrative, and History*, in 1996 before publishing several subsequent texts. Both Caruth and Felman have written extensively on trauma in literature and history. In *Testimony: Crises of Witnessing in Literature, Psychoanalysis, and History*, Felman and Laub focus on the trauma of World War II and the ways in which narrative or the telling and recounting of one's story through literature (stories, narratives, poems) serves as a mechanism to cope with the Holocaust. According to the authors of the text, the trauma of WWII is not "an event encapsulated in the past, but [is] a history which is essentially not over, a history whose repercussions are not simply omnipresent (whether consciously or not) in all our cultural activities, but whose traumatic consequences are still evolving" (xiv). Felman and Laub argue that trauma, therefore, is ongoing and its effects are reflected in the present and can be expected to surface in the future. When a person experiences trauma, she or he becomes a witness to that experience and is compelled to give testimony of the occurrence or remain in silence. "Since the testimony cannot be simply relayed, repeated, or reported by another without thereby losing its function as a testimony, the burden of the witnesses—is a radically unique, noninterchangeable and solitary burden" (3). The authors contend that the person who experiences the trauma bears the arduous and lonely responsibility of conveying the encounter. The witness, they argue, "is a vehicle of an occurrence, a reality, a stance or a dimension beyond himself" (3). This assertion has implications for Frank in *Home*. Frank strives to reconcile the telling of his story, as he is the one who had to bear witness to the deaths he describes and the cruelties he and Cee faced. He is alone with the solitary burden of representation, and he adamantly demands accuracy in the recording of the details. Based on Felman and Laub's analysis, the writer is limited in his role because he has not experienced the trauma and is not the witness; therefore, he cannot interpret what Frank has endured.[1] In one example, Frank's experience is bigger than he is and takes him outside of himself to the point that he becomes a witness and not the actual participant. He separates himself from his actions and associates the acts with some other soldier. His behaviour is a consequence of trauma.

At the same time, Frank's need to tell of his experiences is a form of therapy, even as he seeks to ameliorate his wounds. In *Unclaimed Experience: Trauma, Narrative, and History,* Caruth points out the traumatized person's need to tell stories about the trauma. She says, "it is always the story of a wound that cries out, that addresses us in the attempt to tell us of a reality or truth that is not otherwise available" (4). Frank could refuse to share his story, yet he is compelled to share it, even while inserting such injunctions as "I don't think you, [a mere reporter], know much about love. Or me" (69). More than once he interjects, "When you write this down, know this" (103). His desire to recount his story mirrors Caruth's declaration "that the history of a trauma, in its inherent belatedness, can only take place through the listening of another" (*Trauma: Explorations in Memory* 11). Conveying his story aids Frank in the process of moving forward and working through his trauma.

Shortly after losing Mike, Frank loses his friends Red and Stuff, which pushes Frank to his breaking point. As he relives his experiences, he is plagued by trauma and guilt, which tie into his sense of manhood. In reflecting on the events, Frank believes rescuing his friends would have served as a mark of masculinity. Instead of focusing on the fact that he was by Mike's side to offer comfort when he died, he criticizes himself: "Why didn't you hurry? If you had gotten there sooner you could have helped" (21). His failure to help leads to incredible guilt, which is a symptom of PTSD. Caruth characterizes this experience in the following way: a "pathology [that] consists, rather solely in the structure of experience or reception: the event is not assimilated or experienced fully at the time, but only belatedly, in its repeated possession of the one who experiences it. To be traumatized is precisely to be possessed by an image or event" (*Trauma: Explorations in Memory* 4-5). As Frank recounts his subsequent actions, he is possessed by the imagery and relives it over and over again. He asks himself, "And all of that killing you did afterward? Women running, dragging children along. And that old one-legged man on a crutch hobbling ... you blew a hole in his head because you believed it would ... avenge [Mike's] lips calling mama. Did it? Did it work? And the girl. What did she ever do to deserve what happened to her?" (21). Troubled by what he sees as his ineptness and overwhelmed by the image of urine on Mike's pants, Frank cannot see beyond the negative outcome. He suffers from a pathology of guilt because he outlived those he considered his family.

In an act of aggression, he punishes himself and others by going on a violent escapade, which can be linked to his shift away from brother-mother to his performance of perceived masculine behaviour. Frank's actions are what feminist scholar Michele Wallace refers to as "superficial masculine characteristics—demonstrable sexuality; physical prowess; the capacity for warlike behavior" (xx). Although he does not engage in demonstrable sexuality, Frank does exert physical prowess and the capacity for warlike behaviour. Later he shoots and kills a toothless, Korean girl whose severe poverty leads her to offer oral sex in exchange for food. Frank's conduct is an attempt to conceal the guilt he feels about being aroused by the child's offer, a response he finds detestable. This act of violence goes against everything within him, yet he instinctively shoots her and lies to the reporter, saying that another officer shot the girl and he does not understand why. His description can be likened to what Caruth describes as the wound that cries out to be addressed (*Unclaimed Experience* 4). And as Felman and Laub argue, the trauma causes him to see the encounter in a dimension beyond himself. Frank is struggling to resist a prescribed identity that he fears is beginning to define his life. He is far removed from his caregiving role as brother-mother.

The hardships of war take their toll on Frank; they shift his focus away from his authentic brother-mother identity to patriarchal dominance. Although he was not brave before war, now he is a changed man: "he was reckless, lunatic, firing, dodging the scattered parts of men ... with Mike gone, he was brave, whatever that meant" (98). In light of his experiences, he takes on an aggressive and angry persona indicative of masculine dominance. Wallace criticizes Black men for behaviour such as Frank's, pointing out that "he is unaware that he has accepted a definition of manhood that is destructive to himself and that negates the best efforts of his past" (79). Wallace addresses patriarchy in contrast to a community-centred manhood, which never puts the community in danger of violence just to assert an individual man's power or independence. To use Wallace's framework, Frank was previously operating out of a sense of manhood that prioritized and valued others, namely Cee. According to bell hooks, Frank's former behaviour reflected feminist masculinity. At that time, he was inclined to preserve life and act in humanitarian ways. After his friends die, Frank goes on a rampage, shooting and killing anyone and everyone. The change is consistent with patriarchal interpretations of male dominance and aggression, an interpretation disconnected from that of loving brother-mother.

In *Black Sexual Politics* Collins asserts the following: "Hegemonic masculinity in the United States has several benchmarks. For one, 'real' men are primarily defined as *not* being like women. Real men are expected to be forceful, analytical, responsible, and willing to exert authority, all qualities that women seemingly lack

... male dominance occurs within racial/ethnic categories and is one marker of male power" (188-189). When he loses his friends, Frank uses force to demonstrate his power and control over the situation. His actions parallel Collins's contention that "exercising male authority is a vital component of masculinity" (189). In *We Real Cool*, hooks confirms this viewpoint and expresses some of the challenges black men face as they develop into men and the ways societal notions of masculinity shape their lives. She contends that "Young black males, like all boys in patriarchal culture, learn early that manhood is synonymous with the domination and control over others, that simply by being male they are in a position of authority that gives them the right to assert their will over others, to use coercion and/or violence to gain and maintain power" (88). Morrison chooses not to describe the details of Frank's development from childhood into manhood; however, the historical context of American patriarchy frames Frank's conduct. Collins further clarifies: "In contrast, because so many African American men lack access to the forms of political and economic power that are available to elite White men, the use of their bodies, physicality, and a form of masculine aggressiveness become more important" (*Black Sexual Politics* 190). Although he previously enacted feminist masculinity, Frank begins to use aggression and physicality to contend with his loss and pain.

As he copes with war, he drifts further from a caring and loving brother-mother to a violent man motivated by rage.

Frank learns to perform masculinity as a coping mechanism, a concept that had been foreign to him in the past. As he becomes a young adult, he learns to enact acceptable forms of masculinity. Hooks argues that the performativity of patriarchy is not innate but instead, boys learn early on how to wear a mask over their authentic identities in order to conform. According to hooks:

> Learning to wear a mask (that word already embedded in the term 'masculinity') is the first lesson in patriarchal masculinity that a boy learns. He learns that his core feelings cannot be expressed if they do not conform to the acceptable behaviors sexism defines as male. Asked to give up the true self in order to realize the patriarchal ideal, boys

learn self-betrayal early and are rewarded for these acts of soul murder. (*The Will to Change* 153)

His transition into the patriarchal ideal results from Frank's PTSD. He cannot abate the horrific memories: "as was often the case when he was alone and sober, whatever the surroundings, he saw a boy pushing his entrails back in, holding them in his palms … or he heard a boy with only the bottom half of his face intact, the lips calling mama. And he was stepping over them, around them, to stay alive" (20). He finds himself in a daze: "'Not totally homeless, but close. Drinking and hanging out in music bars on Jackson Street, sleeping on the sofas of drinking buddies or outdoors, betting my forty-three dollars of army pay in crap games and pool halls … I knew I needed help but there wasn't any'" (68). Frank is in a helpless state after the war. He meets and moves in with Lily, who provides solace but even that relationship does not completely heal him or extract him from his trance.

What sobers Frank and realigns him on the path toward authentic self-definition is the correspondence he receives regarding Cee's health and the fact that "she be dead if [he were to] tarry" (8). In spite of his trauma, Frank immediately becomes coherent and devises a plan to retrieve his sister. His brother-mother instincts are ignited by his love for Cee, and he begins his journey from the state of Washington to Georgia, a reversal of the migration narrative. When Frank arrives at the address where his sister resides, he finds her listless and "close to the edge of life" (114). A sense of contentment sets in: "not only because [the rescue] was successful but also how markedly nonviolent it had been … not having to beat up the enemy to get what he wanted was somehow superior—sort of, well, smart" (114). True to his authentic identity, Frank focuses on nurturing Cee and freeing her from victimization using peaceful means. Even as he approaches the home, he briefly wonders if he will have to break in but he cannot "let things get so out of control that it would endanger Cee" (110). His sister is his highest priority, and he governs himself by the principles of a brother-mother.

In keeping with the ideal to protect and nurture his sister, Frank likewise recognizes his limitations. After departing from Dr. Beau's home, he takes Cee back to Lotus—a place where he hoped never to return. His first stop is the home of a woman who is known for her medicinal knowledge and healing virtues. Miss Ethel summons various women who immediately come to Cee's rescue, whereas Frank is "blocked from visiting the sickroom by every woman in the neighborhood ... [believing] his maleness would worsen her condition" (119). Although he has rescued her, Frank entrusts his sister to the "othermothers" in their community. In return, they tend to her as if she were their own child: "Two months surrounded by country women who loved mean had changed [Cee]. The women handled sickness as though it were an affront, an illegal invading braggart who needed whipping. They didn't waste their time or the patient's with sympathy and they met the tears of the suffering with resigned contempt" (121). Not only do they work tirelessly to heal her body, they instill self-worth through axioms and faithful adages:

Men know a slop jar when they see one.
   You ain't a mule to be pulling some evil doctor's wagon.
   Who told you you was trash?
   How was I supposed to know what he was up to? Cee tried to defend herself.
   Misery don't call ahead. That's why you have to stay awake—otherwise it just walks on in your door...You good enough for Jesus. That's all you need to know. (122)

These othermothers resuscitate and save Cee from death. Specifically, "the demanding love of Ethel Fordham soothed and strengthened her the most" (125). The women provide nurture and love and teach her to embroider and crochet, becoming the female mother she never had.

Although Cee will never bear children, she learns for the first time that she has to find and create her own strength. For the first time, "...she wanted to be the person who would never again need rescue" (129). Through the adversities she faces, Cee Money learns the importance of self-love and self-worth. She reflects on Miss Ethel's words: "Look to yourself. You free. Nothing and nobody is obliged to save you but you ... don't let Lenore or some trifling boyfriend and certainly no devil doctor decide who you are. That's slavery. Somewhere inside you is that free person I'm talking about. Locate her and let her do some good in the world" (126). Cee is only beginning her journey toward wholeness, but where would she be without her brother-mother and the othermothers who come to her rescue and provide healing from physical, psychological, and emotional trauma?

ENDNOTE

[1]Other scholars have argued for alternative definitions of witnessing. E. Ann Kaplan in her book *Trauma Culture: The Politics of Terror and Loss in Media and Literature* contends that we can all be witnesses to experiences that are not our own. She sees one of the functions of art as the ability to invite others to bear witness and to invoke empathy. Kaplan explains: "Rather, I suggest that 'witnessing' happens when a text aims to move the viewer emotionally but without sensationalizing or overwhelming her with feeling that makes understanding impossible. 'Witnessing' involves not just empathy and motivation to help, but understanding the structure of injustice—that an injustice has taken place—rather than focusing on a specific case" (22-23).

WORKS CITED

Angelou, Maya. "My Brother Jimmy Baldwin." *Los Angeles Times*, 20 Dec. 1987, http://articles.latimes.com/1987-12-20/books/bk-29958_1_james-baldwin. Accessed 21 May 2017.

Caruth, Cathy, editor. *Trauma: Explorations in Memory*. Johns Hopkins University Press, 1995.

Caruth, Cathy. *Unclaimed Experience: Trauma, Narrative and History*. Johns Hopkins University Press, 1996.

Collins, Patricia Hill. *Black Feminist Thought: Knowledge, Consciousness, and the Politics of Empowerment*. Routledge, 2000.

Collins, Patricia Hill. *Black Sexual Politics: African Americans, Gender, and the New Racism*. Routledge, 2005. Print.

Felman, Shoshana, and Dori Laub. *Testimony: Crises of Witnessing in Literature, Psychoanalysis, and History*. Routledge, 1992.

Gallego, Mar. "Progressive Masculinities: Envisioning Alternative Models for Black Manhood in Toni Morrison's Novels." *Alternative Masculinities for a Changing World*, edited by Àngels Carabí and Josep M. Armengol. Palgrave Macmillan, 2014, pp. 161-173.

hooks, bell. *Feminism Is for Everybody: Passionate Politics*. South End Press, 2000.

hooks, bell. *The Will to Change: Men, Masculinity and Love*. Atria Books, 2004.

hooks, bell. *We Real Cool: Black Men and Masculinity*. Routledge, 2004.

Kaplan, E. Ann. *Trauma Culture: The Politics of Terror and Loss in Media and Literature*. Rutgers University Press, 2005.

Morrison, Toni. *Home*. Alfred A. Knopf, 2012.

Morrison, Toni. "Memory, Creation and Writing." *Thought* vol. 59, issue 4, 1984, pp. 385-390.

Wallace, Michele. *Black Macho and the Myth of the Superwoman*. Verso, 1999.

About the Contributors

Lee Baxter is an independent scholar with a master's degree in gender studies and a PhD (ABD) in gothic and horror literature and film studies. Broadly, her research concerns the representation of wounded bodies and psyches in literature and film.

Veena Deo is professor of English at Hamline University in Saint Paul, Minnesota. She has taught at Hamline since 1991. Her research and teaching interests have been in African American literature, postcolonial literature and theory, diaspora studies—especially the African and South Asian diasporas. She has published literary criticism as well as creative work. Her most recent publication is a translation of short stories from Marathi to English by a Dalit woman writer, Urmila Pawar, titled *Motherwit*. It was by published in 2013 by Zubaan Press, New Delhi India.

Kristin M. Distel is a doctoral student of literature at Ohio University. She is researching modern and postmodern revisions of eighteenth-century ideologies, particularly focusing on the development of feminist communities and gendered spaces. Kristin has recently presented papers at The University of Oxford, The University of Manchester, the Sorbonne, EC-ASECS and many other venues. Her poems have been published in *Coldnoon, The Minetta Review, Flyover Country Review, The Broken Plate, The Stockholm Review of Literature*, and elsewhere. She has recently published scholarly articles on Toni Morrison, Larry Levis, Natasha Trethewey, Phillis Wheatley, and Mather Byles.

Jill Goad is assistant professor of English at Shorter University in Rome, GAA. She is currently pursuing her PhD in literature. Her research interests include feminist revisions of psychoanalytic theory, corporeal theory, and contemporary Southern literature. Jill has published articles in *Southern Literary Review* and *Irish Studies South*.

Jesse A. Goldberg teaches courses on African American literature, theatre and performance studies, and race and U.S. law at Cornell University and in the Cornell Prison Education program. His writing appears in *Callaloo*, *MELUS*, and *CLA Journal*, as well as in the collection *Infrastructures of African American Print*.

Anna L. Hinton is a PhD student in the English department at Southern Methodist University, where she has taught first-year writing courses focusing on disability, race, and gender in popular culture. She is currently completing a dissertation on representations of disability in contemporary African American women's fiction.

Rosanne Kennedy is a visiting assistant professor at the Gallatin School of Individualized Study, New York University. She is the author of *Rousseau in Drag: Deconstructing Gender* (2012).

Barbara Mattar is a PhD candidate at the Australian Catholic University. Her research examines fiction from the late twentieth and early twenty-first century that portray women in pregnancy, childbirth, and breastfeeding. Her work explores fiction for its potential to challenge or reinforce current cultural discourses around the maternal body.

Susan Neal Mayberry is Hagar professor in the humanities at Alfred University, where she teaches early modern and African American Literatures. Her book on the masculine and Morrison, *Can't I Love What I Criticize?* (University of Georgia Press, 2007), received the 2009 Outstanding Book Award from Denmark's Organization for the Study of Communication, Language, and Gender. She is presently writing a monograph on Morrison and the neodomestic/ecocritical environment, tentatively titled *Toni Morrison: Inside and Outdoors*.

Lauren A. Mitchell, MS/MA, is a graduate student in the Department of English at Vanderbilt University. She is a graduate of the Program in Narrative Medicine at Columbia University, a former women's health counsellor, and founder of The Doula Project in New York City. Years of hands-on clinical experience informs her current research in theatre, performance art, and medicine. Her book, *The Doulas: Radical Care for Pregnant People*, will be published in November 2016.

Candice L. Pipes was most recently the head of the Department of English and Fine Arts at the United States Air Force Academy, CO, from 2014 to 2016. Much of her scholarly work concentrates on scenes of violence in African American women's literature and the expression of the trauma of war in literature.

Tosha Sampson-Choma is assistant professor of English at Kansas State University. She has published in CLA *Journal* and conducts research on African American and African diaspora women writers. She teaches courses such as African American literature, Black women writers, African American women and identity formation, and Black American social movements.

Martha Satz, assistant professor of English at Southern Methodist University, holds a PhD from the University of Texas in humanities and an ABD in philosophy from Brown University. She has published widely on such diverse topics as Jane Austen, Richard Wright, Ann Petry, children's literature, and genetics and the disability community. She teaches courses on minority literature, African American women writers, and African American literature. The adoptive mother of two biracial children (African American and white), now adults, she has written frequently about this experience.

Althea Tait is an assistant professor of African American literature at SUNY Brockport. Her current research and teaching interests revolve around twentieth-century black women's literature, black female poets' writings, and political activism as well as black women's and girls' interaction with popular culture. Her most recent published work, "Innocence and Fury: A Reading of the Pink in Rita Dove's *Mother Love*," appears in *Obsidian: Literature and Arts in the African Diaspora* (Spring 2016). She is currently completing a book length study of black women's and girls' negotiations with harmful, racialized beauty norms.

.